Disadvantaged Children in India

Sibnath Deb · Aleena Maria Sunny ·
Bishakha Majumdar

Disadvantaged Children in India

Empirical Evidence, Policies and Actions

Springer

Sibnath Deb
Department of Applied Psychology
Pondicherry University
Puducherry, Pondicherry, India

Aleena Maria Sunny
Department of Applied Psychology
Pondicherry University
Puducherry, Pondicherry, India

Bishakha Majumdar
Organizational Behavior and Human
Resource Management
Indian Institution of Management
Visakhapatnam
Visakhapatnam, Andhra Pradesh, India

ISBN 978-981-15-1317-6 ISBN 978-981-15-1318-3 (eBook)
https://doi.org/10.1007/978-981-15-1318-3

This Springer imprint is published by the registered company Springer Nature Singapore Pte Ltd.
The registered company address is: 152 Beach Road, #21-01/04 Gateway East, Singapore 189721, Singapore

Foreword

Around 39% of India's population of 1.36 billion are children. Of these, millions of disadvantaged children live on the streets, in slums or institutions. They are especially vulnerable to being exploited for child labour, trafficked for prostitution, organ harvesting, illegal adoption, child marriage and begging. They are also susceptible to being recruited into gangs where they commence a life dependent on petty theft and crime and may end up incarcerated. Disadvantaged children are denied access to education, health and opportunity, curtailing their potential as adults and adversely affecting their physical and mental well-being. Young girls from disadvantaged backgrounds fall prey to forced marriages and being trafficked into sex work. All these vulnerable children fall through the cracks of inadequate systems that fail to protect their rights as children, even though India is a signatory to the UN Convention on the Rights of the Child. This book is a call to action to prevent, rehabilitate and support disadvantaged children in India. It provides the evidence base upon which policymakers can act now to save this generation of disadvantaged children, who through no fault of their own live stunted lives with little access to justice, love, education and support. I recommend this extensively researched book written by Sibnath Deb, Aleena Maria Sunny and Bishakha Majumdar to activists, policymakers, students and academics in the hope that something can be done now to alleviate the hardship and suffering of India's disadvantaged children.

Prof. Kerry Carrington
Head of School of Justice, Faculty
of Law Queensland University
of Technology, Brisbane, Australia

Preface and Acknowledgements

We suppose that the constitution of India is meant for all citizens, irrespective of their religion, economic and social contexts. If that is so, it is the obligation of the government to protect the rights of every citizen and ensure that every citizen can lead at least a minimum quality of life. However, the reality is different. A large number of innocent children live in extremely difficult circumstances without any fault on their part and experience neglect, abuse and maltreatment for long, and people of the larger society take the advantage of their helpless conditions and use them. In that case, the very spirit of our constitution that is equality and equality is defeated, for which decision makers, as well as all citizens, are partially responsible. India has made substantial progress in terms of economic development, information technology, international relations and in other domains during the last few decades. However, scientific advancement and economic development did not have any positive impact on the condition of disadvantaged children. Disadvantaged children live in a very sorry state. They require special attention which will in turn, contribute to national growth and development.

Unfortunately, we live in a society where some people enjoy maximum resources of the nation, while the majority somehow manage their lives with the remaining resources. The most challenging question that arises is, whether it is possible to bring equality in a society like India where every individual can lead a minimum standard of life. Among the underprivileged population, children from poor families, orphan and destitute children are the worst victims, although the interests of the children are clearly outlined in the Indian Constitution, in other related legislative measures and subsequently in different policies and programs.

The UN Convention on Rights of the Child (1989) is another international document which precisely talks about the rights of the child, in which most of the nations are signatory. The Sustainable Development Goals (SDGs) also emphasize on the minimum standards of life for every individual. Although the Government of India has come out with several legislative measures and policies for the protection of children from all forms of violence and abuse and to provide them care and support, it did not have much impact in reality. The main problem lies in the implementation. Overpopulation is partially responsible for this. The biggest challenge is that the federal and local governments as well as larger society in the developing countries are not mentally prepared to recognize the rights of the children, not in paper but in practice. There is a general notion that children will grow automatically and there is no need to discuss their rights. This traditional notion should be altered through sensitization by electronic and print media, highlighting the gross violation of child rights across the society and its impact on their career and mental health and long-term impacts on national growth. Until the government and the larger society are sensitized about the issue, the condition of children especially disadvantaged children like street children, slum children, trafficked children, children working as child labour and girl child marriage will not improve. There is an urgent need to allocate more budgets for the welfare of disadvantaged children to ensure that they lead a life of a normal human being with safe accommodation, minimum nutrition, educational and medical facilities and so on. There is also a need to monitor the intervention program for disadvantaged children implemented through NGOs and government welfare homes and evaluate them periodically for improving the situation.

Keeping this background in mind, the authors attempted to write this book titled "Disadvantaged Children in India" under five chapters, covering five categories of disadvantaged children, for sharing their first-hand field experience highlighting the overall condition of disadvantaged children in India and at the end of each chapter, the authors offered a number of suggestions and proposed conceptual models for effective implementation of intervention programs based on evidence.

The authors reviewed different books, published articles, study reports and had informal discussions with all categories of disadvantaged children and with managers of intervention programs of some NGOs in different parts of India for understanding their perspectives of the issues and challenges and also to have a feel of the reality and gained a good understanding and knowledge about the subject. The authors thank all the resource persons for sharing their valuable experiences. The authors had the most valuable experience with disadvantaged children. It was painful to learn from their experience about their sufferings although some of them were unable to perceive their sufferings and long-term impact of the present life. We also acknowledge the valuable contribution of different researchers and academics who wrote good articles in the same area and published them in different journals which benefitted us to a great extent.

We hope the readers and policymakers will find our volume informative, useful and interesting.

Puducherry, India — Sibnath Deb
Puducherry, India — Aleena Maria Sunny
Visakhapatnam, India — Bishakha Majumdar

Contents

About the Authors

Prof. Sibnath Deb, M.Sc, LLB, PhD & DSc is a full-time professor in the Department of Applied Psychology, Pondicherry University (A Central University), India. Before joining Pondicherry University, he was teaching at University of Calcutta. In 1994, Prof. Deb underwent an intensive course on 'HIV/AIDS and Qualitative Research' from the University of Western Australia. During April 2009 to August 2009, Prof. Deb visited the School of Public Health, Queensland University of Technology (QUT), Brisbane, Australia as Visiting Faculty. He is also Adjunct Professor of the School of Public Health and Social Work, QUT, Australia (2014-2019). During 2004-2008, he served the International Society for Prevention of Child Abuse and Neglect (ISPCAN) as a Council Member. He is also an Adjunct Professor of the School of Public Health and Social Work, Faculty of Health (2014-2019) and School of Justice, Faculty of Law (2019-2022), Queensland University of Technology, Brisbane, Australia. In brief, he has 28 years of teaching, research and administrative experience and has produced 19 PhD's in addition to publishing more than 100 research articles in National and International Journals as well as in edited books. Some of the latest books of Prof. Deb are

(i) *Child Safety, Welfare and Well-being (Springer, 2016)*
(ii) *Positive Schooling and Child Development: International Perspectives (Springer, 2018)*
(iii) *An Empirical Investigation into Child Abuse and Neglect in India: Burden, Impact and Protective Measures (Springer, 2018)*
(iv) *Social Psychology in Everyday Life' (Sage, 2019)*
(v) *Childhood to Adolescence: Issues and Concerns (Pearson, 2019)*
(vi) *Distance Education: Prospects, Challenges and Way Forward' (Pearson, 2019)*

The following two books are in press

- *Upholding Justice: Social, Psychological and Legal Perspectives (Routledge)*
- *Delivering Justice: Issues and Concerns (Routledge)*

Current areas of research interest of Prof. Deb include parenting styles, family dynamics, child rights, students' mental health, and adolescent reproductive health. Prof. Deb is recipient of **'Prof. Suhrit Chandra Mitra Memorial Plaque' of the Asiatic Society**, Kolkata (2018) and **'Visitor's Award, 2019'** for his contribution in the field of child protection, student's mental health and HIV/AIDS (sibnath23@gmail.com).

Aleena Maria Sunny, MSc is a full-time PhD scholar under the supervision of Prof. Sibnath Deb at the Dept. of Applied Psychology, Pondicherry University (A Central University). She completed her MA in Applied Clinical Psychology from Tata Institute of Social Sciences (TISS), Mumbai and B.A. in Psychology from Christ University, Bangalore. She has co-authored a book titled "*Childhood to Adolescence: Issues and Concerns (Pearson)*" with Prof. Sibnath Deb. She has one-year teaching experience in UG and PG levels in Psychology. Her research interests include clinical psychology, neuro-cognitive psychology and child development. She has been a freelance writer and columnist in a few national dailies.

Bishakha Majumdar, a fellow of IIM Indore is currently working as an Assistant Professor, Organizational Behaviour & Human Resource Management, IIM Visakhapatnam. She has six years of experience in teaching and research in Applied Psychology and Organizational Behaviour. She has multiple national and international publications in the areas of Human Resource Management, Psychology and Public Health – and has presented her works in major conferences. She is also the Associate Editor of the journal South Asian Survey published by SAGE. Her works have been recognized with, among others, Winner HRM – ISB-Ivey Global Case Competition 2018, William Davidson Institute Best Case Award 2018, IASTEM Excellent Paper Award 2017, an Honourable Mention (ISB-Ivey Global Case Competition 2015), the Best Management Research Award 2013 (National Academy of Psychology), Best Publication Award 2012 (Journal of Indian Academy of Applied Psychology), and the Young Scientist Award, 2011 (Indian Academy of Applied Psychology). Mrs. Majumdar has also been a Master Trainer for HIV/AIDS counsellors under the World Bank GFATM Programme. She has undertaken consultancy projects with Piramal Healthcare and Cummins Turbo Technologies and has also conducted MDPs with organizations such as NHPC, Airport Authorities of India, Employment Exchange, Coal India, Oriental Insurance Company Ltd, Relaxo, and Sonic ZF Pvt Ltd in the areas of HR analytics, mentorship, giving and receiving feedback, employee motivation, time management, and workplace communication. Before joining IIM Visakhapatnam, Mrs. Majumdar has been a faculty at FORE School of Management, New Delhi.

Chapter 1
Street Children: The Paradox of Untapped Human Resources

Abstract Children who are susceptible to street life are estimated to be 100 million globally, comprising of (a) street living children who have migrated either temporarily or permanently and live on the streets without their families, (b) street-working children—who spend most of their daytime working on the streets to earn a living and may return home and (c) children from families dwelling on the streets. These children easily become victims to abuse of all forms, violence, exploitation and inhuman treatment by antisocials and criminals and they remain vulnerable and helpless to further victimization. Challenges they fight with on a daily basis are many—lack of shelter, clothing and food, inaccessibility to education and health care, unaddressed chronic physical illness such as gastrointestinal diseases and STDs and other physical alignments and psychological disturbances, maladaptive personality traits, alcohol and psychoactive drug addiction are some of them. The search for the means of survival often drags them into gambling and robbery, thereby increasing the probability of them maintaining a severe criminal record later in life. A high proportion of the children being raped, kidnapped, trafficked and killed are from the streets and the number is ever increasing. It is inevitable to pay ample attention to such children at disadvantage for two important reasons—(a) to ensure that this valuable human resource is given the right ambience to evolve to its best version and be utilized for nation-building, and (b) to protect their right and dignity as citizen of the nation. This chapter is an attempt to understand the issues faced by these little lives on the streets. With the aid of hands-on experience and case studies, their miserable living conditions, deprivations and challenges are explained along the lines of humanitarianism as well as denial of justice. To understand the situation better, the number of governmental, legislative and constitutional measures taken in line with this social issue are also discussed. The chapter proposes various preventive, interventional and rehabilitative action plans for the betterment of the lives of children on the streets. This chapter closes by recommending a few effective steps to ensure the implementation of needed intervention programs through earnest efforts.

Keywords Street children · Working children · Migration · Abuse · Violence · Deprivation

S. Deb et al., *Disadvantaged Children in India*,
https://doi.org/10.1007/978-981-15-1318-3_1

1.1 Introduction

The phenomenon of innocent children living their lives on the streets is a mounting global concern, which is, very unfortunately, found in both developed and developing countries. Its magnitude is found to be higher in poor nations of the world such as Latin America, Asia and Africa (Mathur, 2009b). Several attempts are continuously being made to estimate their number but the very intricate nature of the matter is making it an unattainable task. Keeping aside the wide mismatches and disharmonies between these gross estimates that comes out, the results of such studies always leave one in an alarming state of mind with the realization that they arrived estimation is just a small droplet from the vast undiscoverable extends of the ocean. Low-income countries in Asia, Africa and Pacific together with the International Labor Organization has assessed nearly 120 million children who are into full-time employment (Omokhodion & Omokhodion, 2004), 48 million in sub-Saharan Africa (UNICEF, 2013) and 25 million in Nigeria (Federal Office of Statistics of Nigeria, 2001). UNICEF, in the year 2006, has accounted for the number of children subjected to violence and discrimination in India to lie between 27.1 and 69 million. The Ministry of Women and Child Development totaled up to 54.5% children on the Indian streets to report incidents of sexual abuse (Save the Children, 2015). India has the largest number of children living on its streets (Gupta, 2012). The proportion of such innocent children is only increasing across all the cities in the country, clearly implying huge proportions of irresponsible and illegitimate parents, family malfunctioning and the starching inability to cope with urbanization and timely economic development that the nation undergoes.

No children choose the street for themselves, rather, several mishaps and unfavourable conditions forces this choice upon them (Institute for Human Development, 2011). Their childhood, dreams and futures are robbed off from them and are pushed into the terrifying world of insecurity, vacillations, crime and exploitation. Several studies have discussed the impact of family ecosystem to be highly influential in children choosing street over their home; abuse and neglect from the families could be due to situations of conflict from the families such as parental separation, abusive and distressful punishments adopted by parents, step-parenting, lack of education and exposure of the parents resulting in unawareness about child growth and development, unsuccessful stress management skills and maladaptive coping skills adopted by parents as well as the family system (Mukherjee, 2014); abuse, neglect, violence, exploitation, household poverty, natural or manmade calamities, lost family contacts, kidnapped and orphaned are a few among other reasons for this pathetic phenomena (Institute for Human Development, 2011). Fast urbanization, high unemployment and highly worsened poverty has significantly contributed to the increase in the number (Mukherjee, 2014). Ignorance can be considered as one of the reasons. Whatsoever it is, all these reasons that force this choice of street on these children need to be addressed with utmost seriousness. "Once the child lands up on the streets they encounter problems like occupational hazards, substance dependence, violence, sexual exploitation, other forms of abuse and psychosocial distress like depression, aggressive behavior and self-harm/injury" (Dabir & Athale, 2011; Dutta, 2018). These children would spend each minute of the day fighting with their intense fears and hardships, all the time being extremely alert and conscious of being victimized. "Poor or NIL housing, sanitation, malnutrition, exposure to infections, high environmental risks, exposure to vagaries of weather, lack of parental guidance and supervision and early childhood labor are endemic and contribute to ill-health of younger children" (Gupta, 2012). This not only questions the physical health, but the moral and psychological health are also seriously under threat in the lives of these children.

Children who are left with no choice, but to be on the streets are further affected by the common man by being labelled as "Street Children". This way of addressing these children have somehow gained international acceptance and have been seen been widely used in public discourses and literatures, thus further subjecting them to multiple victimization and discrimination. However, this chapter attempts to inculcate the norms of collective responsibility from the society's psyche, through whose deeds and thoughts these multitudes have to, paradoxically, find their refugee in the streets across the world. "Children living and working on streets", "Children at risk of street involvement", "Children in difficult circumstances" are a few other redressals that came across, which also serve the purpose. The photos of a Danish aid worker encouraging a Nigerian 'witch' boy (later named him as "Hope"), to drink from a bottle of water and then a year later, his first day at school, taking a million toll across the media is a recent incident (CBS News, 2017; The Independent, 2017), that has passed lessons of humanity across the world. On a similar line, here is an attempt to instigate the sensitivity and responsibility in the minds of people, which are seemingly long lost, but hopefully can be revived back to the exposure of the harsh realities.

Children on- and off-street, as well as children fighting through other disadvantaged situation are in huge numbers; they are the untapped resource of the country whose potentials and capabilities are untapped. The contribution they can make to the country's growth and development is overlook by the government as well as by the civil society that these children grow up in the most unfavourable conditions. The quality of their lives are so degraded and sometimes below the human standards. It is high time that the nation, together with its government and people begin to value these young lives with dignity by ensuring the placement of congenial environment for their development. These children, if provided with the right environment and resources, could be transformed into the biggest strength of the nation. They deserve quality treatment, working along the lines of nation's principles of equity and equality. The deprivation of basic facilities from the children would gradually make them question the meaning behind the much celebrated 'social system'. It would not be surprising if they break rules and become felons, thereby misbalancing the social stability. Since they are alienated from the mainstream of the society, they are involved in deviant social and economic activities from the very beginning of their life. The range of skills these helpless children exhibit is varied, which, if properly guided, can turn into valuable human resources. Since they do not get education, at a later stage, they do find it difficult to manage a decent job for survival and lead an aimless and haphazard life. Antisocials and criminals take the advantage of the miserable and helpless conditions of these children and they involve them in deviant activities. Unfortunately, by and large, our society also considers them as problem creators, street urchins and criminals. A large section of people of the higher and middle class feels that such children should not be seen on the streets, as it looks odd. Change of an attitude of the larger society towards these many children on the streets is needed to bring them into the mainstream of the society. Ensuring the respect and maintenance of their rights would otherwise be a smart move towards a better India.

1.2 Definition and Categorization of Street Children

To define the term 'street children' as it was first presented in 1980s—they are children who spend most of their time on the streets to earn a living for themselves and their family through various occupations that they get into. As can be understood, they are those children who lack parental supervision, support and protection and hence become extremely vulnerable to societal adversities. In other words, a 'street child' is understood as a minor who appears to be without adequate protection on the street. This definition includes, but is not restricted to, a number of those also known under different headings, such as 'abandoned children', 'children at high risk', 'children without families', or even 'children in need of care and protection'. What counts in the description of the target group is apparent and need not require any definition. Stress should be on pavement exigencies. Categorizing them has been challenging since there exists a number of differences among these children in terms of their stay as well as presence and regularity in meeting their parents/significant adults.

Generally, a 'street child', as the description stands for, is a child found on the street that is unsupervised and is at extreme risk of being subjected to violence and abuse. As UNICEF rightly states "street children are those for whom the street (in the widest sense of the word, i.e. unoccupied dwellings, wasteland, etc.) more than their family has become their real home, a situation in which there is no protection, supervision, or direction from responsible adults". The children commonly called 'street children' are best considered as children living and working in a particular urban environment. They are considered inappropriate due to lack of order and involvement from major institutions of importance such as family and education.

Broadly, the street children can be grouped into three categories which are as follows:

- **Children on the Street**: These children form the largest category that has homes in their natives but spend most of their day on the street; they have regular contacts with their family members as they return home on a daily basis.
- **Children of the Street**: Those children who find the streets as a place to stay, to earn a living and to build up social relationships fall under this category. However,

they may or may not have contact with their family; but they find their shelter on the streets even at nights.

- **Abandoned Children**: Children under this category are completely abandoned by their family and have absolutely no ties with their family. They are on their own and completely rely on the street for survival by all means.

A common expression used more frequently about these children is '*children out of place*' which refers to those children who are not involved with any societal or institutional life, family, community or educational institution. The irony that often goes unmentioned is the tremendous involvement of these social systems in causing these children to be labelled as 'out of place'. They are, in fact, the victims of complex situations built and monitored by these same systems. Children out of place are not only part of the urban problems. They must also be seen in other contexts, including international and global scenarios. Political causes and consequences must be addressed. In the last few decades, a large number of poor children worldwide have been labelled 'street children' as they struggle to survive by themselves. However, this cannot be considered a new phenomenon. In the past, such children were reported as vagrants, wandering on the streets and a threat to the society in various countries. Issues of millions of children who live and work on the streets without food, shelter, health care, education, care, comfort and security remain unaddressed till date. Though the physical deprivations faced by them are of a very distressing nature, more damaging are the psychological and social deprivations. Understanding their issues and meeting their needs is the absolute need of the hour. They are to be drawn into the mainstream of our society.

The phenomenon of children on streets is rather universal with all the cities in the countries of the third world. Owing to various reasons children are found on the street of cities especially in the metropolitan cities. In general, street children can be divided into the following categories:

- Children belonging to the families who have migrated permanently;
- Children belonging to the families who have migrated temporarily and would go back to their homes after some time;
- Children who come from the suburbs and adjoining villages of the city in the morning, following some vocations during the day and going back in the evening;
- Children of very poor families lacking care and protection;
- Child workers;
- Unattached children including orphans, abandoned children, maladjusted children, delinquent children, run away children and so on.

1.2.1 Children of Permanently Migrated Families

Commercial centers and market places are the generally relied areas of survival by the children mainly because of the presence of shops, factories and industries. These areas offer the children good employability options. They can also get themselves involved in more than one occupation due to the proximity to the workplaces. Moreover, cities offer more pay than rural areas and so, cities tend to attract children from the villages.

On a general notion, fast urbanization has completely taken a toll on the Indian economy and is majorly associated with these several unaddressed issues that these children face. The families that come to the city in search of a means of life are driven out from their homes for several reasons. Though the most important and pervasive one is poverty, other reasons like natural calamities, litigation in the family, lack of cultivable land also work as contributing factors. The villages around some cities in India are very prone to floods, which is a common phenomenon every year. The natural calamities often force the people to migrate to the city for a better life, in the hope that street would provide them refugee, source of living and shelter. However, not many could find their dreams fulfilled.

These permanent migrants not only come from the suburbs and adjoining villages of cities but also from the neighbouring states. Most of these migrants become permanent residents of the cities in India because they do not have any place to go back, even if they wish to go back. Besides, dire poverty and overcrowding in villages, with need for daily workers in the field gradually diminishing with sophistication and mechanization of the cultivation process, compel a number of families to come and settle in the city permanently, even though they do not get a home there. They either work as daily-wage earners at different construction sites or become rickshaw pullers.

1.2.2 Children of Temporarily Migrated Families

All the cities in India are expanding everyday and thereby because of obvious reasons, the number of high-rise buildings, workshops, flyovers, warehouses and similar structures are being regularly constructed. These avenues also attract job seekers from different rural areas to the city. The typical feature of this population is that they are accompanied by their family and would settle themselves on the street. The whole family would find some occupation or other from the street and would live together in the temporary settlement they make on open areas of the street. As they work over a particular period of time, after the work is over they go back to their native place.

1.2.3 Mobile Children

These are sets of children who are always on move. They come to the city regularly by train/bus and would work as street vendors. They come early in the morning and take their place near stations or in open spaces for selling their goods. Some also go on hawking their wares from one place to another. After they sell off whatever they have brought, they go back to their homes. Not only do these children carry the heavy load of their goods and manage to sneak into the train, ducking the ticket collectors, they also take the risk of smuggling rice and other such items from the suburbs or their villages which is against the law of the country. As a result, they often have to end up in local police lock-ups. Many such children who do not have wares to sell take to rag picking. Metropolitan cities have huge dumping grounds. This ground provides a very important source of garbage, which can be sold in the market for producing new products. This source of income often attracts women and children.

1.2.4 Children of Poor Families

This category of children has their family on the streets, maybe for more than one generation. They, as a family, do not have a house to go back to over the years and have been depending on the street for shelter and survival for years. The children are born and brought up on the streets and are often found to be unmonitored by the parents. They fight with poverty and malnourishment. They are forced into finding their own source of earning from a very early age and are often found to be involved in begging and garbage picking. These children are highly vulnerable and often involve themselves in antisocial activities.

The girl children belonging to this category are very much prone to be victims of sexual abuse and exploitation. Nobody takes care of them or give them protection. They are easily lured into the dark world of immoral means of supporting themselves.

1.2.5 Working Children

'Working children' is an umbrella term since majority of the children on the streets would be working. Due to extreme poverty, these children are compelled to work from a very young age. They involve themselves in a variety of tasks ranging from begging and garbage picking to working in garages and hotels as helpers. Most of them involve themselves in more than one job and so, would end up spending most of their time in a day working on the streets. The child who works as a helper at a tea stall starts working as early as 5 a.m. and by the time he ends up, it is almost midnight. With this routine of 30 days every month, they have no opportunity for doing anything else, not even to spend a few hours for themselves. With the increase in the number of automobiles and two-wheelers in the city, there has also been a sharp proliferation of workshops for their repair and maintenance. To a large extent, these workshops are unlicensed and do not have a regular place of work. So they run their trade on the open streets. These makeshift garages are thriving swiftly in cities, particularly in residential areas as well as places where transport services operate. Almost all these workshops have at least two to three child workers who work from eight in the morning till the evening, spending 9–10 h on the road, thus remaining exposed to obvious hazards of the street along with other material hazards that naturally go with such work. Rag picking is a commonly seen occupation among these children since this does not demand any capital, nor any boss or employer to whom they have to succumb to.

1.2.6 Abandoned and Orphan Children

A pressing reality is that millions of children in India today are abandoned by the parents since a very young age. Poverty, unwanted pregnancy/pre-martial birth, death/natural calamity maybe a few of the reasons for this destitution they face. Abandoned newborn babies in the hospitals across the country in India are common incidents.

This apart, a large number of children becomes the victim of unnatural family conditions. Since these children have no place to go, they are compelled to live on the street and they involve themselves in delinquent activities for survival.

Many children on streets, who are orphans or were deserted by their parents, are often associated with antisocial groups who use them for their vested interests. Many girls have been found to be under the care of elderly women who not only live on their earnings but also engages them in immoral activities in the evenings as they reach puberty. These children obviously fall in the category of high-risk children or latchkey children.

1.3 Prevalence and Magnitude of Street Children

The emergence of street children has been described as a global tragedy. The worldwide numbers of street-involved children is at a rapid increase over the past few years. Most of these children get immobile in the generationally-passed on poverty status which hinder their integrity and quality of living (Duci & Tahsini, 2016). A precision on the magnitude of children on streets is unattainable since they are mostly on the move or they might be working invisibly in unreachable areas as labourers, to later return to the street, or are subjected to trafficking and similar exploitation. Hence, one should not be skeptical of the vague estimates being circulated which may appear to be contradictory or stable even over years.

> The exact number of street children is impossible to quantify, but the figure almost certainly runs into tens of millions across the world. It is likely that the numbers are increasing as the global population grows and as urbanization continues apace. (UNICEF, 2006)

Very unfortunately, every city in the world has children living on the street. 'Estudio de NinosCallejeros', an official study spotted 11,172 children on the street of Mexico City—the world's largest city. The likelihood is that their number will increase with global population growth and urbanizations (UNICEF, 2006). Empirical evidence from a meta-analytical study involving 68,014 children from the streets of Africa, Asia and Latin America portrayed interesting facts. Coercion by families, lack of access to education and overall displeasure with life in Africa were the reasons for children to work on their own on African streets while, in Asia, children were pushed by families to beg/work and act as breadwinners for their struggling families (Alem & Laha, 2016). A regional study conducted in South East European countries like Albania, Bosnia, Herzegovina, Montenegro and Serbia discussed the absence of proper typology, structure and definition of 'street-involved' children internationally. This led to poor understanding of the phenomenon, thereby considering the matters as 'isolated cultural issues' rather than a 'system-related problem' (Duci & Tahsini, 2016). Documentation, intervention and long-term prevention of the issues associated to children on streets would be unsorted as long as this issue is not attended. More or less, they remain under-documented, unseen and unaddressed.

Statistics marks India as the home to 444 million children, clearly calling the country young and full of life. Amidst this celebration, UNICEF highlighted another sobering fact that 11 million of India's children lives on the streets (CHILDLINE India Foundation, 2018). The number at large is also depicting the plight of multitudes of children in difficult circumstances living below poverty line, deprived of their basic rights and excluded from all relevant social systems of the nation. A noteworthy comment is that street children could be considered as a measure/indicator of the country's status on ensuring human rights of its citizens (Institute for Human Development, 2011). A 2011 report by Save the Children cited approximately 51,000 children on streets in Delhi alone and the Institute of Human Development assumes them to be one percent of Delhi's total child population. In the same year, another Census covered 84,563 children on streets from five cities of India namely Lucknow, Mughal Sarai, Kolkata-Howrah, Patna and Hyderabad. The study subjects included children (0–6 years of age) to adolescents (16–18 years) involved in the streets, fighting unimaginable odds in life, ignorant of health, hygiene and nutrition and deprived of protection (Save the Children, 2012). It is important to understand that these estimations are not clear counts and one shouldn't be skeptical about these numbers.

Reports from NGOs working with these children mention the presence of several girls on the streets at night and more than double the number of boys as well. They are found to be relying on the remaining food found in the bins of the railway stations. Plastic bottles and other discarded items are collected to be sold later for recycling. Girls staying alone on the street are comparatively less. Interestingly, the proportion of older girls on street was found to be lesser than the boys; this suggests the involvement of various other factors that would be involved which would take older girls out of the streets (Save the Children, 2012). Only few girls are found on the streets because most of them are trafficked for prostitution. The ones who are still surviving entertain the street boys and gangster men by indulging in sex with them as a return for protection from policemen and touts (Patro, 1997). The number of newborns being abandoned at the hospitals is also no less. The National Crime Records Bureau figures indicate that abandonment of infants has been increasing, with 1093 cases being reported in Maharashtra alone between 2011 and 2015 (Narayan, 2016). A good proportion of these abandoned children ends up on the streets and plays victim to neglect and abuse.

The range of factors such as the children's invisibility and movement, to lack of proper surveillance and intervention by inter-sectoral stakeholders (parents, communities, local bodies and governments) aggravate the condition further. The massive evidence gap that exists in the country makes it nearly impossible to track the movement of these children and they become a commonly occurring but invisible phenomenon around us.

1.4 Causal and Contributory Factors for Accepting Street Life

Children leave home for the most trivial of reasons, such as fear of being scolded or wounded at some imagined insult. Studies showed that it's the intersection of several systemic factors that pushes children out of their home, namely: (a) parental neglect in the form of failing to provide love, affection and care, adequate food, clothing, shelter, denial of medical aids and inadequate supervision; (b) economic factors such as poverty and unemployment, (c) social factors such as crime, violence, abuse and (d) psychological factors such as aftereffects of harshness at home, low resilience capacity, tolerance to stress and personal dispositions (Mugove & Lincoln, 2015). Fear of rejection and punishment would resist them from returning home after realizing the harsh realities of life. At the same time, life on streets is so unbearable that these children would suffer in a double avoidance conflict. The streets, however, are not open repositories for any child who wants to leave home. Those children who left their home to streets for a better life would be the ones who got trapped into an illusionary idea: foods, shelter, employment, quality of life are almost nonexistent for them on the street. Their inner desire to do better in life, to solicit their decision of coming out of home, would push them to further exploitation and damage. They would, in most cases, end up being involved in theft and crime. Some would be victims of drugs, rape and suicide. The ideal solution for a street child is re-unification with the family.

A seven-year old boy from Tirupati had run away from home after being burned with cigarette butts by his father. Should an abusive father be given guardianship? When the case came for hearing in the Juvenile Welfare Board, he was bundled into the next train to Tirupati, Andhra Pradesh as the parents had the right to custody. The law of the land gives custody of children to parents even if they abuse their children regularly. Law doesn't empower children to fight abuse.

To serve the intention of understanding the multi-factorial causes that would lead a child to the streets, Deb and Mitra (2002) carried out a study in Kolkata, India. A group of 40 children, 18 male and 22 female, in the age group of 9–19 years were covered in the present study. Findings disclosed that step-parenting, death/absence of either of the parents, mistreatment from other family members, dysfunctional families, gender bias, poverty/unemployment, neglectful parenting and other situational factors were found to be of significant influence. It was also found that these children who are exposed to the above mentioned stressful experiences would develop a desire for normal living like others and hence would leave their home for a better future. The authors were confident in stating that all these children who have come out of their homes by their own to the streets are prone to abuse, be it physical, emotional or sexual. Evidently, family disintegration is a key causal factor, but the aggravating role is being played by poverty.

There are a range of factors which compel children to leave homes. Personal interaction through informal interviews with some of the street children enlightened the first author about some of the causal factors for leaving home and taking shelter on the streets. For example,

> "*I tried to venture towards urban life and got into a local train and reached Sealdah station, Kolkata two years back. Could not return since I did not know the address*" – *a male child*

> "*I left home because of continuous violence and unhappy situation in the family*" – *a male child*

> "*Somebody offered me a job in the city and then after few days of sexual abuse, one day they left me alone in the railway station*" – *a female child*

> "*Poverty forced me to leave home and come to the city in search of work*" – *a male child*

1.5 Living Condition of Street Children

There is clear difference among the children who completely live on the streets and the ones who return home later at night. Their prognosis is different and so are their conditions of life on the streets. A 2010 survey conducted on Delhi Streets reports that 36.03% of children are from street families, 29.05% work on the streets and 27.91% live alone on the streets. Two out of three children were of the age group of 7–14 and one out of three was of the age group of 15–18. Only 20.5% among them were girls (Institute for Human Development, 2011). A majority of them (63%) live with their families on the street, 14% stay with their fellow mates on the street, 4% stay with their employers on the street and 11% stay alone. Among the children who have left their homes, 88.5% had contact with their families and reported to visit their hometown to deliver money. A noteworthy fact here is that nearly 88% of boys and 81% of girls were winning their share of survival means for their respective families from the streets (Institute for Human Development, 2011). The means of their income generation activities is elaborated in the following session.

Globally, the economically marginalized families tends to place their children in a dysfunctional state, such that they are forced to leave their homes to end up living in unprotected and dangerous life conditions: child abuse and exploitation of children as the breadwinner of the family becomes a common scene in most of the economically disadvantaged families (ODCCP, 2001). Poverty, family breakdown and abusive conditions at home make these children to run away from their homes. The children usually exercise their choice and remove themselves from the environment. Some street children are the victims of kidnapping, abandonment/orphaned or victims of natural calamities or have mistakably lost their parents while travelling.

Usually, no facilities are available for the street children and they have to cope with what they can use as 'free' facilities. A place to sleep at night and escape from the hell of abuse is always a cause of worry for these children. While some have a fixed place to sleep, others sleep wherever they find it convenient and safe. The spatial distribution of pavement dwellers has people on the pavements, tending to gather in a number of places and sleep in shop verandahs, under bridges, trees, in bus shelters, abandoned buildings or just out in the open and railway station platforms. A minority seeks shelter in public places, on the beach or under trees, construction sites. Having no permanent place also means that the children cannot store their possessions in a secure place. However, they often have to contend with the police, who would drive them off the road, the platform or the abandoned building. A large number of children are found living in railway stations, in every corner of the country. Life on a railway station has its own rhythm–mostly characterized by trains whistling in and out and the movement of large numbers of people with trains arriving and departing. Within this floating population are certain elements who are constant features—vendors selling various eateries/drinks, book sellers, others like the railway staff and of course coolies (porters). It is in this environment that children on the platforms eke out their existence: washing, bathing, earning, eating, playing and sleeping. While some on the children live with their family or other relations, many live on their own. Like all street children, the ones living at the railway stations are mobile groups and often do not stay in one place for long.

Informal interviews with the street children in Kolkata helped the first author to have a first-hand feel of the perspectives of the children, of street life and challenges they face on street (Deb & Mitra, 2002). Some of them are unhappy and disturbed while some enjoy the street life. Some of the verbatim responses are worth mentioning here. For example,

> *"There are no restrictions in street life. We can live our life on our own" – a male child*
>
> *"Only one problem we face, that is, interference from the police and sometime when we are unable to earn money through begging for our food" – a male child*
>
> *"We are happy in railway platform since we can view films on platform TV" – a female child*
>
> *"During winter we suffer a lot of problems on the railway platform" – a female child*
>
> *"Street life is better than my home. My father is an alcoholic and used to beat my mother almost every day after taking alcohol" – a male child*

The following case narrates how a 7–8 year-old boy, not by any choice, landed up at a Kolkata railway station:

> ***Case Study 1:*** *Shubhashish was 7–8 years old when he ran away to his mashi's (mother's sister) place. He stayed there for about a week. His mashi insisted that he returns. So one day he caught a train and came to Sealdah. Everyone was getting down at Sealdah, so he also got down. After sometime, he caught another train to go back. That train did not go to Dumdum (mashi's place). It stopped at another station. He got down and walked out of the*

station. He took another train and came back to Sealdah. After that he did not go back to his mashi's place or to his home. He came to Sealdah and stayed there. There was no reason for coming to Sealdah but it happened only because the train stopped at this station (terminal point)'.

The makeshift homes these children make are in such surroundings which are filled with waste disposals. This unhygienic environment is the only choice left for these children since everywhere on the street would give them the same options. In some places in the city, street children sometimes share the common bathrooms and latrines, the living areas, cook and eat in the open due to lack of kitchen space. This makes their living claustrophobic and deprives the residents any sort of privacy. Along with water shortage issues, many water sources are located near public toilets or garbage dumps. This increases the chances of water contamination. Defecation in the open and public places further deteriorates their health conditions: improper sanitation and unmaintained sewage facilities deteriorate their health conditions. Environmental pollution, particularly air pollution also curbs their health condition and hence innumerable health hazards follow. They are virtually excluded from any urban infrastructure and facilities whatsoever and have to rely on roadside amenities for water to be used for drinking and cooking. Children also show tendencies to stay around areas where free food was available such as '*dargas*' or locations where charitable initiatives would serve food. Several children had said that they were well informed about the locations where free food is served on various days of the week (Kombarakaran, 2004). Open space serves for sanitary purposes. Majority of the children on Delhi streets (90% of girl children) have reported to avail the paid access to public toilet facilities which are again unmaintained and unhygienic. The struggle during their monthly menstruation would be above the scope of appropriate explanation.

Inadequate food, unhygienic living conditions and the strain of work affects the health of working street children. From a number of studies, it have been reported that the majority of the children fall prey to physical weakness, fatigue, backache and muscle pain. Also children are affected by respiratory tract infections, tuberculosis, diarrhoea, skin diseases and worm infestations. Usually, private clinics or health services provided by NGOs are the health care access points for these children. A majority of them would not take such medical aids due to unaffordability, ignorance, inaccessibility or even maltreatment by the health care professionals. These are rarely availed owing to the hostile attitude of doctors and hospital staff and public attitude towards them. Exposure to varying weather conditions, filth, smoke and other hazardous materials would gradually deteriorate their health. As a result, a majority of them remain sick from their childhood and a good number of them may even die at a very young age. Along with this, physical and mental disabilities are not uncommon among them which would be seen among children who were abandoned by their parents soon after their birth. Along with this, accidents, abuse, or even intentionally handicapping them to use them for begging, organ harvesting and so on for livelihood are also done. Preventive health also seems lacking. As many as 96.8% of the surveyed street children were not fully immunized. More than 90% of children on streets are undernourished and suffer from moderate to excessive protein and vitamin deficiency as most of them hardly manage to get two meals a day. Unsatisfactory age-height ratio, body-mass index and other physical growth indicators are all matters of serious concerns.

The knowledge about their psychological development is still sketchy. An interesting study matches the street children to that of children from poor financial backgrounds: the level of depression and subjective well-being are found to be of matching frequencies. "The street is not a healthy place to live, even if it does not cause great psychological harm" (Koller & Hutz, 2002). Several studies have validated this opinion by stating the adaptation of these children by effective coping mechanisms in facing these adversities. They are found to master coping mechanisms by making use of the social network they establish over a period of time in their close social circle. Survey reports tell that these children are often subjected to abuse and psychologically remain upset from the fear of being abused again. Aggression, violence, bullying, self-harming behaviours and suicidal tendencies would also be at high rates among these children. Violence and aggressions are everyday occurrences and happen at any time of the day or night. Gang wars between two areas take place almost regularly on every street.

Educational and other essential services are inaccessible to them. Regrettably, 50.5% of children on Delhi streets were found to be illiterate and 20% received very minimal primary education. The proportion of children who received some form of non-formal education is also less than 20%, indicating the lack of intervention for this population (Institute for Human Development, 2011). Access to recreational facilities, sports and games and socio-cultural activities is also very poor. This topic has been further elaborated in a section that follows.

Treatment from the policemen and local municipality are also unpleasant. These children fear getting arrested for crimes they haven't committed. Moreover, once these children are caught for a petty theft, then they would get trapped over and over again. Police also extort a share of money from these poor children as commission for letting them beg or pick garbage. Similar remunerations are to be given to some staffs of the municipalities to ease their rag picking. (Source: National Labor Institution, Noida, U.P., 1992).

One such problem faced by a street child as the price of protection has been narrated below:

Case Study 2: *The police once took Jamir while he was sleeping under a railway ticket counter. Somebody had stolen steel from the staircase and the police accused him of having stolen it and beat him up. At another time, when they caught him and accused him of stealing something, he told them 'I knew who had stolen it'. He gave them a name and ran away from the police station as fast as he could. At the station, there were dadas (big bully) who would demand regular protection money. They would take away whatever money was in Jamir's pocket. Therefore it was useless for him to keep money. So if he had money he used to spend it on movies. The dadas would keep blade in their fingers, and as they walk past children like him, they slash either their face or their hands/legs.*

Addiction, violence and exploitation are matters of day-to-day affairs on the street. Away from protection and guidance, a majority of the children resort to substance abuse as substantiated by studies which proves that an overwhelming number of street children show excessive dependency on tobacco/glue/whiteners/or petrol sniffing as well as locally available drugs such as *pan masala* and *Hashish* (Kanth, 2004). A study identified that approximately 50% of the children were daily consumers, 28% weekly and 20.6% were monthly consumers (Institute for Human Development, 2011). For children who lived with their families on streets, they identify violence on the street and home as a danger that they and other children face most often. On the streets, frequent bullying occurs while at home beating/thrashing happens, mostly by fathers or relatives. A good proportion of mothers, in the families, living on streets would be engaged in prostitution, whose clients would also maltreat these children. They often entice the children in exchange of a small remuneration to buy liquor, pan, cigarettes or drugs for their clients. As mentioned earlier, this exposes the children to the risk of being tempted to try these out.

Most problems of urban childhood have their roots in a country's rural sector. This is especially true for countries like India where thousands of children are forced to migrate from villages to cities to ultimately end up in extremely exploitative situations. Chilly winter nights, mosquito bites, regular theft and violence, susceptibility to bullying, policemen, local *dadas*, passersby's, passengers, railway staffs, *coolie* harassment, accidents, sudden rain showers, absence of dry place to sleep during monsoons etc. are some of the problems these children face who are out on the streets. Given all the hardship, a very few children would like to leave the streets and get back to their homes (Institute for Human Development, 2011). Many street children end up by settling in the city streets, marrying and having a family. In this manner, the street propagates their generation.

In everyday life, they encounter numerous problems like neglect, abuse, exploitation and so on. Constant anticipation of being woken up by abusers, police officers or *dadas* and threats of being beaten up, snatching away of their little savings for tomorrow's living, to be abused, or raped, or maybe drenched by a jet of cold water from trucks, cars or buses lined up for a street wash. Their nights are spent on random unsafe areas on the street, they sleep late and wake up early and would be prone to easy exploitation by any passersby. According to some of them,

"*Common people treat us badly*" – *a male child*

"*During night time, some elder people disturb us*" – *a female child*

"*We all try to sleep at nearby places during night time for safety*" – *a male child*

"*Sometime, we suffer from diarrhoea and fever. There is no place to go for medicine*" – *a female child*

A brief description of the major problems encountered by the street children is given in Model 1.1.

1.5.1 Lack of Safe Shelter

This is the basic problem they face and also a major vulnerability factor for many children. Unfortunately, major Indian cities which are the dwelling place of street

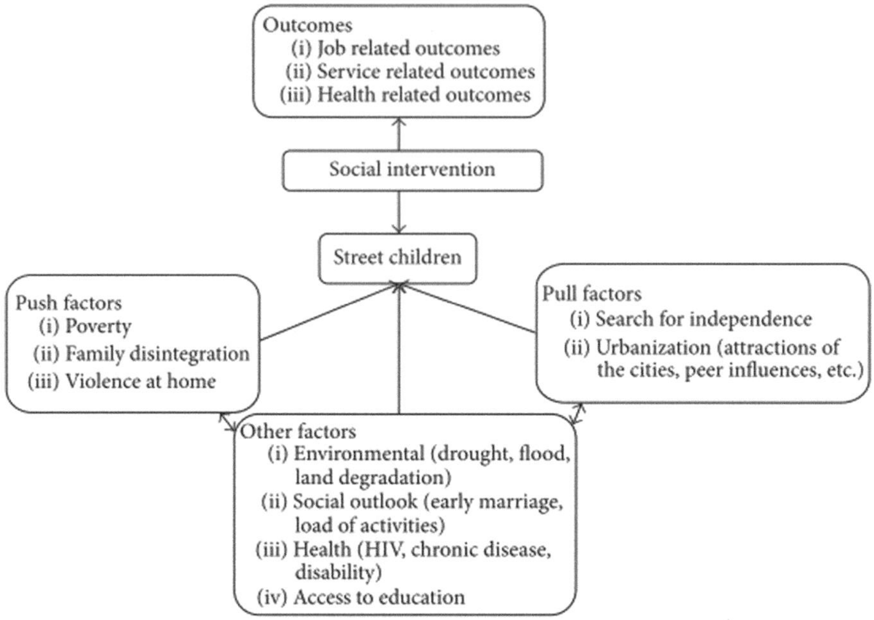

Model 1.1 Conceptual framework on the problems of children on streets from '*Livelihood of Street Children and the Role of Social Intervention: Insights from Literature using Meta-analysis*' (Alem & Laha, 2016)

children are ill-equipped to provide accommodation for such a large number of children (Save the Children, 2012). The same study reports that only 1–2% of children are said to have safety at their night shelter. A Kolkata based study on 600 children showed that 40% live on the roadside, 23% in the bus stands and 21% live in a nearby railway station. The permanent houses of the 2.66% children on the streets were made of bamboo, bricks and plastic, while 71% children lived in temporary houses made of plastic. Rest of them (15%) lived on the roadside and pavements were completely homeless (Mukherjee, 2014). Children on streets were found to be sleeping on footpaths, flyovers and bridges, railway platforms, bus stops, parks and market places and night shelters (Ministry of Women and Child Development, 2007). Wherever they stay and wherever they go, there is practically no safe shelter for them. Everywhere, they are at high risks of exploitation, sexual abuse and harassment. Nowadays, a good number of NGOs have started working for the welfare and rehabilitation of the street children in different parts of the country. A good number of fortunate children enjoy this facility, which is more needed for a girl child.

1.5.2 Inadequate Food

On 2018 World Nutrition Day, Mr. Harsh Mander, the Director of Centre for Equity Studies rightly stated that "Unlike rural children, street children in India do not face hunger. They are typically not food-deprived. But, they do suffer from high levels of malnutrition. One reason is obviously the content of the food that they buy off the street, which is very poor. However, more importantly, their body cannot absorb all the nutrition they eat" (Dey, 2018). A study on children living on the streets of Mysuru (India) validated this comment: anemia (52.5%), underweight (76.5%), stunting (36.8%) and wasting (52%) were reported. Irregular earning and so irregular food habits, poor dietary food consumption are found to have predisposed these conditions in them (Kumar, Chethak, Rama, Bhaktavatsala, & Vikash, 2017). Low BMI (62.4%), protein deficiency (51.85%) and calorie deficiency (60%) were found in children living on Kolkata streets in a cross-sectional study. Health consciousness and substance abuse were found to be prominent influencers for the children's nutritional statuses (Pal, Pari, Sinha, & Dhara, 2017).

As mentioned earlier, leftovers from roadside restaurants and hotels, food stalls, garbage bins or railway/metro stations and parks were found to be the major sources of food (Kombarakaran, 2004; Patel, 1990). Some of them rely on free food available from *durgas*, charitable organizations, weddings or similar functions and have reported to place themselves on the streets accordingly. For earning money, they work hard the whole day as nobody is there to ensure two meals a day for them. Since most of them are illiterate and have no skills, they are mostly involved in casual work against very low wages. Sometimes, some of them are involved in deviant social activities knowingly or unknowingly as influenced by the antisocials for which these innocent children are not responsible. In fact, our social system and structure is responsible for pushing/compelling innocent children in the negative direction. Following are some of the verbatim responses highlighting uncertainty of food:

> "*I am not sure what will happen to my next meal*" – *a female child*

> "*If I am unable to earn money through begging, my friend will share his meal with me*" – *a male child*

> "*I normally wait near roadside food stalls and ask people for money or little food. Some people are good and they give little food after having their food and sometime people give us Rs. 5/or Rs. 10/*" – *a female child*

> "*Sometimes, we depend upon leftovers from roadside restaurants*" – *a male child*

> "*We steal vegetables from the local train when it comes to Sealdah railway platform from the rural areas for the wholesale market and sell it and earn some money for our living*" – *a male child*

1.5.3 Lack of Medical and Educational Facilities

In case of any health problem, most of the street children remain unattended, except a lucky few who are under the intervention program of NGOs. Sometimes, they visit nearby/local Govt. Health Centers for treatment and get free medicine. Since nobody is there to follow-up whether they are taking medicine on time or not, and since there is no secure and safe place to preserve medicines, after one or two days, they do not take the medicine regularly. Hence, a large number of street children suffer from different health problems throughout the year.

Educational level of children on the streets should be closely analyzed in terms of their literacy as well as attendance. The findings of a study conducted in 5 areas of India found that 63% of the children were illiterate. This rate was observed to be higher among working children highlighting how earning for survival is actually hindering their learning opportunities. However, the situation were not different for children who stayed with their parents either (Save the Children, 2012). Most of them do not get the opportunity to study. As a result, in future, when they become older, they do not get better jobs. Their whole life, they work as unskilled labourers. In a following section, the educational status of the children on streets is elaborately discussed.

1.5.4 Physical and Mental Health Problems

Innumerable are the physical and psychological problems that these children face, which are the result of circumstances that left them on the streets as well as the direct effect of street on them. Most of these children have nobody to look after them and most of them have no knowledge of medical facilities, which they could avail of. As a result, in case of any health problem, they mostly remain unattended. Nowadays, a number of NGOs are extending health services to the disadvantaged children but these are inadequate and follow-up is also very poor.

Streets are obviously not hygienic places to live. Street activities that these children indulge in make them even more vulnerable to health problems (Di Giglio et al., 2014). These children are often found unclean, in unwashed misfit clothes, filthy hair and faces and often without footwear. Leftovers from roadside restaurants and hotels, food stalls, garbage bins or railway/metro stations and parks were found to be the major sources of food (Kombarakaran, 2004; Patel, 1990). Inadequate shelter, poor quality diet or very occasional starving, inaccessibility to health care facilities, high socio-economic as well as environmental risks at living and working conditions tremendously contribute to the ill-health of children on street (Gupta, 2012; Mathur, 2009a). Health problem associated with rape, unplanned pregnancies, reproduction, birth-giving, abortion and violence is in itself an unending struggle for survival. STDs are very common among them; so are pregnancies. Health problems related to pollution are quiet common with high incidences of asthma, tuberculosis and skin disease. High rates of drug and alcohol abuse as well as high rates of depression and suicide are found among this set of children.

Illness conditions like "malaria, tuberculosis, cold and cough, water-borne diseases and skin diseases" were commonly reported among children on Kolkata and Mumbai streets, mainly due to unhygienic environment of living; inadequate sanitation facilities is the pronounced problem which also results in issues related to lack of privacy, particularly among girl children (Dutta, 2018). Strikingly disheartening statistics produced on the children of Khammam city, Andhra Pradesh (India), showed very poor maintenance of personal hygiene. Various ill-health statuses such as malnourishment (64.7%), Scabies (6.7%), anemia (30.66%), Vitamin A deficiency (46%), Vitamin B deficiency (17.33%), visual and hearing impairments (34.7%), dental problems (60.66%) psychiatric conditions (5.3%) and addictive behaviours (42.66%) were also brought to light, They were found to be underweight and stunted; very few children were vaccinated (Berad, Momula, & Kumar, 2014). Similar findings were seen in the neighbouring country of Bangladesh where nearly 87.2% of children have suffered from conditions like accidental injury, skin infection, hepatitis, STDs and worm infections (Chowdhury et al., 2017). Heat boils and chickenpox were reported among 27.7% of children on Delhi streets; it was noticed that they do not report any skin-related problems unless probed because it was very common among all of them and they were least concerned about treatment (Institute for Human Development, 2011). Interestingly, similar attitude among children was discussed in studies conducted in Cairo and Alexandria, Egypt. The children ignored illness as 'minor or normal' as long as they can move and function to meet their needs (ODCCP, 2001). Therefore, most of the time, due attention was not paid to seeking medical assistance unless they are not able to move or work.

Substantiating aforementioned data, a study on the children on Sangam Vihar (it is an unauthorized colony in South Delhi) also exposed unwelcoming findings. About three-fifth (59%) of children in the study reported having minimal to no space for bathing and 41% didn't have toileting and washing facilities. They relied on nearby water sources to bathe once or twice a week. In line with findings from other streets, skin diseases, fever, cold and cough, diarrhoea, tuberculosis and STDs were common among them. Many among them reported to be spending hours in queuing up for collecting drinking water from the municipality water supply, and girls reported to pay and use poorly maintained public toilets during menstruation (Gupta, 2012). Malnutrition can be understood as the root cause of several illnesses, which can arise due to the intake of tainted food, inadequate dietary intake of essential nutrients, faulty dietary habits and repeated illness (ODCCP, 2001). The chronic health conditions that accompany malnourishment would increase the demand of nutritional needs in children, making their health status dicey. This is a vicious cycle which takes a toll on the children's immunity system and thereby overall health.

WHO reports the curtailing effect of abuse, exploitation, neglect, discrimination and harassment on the overall development of the individual. It also emphasizes the likelihood that human rights violation could function whenever there can be mental health issues in such vulnerable populations (Null et al., 2010). Added to this is the distressful personal relationship within children who live together on the streets:

abuses such as 'calling names, exchanging abusive words, passing inappropriate comments, ragging and bullying younger siblings and overall discouragement were also reported (Dutta, 2018). Those who attempted to eke out an honest livelihood by doing odd jobs or rag picking etc. are most of the time underpaid. They end up being exploited for their vulnerability. Their hard-earned money is also stolen or forcefully taken away. A relevant statement in this context in the document Education for Street and Working Children in India follows:

> Street children are susceptible to drug/alcoholic addiction and to inhalants to offer them an escape from reality, take away hunger and cold and give them the 'courage' to steal and engage in survival sex. As a result, they get into a lot of physical and psychological problems. (UNESCO, 2001)

Many children on the streets prefer not to save money for these reasons and therefore spend almost the entire amount of what they earn, mainly on food, gambling, addictions and vices. Children on the streets are also used as drug peddlers and pushers (injectors). The lure of money is high. The drug trade (involving heroin and its derivatives) flourished during the late eighties and the early nineties attracting a number of children and youth to the trade as pushers and consumers. Drug addictions, depression suicidal thoughts/attempts, are prominent among children. A study explained behaviours like addiction, smoking, visiting prostitution etc. as maladaptive coping to the unsafe, unpredictable and risky behaviour they face on the street. Children are reported to have addiction to substances like "petrol, glue, photocopier solution, nail polish, valium, marijuana, hashish, heroin and opium' (Kombarakaran, 2004). Peer influence is another important triggering factor in trying out their experiences with these substances. Substance abuse can "damage vital organs and cause respiratory, digestive, oral, facial and heart diseases; HIV AIDS, STIs, violence and crimes are the social effects of substance abuse" (Sharma & Joshi, 2013). Note the words of a 12 years old boy near Easamina Bazar, Hyderabad—"*we keep some money for Lodex and Corex, as they instantly energies us without harming our health*" (Save the Children, 2015). Gambling in the form of *satta* and playing cards is most common among all age groups of males including boys and they can be seen playing cards in the park and on every street of the cities.

Clearly, psychosocial distress among children on the streets of India is alarming, even though attempts to document the same are only few. A Mumbai based study proved that psychosocial distress among children on streets range from moderate to severe, after being subjected to maltreatments, rejection and abuse (Allen, Balfour, Bell, & Marmot, 2014; Guernina, 2004; Savarkar, 2018). Adding to this are factors like persecution and violence at work, workplace sexual harassment and distress associated to poor wages and long working hours at young ages, that can alleviate the vulnerability (Agarwal 2017; Audu, Geidam, & Jarma, 2009; Caglayan, Hamzaoglu, Yavuz, & Yüksel, 2010).

Along the lines of family upbringing and parent-child behaviour, a noteworthy feature is about the unsupervised family environment of children who live with their families on streets. Mostly, these are incomplete households where the mother is alone with her children, or the father, or the children are left to grandparents, aunts, uncles, etc. Usually, these are mainly women who are separated from their husbands rather than unmarried females, who have never experienced a stable marital relationship before.

Following is the case study of a child who ran a high risk of abuse found on the streets/platforms of Kolkata city:

> ***Case Study 3:*** *Ramesh was 4 year-old when his mother eloped with another man. His father, unable to bear the stress of bringing up his children took to drinking. In this drunken state he would beat the children frequently. Gradually, Ramesh (and his sister) took to staying away from school and stealing money from his father to spend. Ramesh would often run away from home and would be found by the police, wandering about, begging or stealing at various railway stations. Their father had their so-called 'aunt' living in with him. In 1990, when he was twelve, unable to take any more thrashings or humiliations from his father, Ramesh and his sister finally ran away from home for good. He was 'pretty' in appearance, enjoyed wearing female apparels and ornaments and hence became a target of sexual abuse for older boys and men.*

Another study states the fact that socio-emotional development, which can influence the child all throughout his/her life, is the quality of parent–child relationship. In line with attachment theory, the study argued that the threat that has happened in the child's relationship with his/her parent at such a young age that it would adversely affect any social relationship later in life. This has the potential to develop serious social-emotional difficulties in the lives of the children (Teta, 2002). The comprising picture points the high incidence and prevalence of mental illness such as post-traumatic stress disorder, suicidal behaviour and depression (Kidd, 2004; Whitbeck, Hoyt, & Bao, 2000) with 12–40 times more mortality rates than the normal population (Shaw & Dorling, 1998). Not surprisingly, suicide is found to be the leading cause of death (Roy, 2004).

Despite the obvious need for medical services—both physical and psychological, they also suffer from lack of knowledge in relation to unawareness on clinic sites, confidentiality issues and fear of approaching for medical supervisions. Improvement in the access to appropriate health care facilities should be done at the earliest, by making use of available community resources. Advocacy by a responsible other would always make difference in terms of reaching the authorities in providing services to this disadvantaged population (Feldmann & Middleman, 2003). This is an area that has to be addressed with utmost urgency and care.

1.6 Education of Street Children

The majority of the street children are illiterate. They can neither read nor write their name. The children who run away from the families they can read and write. A 2011 survey based on Delhi streets has produced precise statistics on the educational status of the children. Among the children who claimed to be school educated, nearly 50% of them had actually received school training till class II, 19% had attended till class V and the percentage of children educated beyond primary school was very minimal. The interesting part of the study is the estimation it took on the number of children who wanted to be educated in one way or the other: 64.2% sought for skill training, 43.7% wanted school education and 17.4% wanted both; and over 55% preferred evening classes (Institute for Human Development, 2011). Over 100 children among the 50,923 participants of the same survey remained on the street despite completing their secondary education. This opens up the need for further socialization and support from the larger society. Parallel findings were found in other cities of India too, where not more than 35% children had gone beyond upper primary. They were irregular in school and so, not surprisingly, poverty remains the foremost reason for school dropouts. The study found that non-enrolment of children and early dropouts were the key issues to be addressed in order to run the RTE Act in the cities (Save the Children, 2012).

The trend in Turkey would provide an international perspective to the matter. A great number of children there start to work at early ages, either to support them or to contribute to the family income. Despite the fact that five-year primary school is compulsory, some of these children work on a full-time basis, starting at very young ages and some of them work, during off-hours and vacations on a part-time basis or as seasonal workers. The children work in agriculture, manufacturing industry and service sectors such as trade, restaurants and hotels, while a large portion of them work in the marginal sectors. Turkey is in a period of transition, characterized by rapid urbanization with a high birth rate. In the urban areas, employment of child labour has, to a great extent, shifted outside, away from the family. The children are mostly found in workplaces where vocational skills are transferred through the master-apprentice set up. This trend is prominently seen in housework, service sectors and to a great extent, in the marginal sectors. Parallel to the rise of globalization, the growing numbers of poor marginalized urban children and street children, in particular, became a matter of public concern.

As the numbers shows, children on the streets generally do not attend any form of education whatsoever, which in itself almost condemns them to persistent poverty. When asked about the reason for not going to school, the answers generally relate to three types of factors:

(a) The requirements of the educational bureaucracy (birth certificates, parent's documents and parent's contribution to the cost of schooling, books and uniforms).
(b) Discrimination (beggar-children, outcasts as them are not easily admitted to any kind of schools, whether they comply with the rules and regulations or not).
(c) The impossibility of conventional schools to respond to the very peculiar situation in which street children have to study and adjust their program accordingly.

This third factor appears as the most serious issue. Not surprisingly, attempts to coerce street children to attend school have been largely unsuccessful. The education system, obviously has quite a lot to answer for education, which one hopes to be the engine for social mobility of the urban poor but, today's street children remain largely deprived of it. '*Deprivation of*' does not simply mean without it, because, nearly all indicate their willingness to go to school, if only it could be made possible. Therefore, to enable them to undergo a form of training appears to be of great importance. Needless to urge that this training should match their possibilities. The newly proposed National Education Policy captures special attention regarding this matter, as one of the main target of the policy is to ensure quality in the early childhood care (The Hindu, 2019). More relevant to this context is the intention of widening the range of applicability of the Right to Education Act from 3 to 18 years by 2030. Both these targeted provisions in the policy are capable of making remarkable changes to the lives of these street children. It has to be appreciated that, under this proposed policy, the probability of street children to get access to education and care facilities would expand at least in relation to their rights. But, the questions that demand brainstorming and practical answer is how this aims can be put into practice among street children. The reality is so distorted that, ensuring that their rights are preserved in terms for education is a tremendously challenging. One of the most probable solutions could be the institutionalization of street children as this can bring a structure, order and flow to the execution aspect of this policy. Once the children are brought under the shelter of an institution, the challenges in relation to bringing education to them could be minimized to a greater extent. Hence, it is highly recommendable that the government should take initiatives to ensure institutionalization of the street children to maximum feasible extent, thereby taking an effort to actually bring the policies on papers to practice in their lives.

School dropouts continue to be one of the biggest problems in the primary education system of India. It is estimated that nearly 50% children dropout of schools before completing their Vth grade. Often it is argued that a majority of the children leave school for economic reasons, as they have to support their families. However, lack of conclusive evidence failed to determine the degree to which gainful employment resulted in school dropouts. Nonetheless, it remains a fact that education is yet to reach most of the children living in difficult circumstances. A survey was conducted in 450 villages/urban pockets to examine among other issues, the activity status and type of employment, earning, health, physical condition, aspiration and achievement level of children dropping out of primary schools. The study also explored the reasons for dropouts. The findings indicated that, in general, less than 10% dropouts were engaged in gainful employment. However, the chances of dropout due to employment varied from place to place, indicating significant linkages with the employment opportunities. Poor quality of education was suggested as the most important reason for dropout. If education is made relevant and meaningful to the economic needs of the community, it has greater chances of attracting and holding children. Education of children on the street gets affected because they receive more positive reinforcement from street activities than from the school activities because the money they earn has a high positive value for the family. Pedagogies designed for these clients, which are nowadays widely agreed upon, calls for a thorough understanding of the child's emotional needs and socio-economic environment. Another factor that affects children is parental support: illiterate parents, being unaware of the importance and various possibilities of education, kept their children away from schools. Moreover, an educational ambiance and pro-educational environment would not be present at home for the children who were fortunate to be part of any social intervention.

For girl children on the streets of India, victimization is not only in the form of atrocities such as rape or incest. It is often subtle but nevertheless shackling which prevents her from attaining her full potential as an individual. Cultural practices and poverty ensure that the girl child drops out of school at a very young age. Girls form more than half of the illiterate children in the age group of 5–9 years and 65% in the 10–14 years age group. Nearly one-third of the number of girls who manage to enter formal education in Class I drop out by Class II. Lack of awareness of educational opportunities was present among guardians and children, especially among girl children. A majority of them began to show interest in educating themselves and towards 'dreaming big' once they got exposed to it. A follow-up study done in Delhi found that this trend was more among older girls who reside in shelter homes and are at constant engagements with similar social interventions (Dutta, 2018). The number of dropouts and stagnation cases in girls is nearly twice than that among boys. The dropout rates of rural girls are higher than urban girls. Along with this, the dropout rates of street girl children are more than that of non-street ones. The reason is not far to seek. Girls are expected to look after their siblings. Parents are also worried about the girls being sent to far away or co-educational schools after they attain puberty, even if the girls are eager to learn. One such case is narrated below:

> ***Case Study 4:*** *Rina Pawar was merely 13-years-old but her sights were set on goals that go beyond the narrow confines of her little village of Talegaon, Maharashtra. She studied up to the Vth Standard. Rina would have loved to continue education but her parents took her out of school. She now cooks and cleans at home and looks after her younger siblings. She said with stars in her eyes, 'I want to study much further, and I would like to take courses in knitting and sewing'. Will she be able to attain her goals is a question yet to be answered. (the girl child oblivion; nagpur-streeadhar Kendra).*

Nowadays, due to intervention programs undertaken by various NGOs for the welfare and rehabilitation of street children, a good number of them have got the opportunity to get basic education and they can at least write their names and read simple things in the local language. Appreciable efforts have been taken by several NGOs in providing access to education to these children but the outcomes were not as it were expected, for several reasons. As per the reports of a Kolkata based research, in-house informal education was provided to them by providing tutoring and home assignments, but once the children went out of the sight of the trainers/NGO volunteers, they acted irresponsibly. Absenteeism, below par involvement in studies, losing study materials such as free books, bags and stationery became a routine. It appeared that the easy availability of such amenities were taken for granted and so expected outcomes couldn't be produced (Dutta, 2018). Of course, streets would not provide a congenial environment for studies and added to this were the unavailability or inattention from the parents in providing assistance to the children in making use of the opportunity.

There are several such children as portrayed in those cases, who desire to go to school, even if they are on the streets of Kolkata and other cities of India. The society at large poses a barrier in some form and tries to keep these children in the dark. Eventually, '*for every darker side there is a brighter side*'. Various initiatives have tried to educate these children through NGOs, mobile schools, through educated and willing neighbourhoods and night schools. Skill training is another option which had dual effects: it would enhance the capacity and skills required for jobs of interest and also provide basic literacy skills. Boys were found to seek skill training while girls demanded for school training (Institute for Human Development, 2011). "Helping illiterate become aware of educational opportunities seems to be one of issues most in need of social interventions" (Dutta, 2018). Through smart usage of internet and awareness campus, this issue can be tackled and thereby a right spirit can be inculcated among the children on streets and their families.

1.7 Occupation of Street Children

The worldwide picture shows that the largest numbers of the child labourers are in Asia, 44.6 million; followed by Africa, 23.6 million and Latin America, 5.1 million. Estimates by country showed that even the developed European countries are not immune to this. Among 10–14-year old children, the working rate is 41.3% in Kenya, 31.4% in Senegal, 30.1% in Bangladesh, 25.8% in Nigeria, 24% in Turkey, 17.7% in Pakistan, 14.4% in India, 11.6% in China, 11.2% in Egypt, 6.7% in Mexico, 4.5% in Argentina, 1.8% in Portugal and 0.4% in Italy. This is only the tip of the iceberg. No reliable figures for workers under 10 years are available, though the numbers are significant. Over 73 million children aged 10–14 years were reported to be working according to a survey conducted by International Labor Organization. In the Indian context, the estimates on the magnitude of child labour falls short of the actual and factual figures for a number of reasons like multiplicity of definitions, different approaches of computation, diverse sources of data and lack of correct information. Still, Human Rights Watch, 1996 estimated that 60 and 115 million working children are in India, the highest number in the world. India is the largest example of a nation plagued by the problem of child workers (Walolkar, 2003).

For the healthy development of children's minimal facilities like adequate food, safe shelter, basic education and medical care, congenial environment and affection are the primary needs for survival. Unfortunately, street children are deprived of all these basic minimal facilities and, moreover, they have to struggle every day for earning their bread and butter. Parents of such children are found to see these streets as affordable places for their children to work towards the survival of the whole family. Hence, they encourage their children to support the family in their economic crisis. In some families, children were expected to start contributing to the family income once they were judged to be old enough. In many instances, child street workers and their families can be thought of as winners, losers and survivors. Street work cannot be evaluated every time in terms of a simplistic dichotomy of 'good' or 'bad' in terms of its effects on the children and their families. In cases where street life involvement brings positive benefits to the child and the family, these children can be regarded as winners. For some children, participation in street life brings negative results. This may be due to environmental factors (a child gets knocked down in a traffic accident) or personal characteristics of the child (he/she does not have the cognitive or social skills for the demands of the street work or are unable to restrain them from being abused). Many children are unable to develop a street sense due to their ability to deal with the demands of the busy street environment, particularly the traffic, is not adequate.

A Delhi-based survey report observed the children to be working for six days a week for around six and a half hours per day on an average. Over 87% of these children (Boys—88% and girls—81%) were involved in some works that would give them money for survival. Further, almost half of their income was usually given to either their parents or supervisor/gang leader or unfortunately, the police. The survey assessed their average monthly income to be Rs. 2240 (Institute for Human Development, 2011). A study conducted in five prominent cities excluding Delhi found that these children who, on an average work for 10 h a day earns only up to Rs. 500. (Save the Children, 2012). Findings of a Surat-based study left an elaborate and clear picture of the situation. About four-fifth (79.8%) of children start as beggars to soon swap into other occupations based on their age, capital, interest, physical conditions and available opportunities. Assisting in eat-outs and tea stalls, begging, sweeping, hawking newspapers and magazines, shoe polishing, selling water bottles and soft drinks and rag picking were reported to be the prominent occupation options. Prostitution by girl children and illicit alcohol transport by older boys were the lucrative activities (Abraham, 2015; Patel, Desai, & Bansal, 2011).

The earlier they start working the better is attitude these children and sometimes their families have, in order to face the extreme economic hardships. Hence, they get involved in more than one job and work the whole day. They seek guidance from the peers and elder gang leaders and take up any job like begging, rag picking, massage work, loading and unloading, helping in hotels and workshops, etc. Children were involved in more than one activity like rag picking, begging and hawking varied things along the road. These were found to be the most prominent primary activities for earning income (Save the Children, 2012). These were seasonal or temporary daily-wage jobs of unpredictable nature. They lived a life which lacked discipline and order. They remain unequipped and untrained for any skill related job. They would not prepare any routine or discipline and would continue living an anarchic life. Their behaviours and languages are often rough. Duties and responsibilities would suffocate them. They would target making huge money within short periods of time and would not favour the idea of saving the money for future use. The street seemed better to them. Involvement of street girl children as maidservants to supplement the family income is a common practice among the migrant population in developing countries, especially in the SAARC region. India is not an exception to that. Domestic work is one of the largest categories of child labour in the world and is often equivalent to slavery. We continue to know very little about this most hidden and marginalized group of female workers.

The children, who work on the streets and are 12 years old or under and are working for economic reasons, often earn near to the minimum legal wage. They belong to families with many children living in overcrowded conditions. The children generally work on weekends, during summer vacations and at any time of the day as the need arises. They start working early in the morning and may continue until late in the evening. The children experience difficulties due to the kind of work they perform, the weather, the police and the municipal people. The majority of them have been taken to a municipal police station at least once. The children quarrel with their friends over stealing clients, swearing at and making fun of each other. They get angry with, or may be frightened by, other street children, adult street workers, clients, gangs and pickpockets. Children who begin to work from a young age also get exhausted at a very young in their lives. The exhaustion would harm all realms of their lives and they would look for other sources of money-making even when employment is available "Born to parents who themselves were uneducated child workers, many child workers are forced to continue a tradition that leaves them chained to a life of poverty" (ILO, United States Policies to Address Child Labor Globally 2010); and thus the vicious cycle restarts when they want their children to work instead of them.

No amount of legislation is enough to solve the problems of the street children, nor can any amount of NGO intervention programs make a significant dent on the mountain of problems of the street children. Nothing short of a collaborative movement between the Government and NGOs can root out the most heinous surge of modern civilization—the phenomenon of street children. The sight of the ill-clad starving street children may give you an opportunity to indulge in the Wordsworthian poetic sensibility to say in a pseudo-tragic tone: 'see what man has made of man; inhumanity oozing out of humanity' or an opportunity of political oratory in the Churchillian fashion: 'O! Never before in human history has so many been exploited so much by so far for so long.' The spirit of the suffering of street children pricks our conscience and nags us with a queer sense of uneasiness and with a 'smart' crow-like closing of the eyes, we hide the sight from our conscience and move away from the scene, conveniently rationalizing that it is someone else's job to set right what has gone wrong with our society. Modern man lives in his cocoon of 'enlightened self-interest with a dead conscience.' The world is not as it could have been made, but it is as it is, not because of the reckless 'action' of the rascals and criminals but because of the 'inaction' of the generally good people like any one of us. The failure of the good people to make their mite of contribution towards the world as it could have been made has turned them into criminals by default. The resurrection of the modern man from the grave of dead conscience alone can bring into existence a 'people's movement' fueled by passion to clean the society of all crimes, the worst being the phenomenon of street children.

1.8 Abuse/Maltreatment of Street Children

Child abuse and neglect is a worldwide social problem that can exert a multitude of short- and long-term repercussions on the children (Saini, 2013). Statistics says children on streets are highly subjected to all forms of abuse and maltreatment since most of them do not have any guardian and/or safe shelter. They are constantly being intimidated and threatened by adults, taking advantage of their helplessness (Sharmila & Kaur, 2014). According to some of the street children,

> "*Neglect is a common phenomenon since nobody is there to take care of street children and arrange their food*" – a female child

> "*Elderly people sometimes attempt to sexually abuse us. Some of our friends experienced the same several times*" – a male child

> "*Some of us work in tea stalls and or in street side small hotels. Sometimes, other than food, they do not give us any money although they agreed to give some money at the end of the month. However, since we get a place to sleep and eat, we do not ask for the money*" – a male child

People of the larger society, especially antisocials, small and petty businessman and even educated people, takes full advantage of their helplessness. The society has a negative attitude towards them. Insensitivity towards the security and rights, the law and order of the country are hesitant to take any action to better the situation: the overburdened police department is found to be treating these children as problematic. In fact, little sympathy of the general population towards street children could be of great help for them to lead a reasonably better life and to get merged into the mainstream of the society. To understand the effects of violence on children, it is important to carry out multi-disciplinary researches to understand the issue holistically.

Children on the streets are constantly subjected to physical abuses by the family members, policemen and other adults. A study revealed that the overall incidence of physical abuse to which these children were subjected on the streets were nearly 70%, while that reported on sexual abuse was 55% (Ministry of Women and Child Development, 2007). Sexual assaults (6.53%), forcefully making the child touch one's private body parts (17.73%), exhibitionism (15.10%), being photographed in nude postures (5.39%), kissing the child forcefully (21.99%), sexual exploitation during vulnerable situations such as travel (26.16%) and exposing children to pornographic materials (31.06%) were the commonly encountered forms of abuse in the study. Another study based in Jaipur also reported that 62% children on the streets reported the experience of moderate degree of abuse, while 36.6% reported being subjected to severe and very severe abuse (Mathur, Rathore, & Mathur, 2009). *"My sister's husband wanted to massage my body part every night" reported a girl living with a caregiver in Jaipur* (Save the Children, 2015). In general, girl children are born in India into an inhospitable environment. Discrimination starts right from birth in case of girl children. Child rape and incest are increasingly being perpetrated on the girl child with the law not adequately protecting her. The following case is that of a girl child living on a railway platform:

> ***Case Study 5:*** *Bharati stayed on the platforms of New Delhi railways stations for years now. She remembered; it was nine years old when a gang of homeless boys raped her for the first time. Homeless and helpless, she was subjected to rapes and assault several times after that, she became pregnant and delivered a stillborn child on the platform. The 14-year-old has been detected with tuberculosis as well as HIV AIDs. She is found not be persistent with the medication. Bharati collected used plastic water bottles and glasses for a living. She made*

about 60 rupees daily (36 rupees to a dollar) from the sales, enough to feed her and pay for her treatment.

Several NGOs and activists who work for these children commented about the extreme vulnerability of girls towards getting raped and abducted for prostitution. Rape is being used as a weapon to threaten them. Sometimes, these girls are asked to repay through returns involving compliance to the sexual needs of the powerful. Sexual abuse is, however, not limited to just girls on the streets. Along with them, the boys are also subjected to rape and sexual exploitation and there have been instances of boys getting beaten up if they refused. A report states that more than intravenous drug use, which is another daily habit of the street children they are more at risk from unprotected sex.

Indian street children are routinely detained illegally, beaten and tortured and sometimes killed and are viewed as vagrants and criminals by the police. While the extent of juvenile crime is unknown, however, along with their tendency to get involved in crime, other factors like the perception and attitude of police towards these children, issues like corruption, non-implemented legal safeguards and heightened insensitivity of the personnel of law and order, further intensifies these issues. In a study based on children on the streets of Varanasi, children reported police (25.5%) as the most important perpetrators on the street (Srivastava & Shareef, 2016). The verbatim that follows is by a girl living near Bainsgodam flyover, Jaipur (India)—"*many a times, the policemen on night vigil come to us and engage us in sexual acts. When we hesitate, we are beaten black and blue*" (Save the Children, 2015). Ever-increasing number of children on streets, the perceived criminal profiling given to these children and lawlessness of the keepers of the law would all club together to result in police abuse of these children.

UNICEF (2004) found the interference by the police to be the most pervasive form of abuse faced by street children. Children are beaten up badly and are forced to obey the police. Girls have reported to be raped by some police; they take money from the children, accuse the children of any unresolved crime and torture them. The police apparently take the attitude that any child or youth on the street is automatically a delinquent and in their efforts to protect the material belongings of the sections of society, which possess them, they take the children into custody. Several factors were found to be adding up to cause this phenomenon, like, "police perceptions of street children, widespread corruption and a culture of police violence, the inadequacy and non-implementation of legal safeguards and the level of impunity that law enforcement officials enjoy"(Ministry of Women and Child Development, 2007). While it is true that street children are sometimes involved in petty theft, drug-trafficking, prostitution and other criminal activities, the police tend to assume that whenever a crime is committed on the street, street children are either involved themselves or they know the culprit. Their proximity to a crime is considered reason enough to detain them. This abuse violates both the Indian domestic law and international human rights standards. Following is the report of a study, which, was conducted, on police personnel in Delhi in 1992 (Human Rights Watch). The police would accuse the children for some of the unresolved petty cases such as stealing, and they would be asked to pay these policemen to be saved from the case. Scapegoating is an often observed phenomenon when these policemen resort to financial incentives. The most common complaint of street children without families is about the money police claim from them, they were beaten up on the street for money. They are forced to bribing the police in fear of being taken to the jail. The threat of severe punishment at the police station would make them pay the police rather than suffering the aftereffects.

Case Study 6: *Five police officials, one at Connaught Place and four at New Delhi railway station, were interviewed to find out their perception of these children and their experiences in dealing with them. The police invariably were quite critical about these children-except for one officer, who was quite sympathetic. According to the three police officers at the railway station and one at Connaught Place, these children were anti-social elements. They perceive them as thieves, rogues and drug addicts who have to be remanded in institutions and disciplined. They feel there might be only 2–3% who are 'honest' and are at the station and the streets to earn a living.*

Violence is a recurrent event in the daily life of most street children and is caused by misery of an extreme order at their former home. From the recent increasing crime scenario in India, it has been observed that most of the crimes are committed by those youths who are neglected, abused and deprived of their basic rights in their formative years of life. Street children, being fragile, ignorant and poor are easy targets to violence. Absence of a strong parental figure for defense would further ease the process in no time. They are very unlikely to lodge any complaints despite severe abuse and threatening. Therefore, they are very easily used by criminals, drug distributors, traffickers and pimps. There is also evidence which says that these children fall prey to the threat of a little older child, as in, an adolescent who is treated as the gang leader. Not only is the situation prevalent in New Delhi station but also innumerable cases are available worldwide. The frequent intervention of the local *dada* or gang leaders who bully the working child and often ask for a share in their earnings is a regular disturbance on the street. In one study conducted among African street children in Rwanda, it was found that mostly, they were adolescent boys, almost half of whom were homeless (42%), with a high proportion of orphaned children or children who had lost at least one parent. Two variables predicted homelessness: child's guardian and reason for being on the street. Qualitative accounts of children conveyed the impact of death of family members, repatriation, imprisonment of parents and poverty of their lives. The analysis highlighted the need for community-based support for children in alternative guardianship care and for policies to support the re-integration of male youths as prevention strategies for street migration (Source: Veale and Dona, 2003). Thilagaraj and Priyamvadha (2000) observed that "street children are used as the instruments of professional conmen to evade police and vigilance in a state." These children are increasingly being used in different ways to meet the interest of the rich, who are involved in organized crimes. They are easily manipulated and trained to tactically commit several crimes. These pavement dwellers directly or indirectly are exposed to drug peddling, vandalism, robbery, murder, sexual commitment, petty theft, addiction, delinquency, bullying, fighting, etc. Extensive literature review indicates that no such local study has so far been reported and published revealing street children's creative potentiality, cognitive ability and personality characteristics. Hence, there is a need to carry out studies on this issue for developing need-based rehabilitation program for the street children.

1.9 Community Perception About Street Children

The painful fact remains that the law lashes the child often but seldom comes to his/her rescue. The Indian mindset strongly believes that any child not living with the family is a potential criminal, a threat to the society. So, keep them in a home or institution or someplace where they can never be seen. The Delhi Corporation passed an order that no child should be seen begging at traffic signals because it is an insult to the city. This is the condition of the street destitute. These children are perceived as criminals and thieves by the community, thereby creating a hostile, stigmatizing and criminalizing climate when it comes to the street children, which get transferred to the whole society (Scheper, 2006). The all India scenario also shows that the place for street dwellers is like that of prisoners, where they are treated as '*incorrigible criminals*', and remain the recipient of some charity. It is found that most street children have more than one instance of mindless police atrocity against them, so much so that they perceive police as their biggest danger. Some of the stories of police atrocities against them are truly heart-rending.

> We do get some job or the other, but we are needed just for that job, but otherwise we are treated as garbage by the people—says a 16 years old boy on Hasanpura street, Jaipur (India). (Save the Children, 2015)

In our country, several Children's meet are held regularly to make the society aware of their protection and safety. One such 'Girl Child Week' campaigning was organized in New Delhi, during September 18–24, 2001 by *Global Movement for Children,* (GMC) who stated that like adults, children also want to express their feelings but no one listens them. They came out with a slogan of '*Say yes to Children*'. The unwelcoming attitude of the general public and the authorities shows their own inadequacy and failure (Tipple & Speak, 2004) and hence it is important to re-shape the perception of the community towards these homeless people to successfully frame any intervention strategies.

1.10 Role of Media

Media can take an active role to sensitize the larger society about the problems of disadvantaged children in general and street children in particular which will in turn help in developing a sympathetic attitude towards street children. Public awareness about the living conditions of these underprivileged children living on streets can bring an attitude change in the perception of the society towards these children. Similarly, parents can also be sensitized on the importance of child care and protection, proper parenting and monitoring. Children's active participation and skills as well as their rights should be appreciated and acknowledged as an important factor in the society, so that they must be treated with care. Media has a very crucial role to play in this regard. "Beyond rationalization of existing laws, the main challenges in India remains their enforcement and the fact that there is a certain degree of impunity for those violating the law" (Seth, 2013). Responsible and sensitive media can reach even the rural part of the country and provide information about the existing legislative measures in the country with the help of which issues related to these underprivileged children can be tackled. Cases/issues that need immediate attention can be brought to the notice of the government and the public through media coverage. Media can also create platforms for active discussions and negotiations on such issues which would improve public awareness along with creating new ideas from sensitive citizens. They can also encourage childless parents to adopt these children, which is an alternative approach to rehabilitate the street children.

1.11 Prevention, Intervention and Rehabilitation of Street Children

1.11.1 Prevention

Primary prevention should be the target in terms of being watchful about the number on the streets. The following steps could be adopted:

- The rapid growth of street children in almost all cities is the result of rapid urbanization through migration. Hence, migration should be checked by arranging basic amenities and employment opportunities in the rural areas.
- Poverty is one of the main causes behind a large number of children coming to the city for finding the means of life. In the rural areas, awareness should be generated about the sources of financial support from the banks for cultivation, income-generating activities and/or for small businesses.
- In some families, the parent-child relationship is not healthy. As a result, a good number of children leave home on account of differences of opinion with the parents. Hence, it is important to launch intervention programs in the rural areas to create awareness about child-rearing practices and the importance of cordial parent-child relationships. In the urban areas, NGOs should identify run away children and reintegrate them with the family.

A conceptual model (Model 1.2) for the prevention of the increasing number of street children is provided below for the NGO activists, international organizations and other government officials involved in child protection program and child safety.

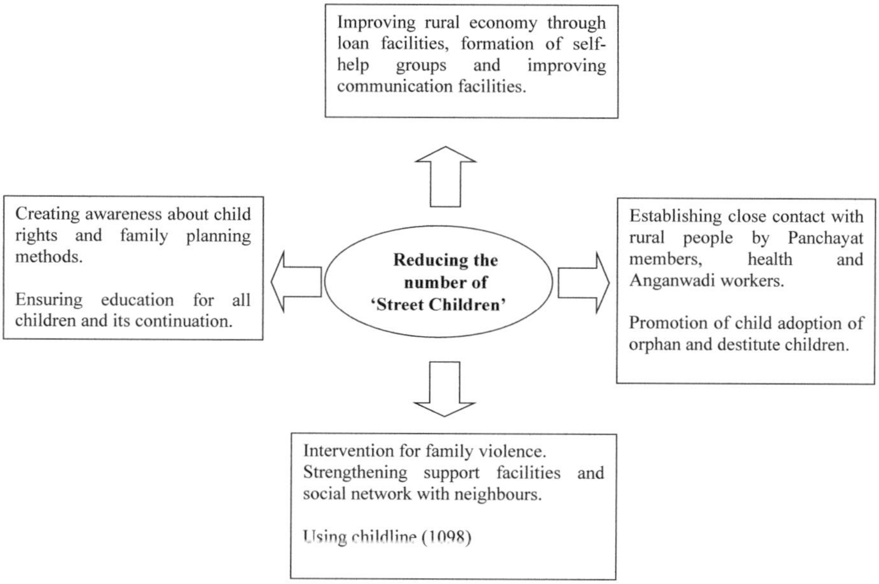

Model 1.2 Prevention of increasing number of street children

1.11.2 Intervention

For the normal and healthy mental and physical development of children, basic amenities like adequate nutrition, safe shelter, health care facilities and education should be provided. In case of street children, more and more NGOs should come forward and provide these facilities.

Non-formal Education

Basic and/or minimum literacy is needed for each and every child for leading a better and well-adjusted life. In general, street children do not give importance to education owing to the lack of guidance and exposure. Hence, some provisions of non-formal education for the street children should be arranged in the form of evening or holiday schools for which infrastructure of the Government schools could be utilized with due permission from the authorities of those schools. With the involvement of local self-government and other senior community members, non-formal education can be run in the government schools on an ongoing basis (Seth, 2013).

In this regard, the Ministry of Human Resource Development, Government of India launched the non-formal education scheme for the children in streets which were partially successful in the rural areas. In the urban areas, it did not get much success owing to the lack of infrastructure. NGOs should launch this program through partnerships approach with the Government and Private schools in the urban areas.

For imparting effective non-formal education to children on the streets, services of retired teachers and/or educated people and youths could be utilized. In fact, it would be more beneficial for the NGOs as well as for the needy children. Likewise, a lot of public and private spaces remain vacant/unutilized, which can be utilized for a good cause. For this purpose, NGOs should take initiatives to explore all these resources and utilize them properly. Sometimes, people used to say that shortage of fund is the main barrier to initiate welfare activities. It is not always correct. NGOs should be innovative enough to generate resources and utilize underutilized resources for the welfare of disadvantaged children.

Vocational Training

It is important to mention that in case of street children, emphasis should be given more on vocational training as per the aptitude of the children so that they can find the means of life and lead a better life. There is one problem though. Since these children are occupied in different activities, which are essential for their survival, they can neither afford time nor money for such training. Hence, the Government should introduce a special vocational training program for the street children and it should be arranged in such a way that these children can continue their present economic activities, if it is not a deviant social activity. The street children who are working in automobile or two-wheeler repair shops, electrical shops, tailoring shops, etc., can be given training in their respective trades to develop specialized skills. The children who work as rag pickers or do odd jobs with no skills can select a suitable vocation after ascertaining their aptitude.

For the welfare and rehabilitation of street children, a number of NGOs are working in different parts of the country and some of them are working effectively while majority of them lack proper planning and do not know how to implement the program. They also lack basic knowledge and expertise about monitoring and documentation. As a result, it is very difficult to understand the efficacy of the program.

Special Arrangements and Night Shelter for the Children on Streets Especially for the Girl Children

Children on the streets are subjected to all forms of abuse and maltreatment in everyday life. Besides other harassments, girl children are more prone to sexual abuse. Hence, a safe night shelter is urgently needed for these children, especially girl children, to protect them from antisocials and pimps.

This apart, an arrangement for keeping the belongings of children is required. So, night shelters should have the same arrangements.

Lack of adequate clothing is another problem faced by these children. In order to solve this problem, NGOs should take initiative to collect used and old cloths from the high and middle-class families and distribute the same to the children.

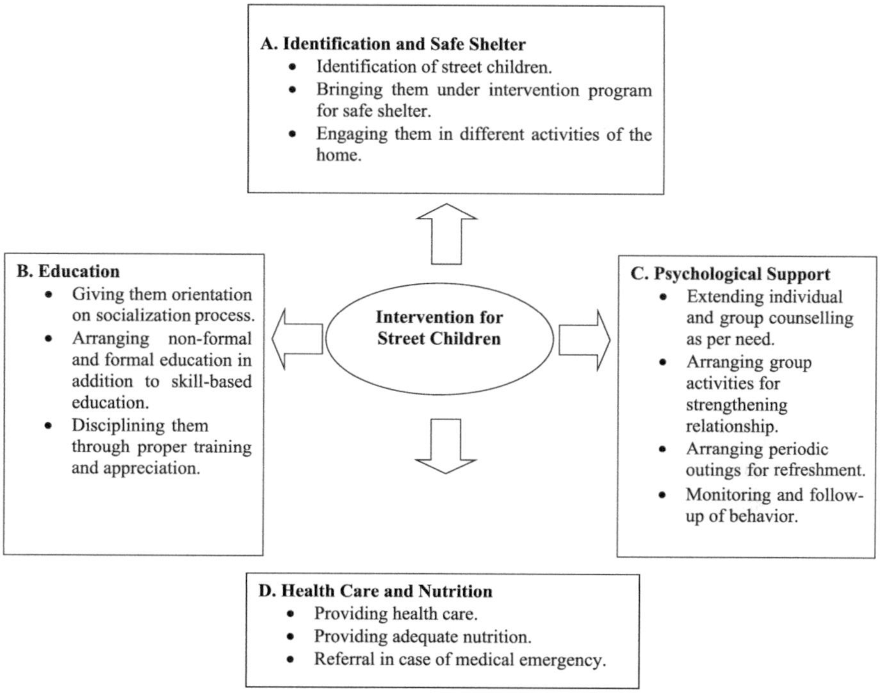

Model 1.3 A conceptual model for intervention

Resource Generation and Referral

For taking up different programs for the children on the streets, resources are required. Besides resources of government and international funding agencies, NGOs should initiate dialogue with private agencies like industrialists, business houses and trust bodies to motivate them for funding various programs for these children.

In case of a special child with some challenges, he/she may be referred to another NGO working with similar children. Therefore, every NGO and social welfare department should have a list of all NGOs working with children.

Apart from financial resources, students and teachers should be motivated to take up social work programs both individually and collectively for street and working children like organizing literacy camps, recreational meets and cultural programs in collaboration with voluntary organizations (Model 1.3).

1.11.3 Rehabilitation of Street Children

The plight of disadvantaged children is such that, efforts to rehabilitate them are extremely challenging. They have no education or job skills, are subjected to all forms of abuse, neglect and maltreatment (Seth, Kotwal, & Ganguly, 2005). Hence rehabilitation should be multi-dimensional. Provision for their basic demands should be laid down through programs such as mid-day meals; basic hygiene and sanitation facilities; non-formal education and vocational courses; nutritional screening and free medical care, vaccinations, health education and monitoring; counselling services to address substance abuse, HIV/AIDS and other psychological disturbances (Seth, 2013). Child protection responsibility is an enormous one and can be effectively broken down and assigned to the proximate community and governments. Enlightening parents on effective parenting is the most effective of all, but in the case of children on streets, this measure wouldn't be as effective as it is expected to be. Hence, for those children who are not practically present and sensible about such issues, the nearby community and the elected representatives at the village panchayats as well as senior community members should take up the responsibility. They should ensure that every child is getting educated, receives basic health care and is protected from child abuse and neglect (Srivastava, 2008). Now, there is a general feeling among people of all works of life that children on streets should be helped and rescued. They should be provided with proper food, clothing and safe shelter in the form of an orphanage. For giving shelter to these neglected and abused children, and to take care of their basic needs, a lot of national and international funding agencies have come forward with their commitments. Side by side, local NGOs are also working for the rehabilitation of these children. Taking into account the large number of children who are in need of these services, the great work done by these NGOs are showing only marginal impact. Nevertheless, their efforts have made huge differences in the lives of children to whom they have reached.

In the recent decade, problems of disadvantaged children, especially street children drew the attention of academicians and researchers. A number of studies on different dimensions of street children, especially for rehabilitation of the street children, have been carried out in India by the researchers. In this regard, in a follow-up study, Deb et al. (1997) found that supportive counseling and continuous efforts brought some positive change in the outlook of street children, resulting in moderate improvement in interpersonal relationships and some interest in vocational training. The findings of that study suggest the detachment of street children from pathogenic parental influence during rehabilitation. It has also been observed that street children have developed a daredevil attitude towards the society because of prolonged deprivation (Deb, 1996a). In another action research study, Deb (1996b) observed that 7 out of 10 street children were successfully institutionalized and they pursued their studies satisfactorily while the remaining three children were unable to settle down to institutions and became dropouts due to certain personal and environmental factors like unfavourable parental influences, pathological and deviant behaviour of either of the parents, low intelligence, organic impairment and uncongenial living environment.

Findings of a study suggest that for merging street children into the mainstream of the society, they should be oriented with the socialization process first. For bringing positive changes in street children's behaviour, encouragement towards their performance and introduction of reward system should be initiated. For facilitation of

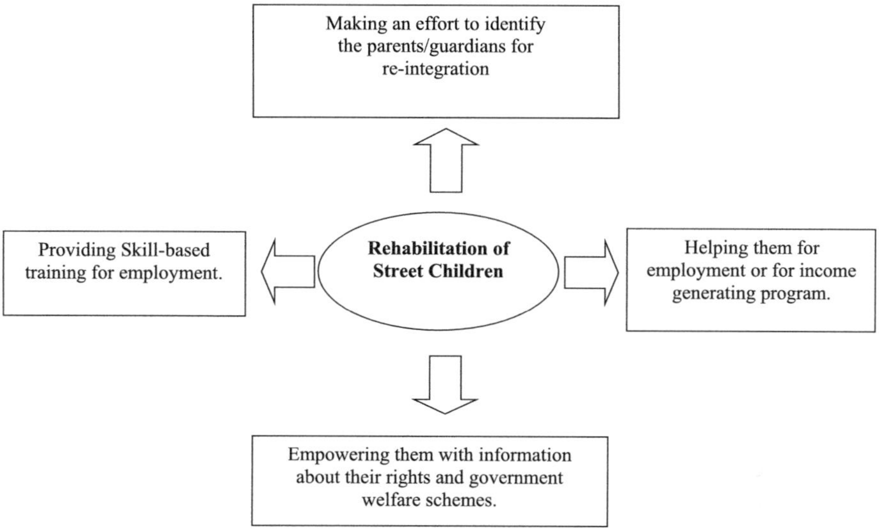

Model 1.4 A conceptual model for rehabilitation of street children

the rehabilitation process, cooperation of guardians, if available is urgently needed. The Welfare Agency should hold periodic meetings with the guardians to make them understand about their important role in motivating children towards studies. Feedback about children's performance and conduct should be given to the respective guardian. Linkages should be established with the guardian who does not visit the child at all. Authorities of welfare organizations should initiate dialogue with the authorities of residential schools for facilitating the admission of these children (Deb & Mitra, 2002). A conceptual model for rehabilitation of street children is provided in Model 1.4.

1.12 Strengths of Street Children

How do these children at disadvantage survive through their plight on the streets every day of their lives? The strengths of street children are many, which usually go unappreciated. The simple fact that they manage to adapt to the unimaginable extremities and odds of the street life, falling victim to harsh realities of their day-to-day experiences and coming out of them with the spirit of overcoming. Their resilience capacity and coping skills are commendable, and are undoubtedly, the fuel for thriving more. However, most of the times, their strengths go unnoticed and is more preferred to be seen as vulnerable who is waiting for the mercy from privileged session of the society. The understandings drawn from a few focus group interviews on street children in South Africa transforms this understanding to a great degree; street children were found to 'negotiate resilient trajectories' which is enhanced by their strong peer group support and religiosity (Malindi & Theron, 2010). A study among homeless youth to understand their resilience capacity highlights their reliance on "informal social networks for survival"; apart from this, a good association between spirituality, mental health and creativity with their coping skills was also observed among this population (Cronley & Evans, 2019). These children are actively involved in the learning process which helps in the development of their problem solving and decision-making skills; their group dynamics are found to be their strength on which they keep them going. Following is a case study highlighting the positive adaption of street children

Case Study 7: *Sumanth, a 7 years old boy, who lived on the streets of Mumbai could be found busy in rag picking during the day. He had to undergo various harsh moments including poverty, abuse and violence and several other challenges of street life. However, he spent his later evenings and nights with his peer group, by enjoying the moments with his friends in their own ways, and sharing the food and sleeping space amongst each other. The feeling of belongingness that he had received from his peer group was his biggest strength and had enhanced his coping patterns.*

As can be understood, the peer group is, in fact, the supporting environment the children have upon which they learn to survive the odd circumstances in a more adaptive and creative manner in line with the demand of the situation.

1.12.1 Community Support for Street Children

Overall street children are subjected to negativity and avoidance by the general public. However, there are also reported instances where communities/institutions have been inclusive and responsible towards these children at disadvantage. The first author was involved in a six-year-long action research conducted among the street children of Kolkata living in and around Sealdah Railway Station during 1990–1996. The project was funded by Save the Children, UK.

An NGO called 'CINI-Child in Need Institute' located in Kolkata addressed the basic needs of street children living in and around Sealdah Railway Station. This NGO could arrange a room in the railway station with the permission of railway authority for providing services to the street children. First, they identified some elder street children and established good rapport with them. These children were used to identify and bring other street children living in and around the Sealdah Railway station to the centre. Second, their needs were assessed through qualitative data collection approach and came out with a need-based program for their welfare. Third, some indoor games were arranged for attracting the children. Fourth, when children were coming to the centre, non-formal education was introduced to them. In addition, these children were served food, provided the provision to bath and wash clothes as well as a locker to keep their belongingness and money safe. Slowly they were also trained in basic literacy and numeracy, did proper disciplining, brought order to their daily living activities and trained them in socialization skills. The children who showed interest in getting educated was shifted to a halfway home, from where they were enrolled into formal schooling system. Except for a limited case, all the children who were involved in this intervention showed significant improvement in their knowledge and understanding as well as attitude towards Life. This is one good example to show how minimum care and attention could alter lives of disadvantaged children for betterment.

At the same time, support from educational institution was found to be instrumental in improving the quality of life of street children in Kolkata. For example, Sister Cyril—the Principal of Sealdah Loreto School opened her school door for street children. Any time these children could come inside the school and go out. She engaged the students of Loreto School on rotation basis as part of their extra-curricular activities to teach basic lessons to the children and address their other issues. In addition, street children were provided medical care and allowed to make use of the facilities offered at the school such as their washrooms to take shower and wash their clothes. An example of such dignity and class, nothing more could be quoted here, to prove the unparallel contribution a community can do towards the betterment of these children at disadvantage. The same concept may be replicated elsewhere to address the basic needs of disadvantaged children giving them a hope of new life.

1.13 Socio and Legal Measures for Welfare of Disadvantaged Children

"The right of the child to freedom from all forms of violence" is the demand of the United Nations Convention on the Rights of the Child (2011) in its General Comment No 13 (GC13):a paradigm shift was encouraged through a right-based approach by "securing child's right to survival, dignity, well-being, health and development, as well as participation and non-discrimination"(National Disaster Management Authority, 2014). Accordingly, various legislative, administrative, social and educational measures were taken by the Government of India in order to protect these innocent children. The Juvenile Justice Act 2000 (amended in 2006), Prohibition of Child Marriage Act (2006), constitution of National Commission for Protection of Child Rights (2005), National Plan of Action for Children (2005), the Goa Children Act (2005), The Child Labor Act (1986, 2006 and 2008), Integrated Child Protection Scheme (2009), Right to Education Bill (2009) and Prevention of Children from Sexual Offences (POCSO Act 2012) are the various governmental interventions (Ministry of Women and Child Development, 2013). The wide gap between the implementation and enforcement is a matter that requires heightened attention.

1.13.1 Integrated Child Protection Scheme (ICPS) Under the Ministry of Women and Child Development, Government of India

For the welfare and rehabilitation of street children, there was a scheme in India titled "An Integrated Program for Street Children" prior to 2009–10 under the Ministry of Women and Child Development. The same ministry has come out with another scheme called the "Integrated Child Protection Scheme (ICPS)" into which, the earlier scheme that is "An Integrated Program for Street Children" has been merged. ICPS has been introduced in 2009–10 with an objective to provide safe and secure environment for the overall development of children who are in need of care and protection and children in conflict with the law. ICPS also emphasizes on establishment and maintenance of Children's Homes, Open Shelters in urban and semi-urban areas and Specialized Adoption Agencies (SAAs) for children in need of care and protection including destitute/orphan/street children.

There is a need to monitor the implementation of the scheme in reality across the states and Union Territories in India as well as evaluation of the schemes to ascertain effectiveness of the program and its shortcoming, if any, for taking correctives measures. Without monitoring and evaluation, it is very difficult to comment on its quality of implementation.

1.13.2 The Juvenile Justice (Care and Protection of Children) Act, 2015 (JJ Act, 2015)

This latest revised legislation (JJ Act, 2015) is a very comprehensive law taking care of all possible legal and social measures for two broad categories of children. These include children in need of care and children in conflict with the law. It is the obligation of the state government to implement the law in the truest sense for the best interest of all children. In the beginning of the law, the general principle of care and protection of children are clearly outlined. They include the principle of presumption of innocence (i.e. children are innocent and they may not commit any crime with a motive), principle of dignity and worth (i.e. children deserve equal dignity and rights like elders), principle of best interest (i.e. all decision concerning a child should be taken keeping the best interests of a child), principle of family responsibility, safety, positive measures, equality and non-discrimination, natural justice and so on. In other words, it might be stated that children should enjoy all rights as enjoyed by the elders.

As per the law, every state should constitute one or more Juvenile Justice Board for each district to address the issue of children in conflict with the law. Similarly, at least one Child Welfare Committee should be formed for each district of a state to look into the care and protection issue of the children in need. The members of the said committee should be sensitized about the issues related to children so that they can discharge their duties sensitively for the best interest of the children.

The law clearly elaborated about the procedure in relation to children in need of care and protection in Chapter VI of the JJ Act 2015. Therefore, NGOs working with disadvantaged children can use the same provision for sending street children in the government-run observation homes or homes recognized by the government for safety and other basic needs of the children like nutrition, medical care, formal and vocational training. In turn, a child in need of care will get all the basic facilities for his/her normal growth and development including skills for leading an independent life with dignity and self-respect. However, it is very important to ensure basic facilities in the observation homes as outlined in the law and its effective implementation.

The same law has a provision for mandatory reporting regarding a child found separated from the guardian. This provision of law is highly applicable for street children especially who live on the street by themselves. Although this is a good provision, it does not benefit much in reporting such cases since a good number of people who are mandated by the law are either not aware of this provision or they are reluctant to report such incidents because of perceived harassment that gets accompanied for this purpose. There is an urgent need to create awareness about the issue of mandatory reporting of neglected children, especially among police personnel, nursing or hospital staff or staff of maternity homes so that they pass on the information to the Childline or Police or Child Welfare Committee or to the District Child Protection Unit for child safety and welfare. The law also clearly mentioned the penalty for non-reporting of such cases (section 34). At the same time, sensitization program for the concerned social agents and penalty provisions should be communicated to them.

The law further specified the provision for rehabilitation and social re-integration of children in need and care under Chapter VII. Section 39 talks about the process of rehabilitation and social re-integration that is children in conflict with the law and/or in need of care will be placed in the government-run observation homes while section 43 mentioned about Open Shelter in every state for children in need and care. In particular, the Open Shelter "shall function as a community-based facility for children in need of residential support, on short-term basis, with the objective of protecting them from abuse or weaning them, or keeping them, away from a life on the streets." There is a need for close observation of the functioning of open shelters to ensure it does not become a place for further victimization.

Likewise, Foster Care concept (section 44) and child adoption (section 56) as mentioned in the JJ Act 2015 may be promoted for giving a home to a homeless child and a child to a family without children. It is very important to see that the family or a couple is capable to take care of a street or orphan child for his/her best interest in terms of career growth and development.

Disadvantaged children living on streets, slums and other backward areas often experience corporal punishment with or without reasons. For prevention of corporal punishments, appropriate measures have been prescribed in the JJ Act 2015.

Overall the JJ Act 2015 is well-designed for the best interests of the children in need and care and now it is the job of the respective state governments to implement it effectively. The effective implementation depends upon sensitivity of the concerned Social Welfare Minister, Secretary of Social Welfare Department and/or Director of Social Welfare. If all the concerned people are serious about the issue, it is possible to ensure safety, care and protection for all children, especially disadvantaged children. Seriousness about the issue on the part of policymakers and administrators will make others to take up the issue seriously, especially those who are working in the field and finally, disadvantaged children will enjoy better quality of life to act as a responsible citizen in the future.

1.14 Steps for Effective Implementation of Intervention Programs

The following steps are suggested for effective implementation of intervention programs for the disadvantaged children in general and street children in particular on the basis of the author's first-hand field and research experience:

- Identification of disadvantaged and/or street children.
- Listening to their problems, basic requirements/needs and trying to contact with the family members for re-integration.
- Thorough medical examination should be done and extending medical services, if required.
- Extending individual and group counseling for establishing trust-building relationship and to develop fellow feeling and improve group cohesiveness.
- Extending family counseling, if parents or either of the parents are available and seek their cooperation for future career of the child.
- Providing non-formal education to the disadvantaged/street children to make them familiar with the socialization process.
- Providing formal education at least up to primary level and more in case of better performance.
- Ascertaining the aptitude and interest of the disadvantaged/street children for providing need-based and potential vocational training.
- Follow-up and monitoring of performance and movement of these children as they are likely to be involved in deviant activities again under the influence of peer group members and may run away from home and/or residential school.
- Organizing outings and cultural programs for the children for recreation and to develop a positive feeling about life.
- Giving feedback to the children periodically about their performance, which will motivate them to perform better.
- Reward system should be introduced to reinforce their motivation and active involvement of the children in various activities of an intervention program.

- Precautions should be taken while selecting staff/personnel for dealing with disadvantaged/street children. Efforts should be made to select personnel with child-friendly attitude and preferably female candidates with motivation and interest in this work. Otherwise, despite all other proper arrangements, one may not get the better and/or expected results from the program.
- Monitoring of performance of staff/counsellors who directly deal with the children and to take appropriate measures. In this regard, it is important to speak to the beneficiary children to gauge their perception about the behaviour of the service providers/counsellors/trainers.
- Developing coordination and partnership with other similar agencies/NGOs for sharing of resources and for working together so that basic needs of the children are addressed. One organization may not have all the facilities. So, coordination and partnership with other similar agencies/NGOs will help to fill up the gaps.
- Periodic evaluation of intervention program for effective implementation of the same by an outside agency. Evaluation does not necessarily mean to criticize the designer of the program and/or to find out the faults of a program. Rather, it helps to understand the shortcomings in service delivery, if any and thereby helps in taking course corrective measures.
- Attending and sharing the learning experience, whether positive or negative, in seminars/workshops/conferences so that others can learn from that experience and replicate the positive results, if necessary.
- Dissemination of information and/or outcome of an intervention program through publication of papers in the journals and in periodicals for wider coverage of audiences.

1.15 Conclusion and Implications

The increasing number of street children across all the cities has become a big challenge for the policymakers in India. It is important to prevent the problem by adopting multiple strategies and they include family-based intervention in the rural areas for improving the economic condition and ensuring harmony in the family, improving rural economy for prevention of rural migration and creating awareness about family planning methods. More and more NGOs should come forward to ensure safe shelter for street children in addition to taking up various activities for their healthy growth and development. Towards this end, formal and non-formal skill-based education should be arranged. Efforts should be made to connect the child with their family. For rehabilitation of these children, foster care and child adoption approaches could be promoted following the rules and regulations related to the identification of genuine families. Over and above, children at disadvantage should be considered as the treasured human resource of the nation who should be provided with nurturing grounds of growth and development; their rights are to be respected and dignity should be upheld. The nation should holistically involve in the creation and maintenance of acclimate that is at par with the principle of equity-equality the nation urges to provide its citizens. If appropriate preventive and intervention programs are not taken at the earliest, every not will lose huge human resources and incur additional burden of crime in the society.

References

Abraham, M. (2015). Situational analysis of street children in Guntur, Andhra Pradesh: A study. *TechnoLearn: An International Journal of Educational Technology*, *5*(1 and 2), 27. https://doi.org/10.5958/2249-5223.2015.00005.4.

Agarwal, S. (2017). Impact of child labour on the nutritional level and developmental 9–12 Years. *Journal of Textile Science Engineering, 7*, 300. https://doi.org/10.4172/2165-8064.1000300.

Alem, H. W., & Laha, A. (2016). Livelihood of street children and the role of social intervention: Insights from literature using meta-analysis. *Child Development Research*, 1–13. https://doi.org/10.1155/2016/3582101.

Allen, J., Balfour, R., Bell, R., & Marmot, M. (2014). Social determinants of mental health. *International Review of Psychiatry, 26*(4), 392–407. https://doi.org/10.3109/09540261.2014.928270.

Audu, B., Geidam, A., & Jarma, H. (2009). Child labor and sexual assault among girls in Maiduguri, Nigeria. *International Journal of Gynecology and Obstetrics, 104*(1), 64–67. https://doi.org/10.1016/j.ijgo.2008.09.007.

Berad, A., Momula, S., & Kumar, B. P. (2014). Study of health status of street children in Khammam City of Andhra Pradesh. *International Journal of Research in Medical Sciences, 2*(4), 1500. https://doi.org/10.5455/2320-6012.ijrms20141147.

Caglayan, C., Hamzaoglu, O., Yavuz, C. I., & Yüksel, S. (2010). Working conditions and health status of child workers: Cross-sectional study of the students at an apprenticeship school in Kocaeli. *Pediatrics International, 52*(1), 6–12. https://doi.org/10.1111/j.1442-200X.2009.02881.x.

CBS News. (2017). One year later, Nigerian "witch boy" healthy, heading to school. Africa. Retrieved from https://www.cbsnews.com/news/one-year-later-nigerian-witch-boy-healthy-headed-to-school/.

CHILDLINE India Foundation. (2018). CHILDLINE India Foundation.

Chowdhury, S., Chowdhury, A. S., Huq, K. E., Jahan, Y., Chowdhury, R., Ahmed, T., et al. (2017). Life style and risk behavior of street children in Bangladesh: A health perspective. *Health, 09*(04), 577–591. https://doi.org/10.4236/health.2017.94041.

Cronley, C., & Evans, R. (2019). Studies of resilience among youth experiencing homelessness: A systematic review. *Jounral of Human Behvaiour in the Social Environment, 27*(4), 1–5.

Deb, S. (1996a). Perception of juvenile delinquents towards the society. Paper presented in the *4th Asian Conference on Child Abuse & Neglect*, organized by the Indian Institute of Psychological and Educational Research, Calcutta, India held between November 25–27, 1996.

Deb, S. (1996b). Institutionalization of abused street children: An in-depth study. Paper presented in the *11th International Congress on Child Abuse and Neglect*, organized by the University of Dublin, Ireland between August. 18–21.

Deb, S., Datta, K., & Ghosh, M. (1997). Modification of a deviant street children's behaviour: An in-depth case study. *Indian Journal of Criminology, 25*(1), 15–22.

Deb, S., & Mitra, K. (2002). Deviance among disadvantaged children in Kolkat and reasons thereof. *Indian Journal of Criminology and Criminalistics, 22*(1), 41–59.

Dabir, N., & Athale, N. (2011). From street to hope: Faith based and secular programs in Los Angeles. *Mumbai and Nairobi for Street Living Children*. https://doi.org/10.4135/9788132107651.

Dey, S. (2018, May 28). World nutrition day : What do the street children of India eat ? *CNN-News 18*, pp. 1–11. Retrieved from https://www.news18.com/news/india/world-nutrition-day-what-do-the-street-children-of-india-eat-1762007.html.

Di Giglio, S., Kore, Z., Bolduc, E. K., Bocaj, J., Majko, A., Hima, F., & Jonuzaj, M. (2014). *National study on children in street situation in Albania*. https://doi.org/10.1002/anie.201106048.

Duci, V., & Tahsini, I. (2016). Regional Research on prevalence of street children phenomenon in Albania, Bosnia and Herzegovina, Montenegro and Serbia proofreading: Save the Children.

Dutta, N. (2018). Street children in India: A study on their access to health and education. *International Journal of Child, Youth and Family Studies, 9*(1), 69. https://doi.org/10.18357/ijcyfs91201818120.

Federal Office of Statistics of Nigeria. (2001). *National modular child labour survey country report: Nigeria*. Nigeria.

Feldmann, J., & Middleman, A. B. (2003). Homeless adolescents: Common clinical concerns. *Seminars in Pediatric Infectious Diseases, 14*(1), 6–11.

Guernina, Z. (2004). The sexual and mental health problems of street children: A transcultural preventative approach in counselling psychology. *Counselling Psychology Quarterly, 17*(1), 99–105. https://doi.org/10.1080/09515070410001665721.

Gupta, A. (2012). Social determinants of health—Street children at crossroads. *Health, 04*(09), 634–643. https://doi.org/10.4236/health.2012.49100.

Institute for Human Development. (2011). *Surviving the streets*.

Kanth, A. K. (2004). Street children and homelessness.

Kidd, S. A. (2004). The walls were closing in, and we were trapped. *Youth & Society, 35*(3), 341–365. https://doi.org/10.1177/0044118X03257030.

Koller, S. H., & Hutz, C. S. (2002). Street children: Psychological perspectives, University of Rio Grande do Sul Porto Alegre, Brazil.

Kombarakaran, F. A. (2004). Street children of Bombay: Their stresses and strategies of coping. *Children and Youth Services Review, 26*(9), 853–871. https://doi.org/10.1016/j.childyouth.2004.02.025.

Kumar, K. J., Chethak, K. B., Rama, H. V., Bhaktavatsala, H. R., & Vikash, V. (2017). Prevalence of anaemia and undernutrition among street children in Mysuru, India. *Sri Lanka Journal of Child Health, 46*(1), 44–47. https://doi.org/10.4038/sljch.v46i1.8105.

Malindi, M. J., & Theron, L. C. (2010). The hidden resilience of street youth. *South African Journal of Psychology*, 1–2.

Mathur, M. (2009a). Socialisation of street children in India: A socio-economic profile. *Psychology and Developing Societies*, *21*(2), 299–325. https://doi.org/10.1177/097133360902100207.

Mathur, M. (2009b). Socialisation of street children in India. *Psychology and Developing Societies, 21*(2), 299–325. https://doi.org/10.1177/097133360902100207.

Mathur, M., Rathore, P., & Mathur, M. (2009). Incidence, type and intensity of abuse in street children in India. *Child Abuse & Neglect: The International Journal, 33*(12), 907–913.

Ministry of Women and Child Development. (2007). *Study on child abuse : INDIA 2007*. New Delhi. Retrieved from https://www.childlineindia.org.in/pdf/MWCD-Child-Abuse-Report.pdf.

Ministry of Women and Child Development. (2013). *Third and fourth periodic reports of States parties due in*. Retrieved from https://www.refworld.org/pdfid/528212bb4.pdf.

Mugove, K., & Lincoln, H. (2015). Why children leave their homes for the streets? The case of Harare. *International Journal of Scientific and Research Publications, 5*(10), 1–5.

Mukherjee, C. (2014). A study on socio-educational and rehabilitation status of street. *IOSR Journal of Humanities and Social Science, 19*(7), 65–102.

Narayan, V. (2016, September 3). Most kids abandoned or killed in Maharashtra, reveals NCRB report. *Times of India*, pp. 1–32.

National Disaster Management Authority. (2014). *Managing crowd at events and venues of mass gathering: A guide for state government, local authorities, administrators and organizers*. Retrieved from https://ndma.gov.in/images/pdf/managingcrowdsguide.pdf.

Null, C., Stewart, C. P., Pickering, A. J., Dentz, H. N., Arnold, B. F., Arnold, C. D., … Colford, J. M. (2010). Effects of water quality, sanitation, handwashing, and nutritional interventions on diarrhoea and child growth in rural Kenya: A cluster-randomised controlled trial. *The Lancet Global Health, 6*(3), 316–329. https://doi.org/10.1016/S2214-109X(18)30005-6.

ODCCP. (2001). *Rapid situation assessment of street children in Cairo and Alexandria. United Nations Office for Durg Control and Crime Prevention* (Vol. 91).

Omokhodion, F., & Omokhodion, S. I. (2004). Health status of working and non-working school children in Ibadan. *Annals of Tropoical Paediatrics, 24*(2), 175–178. https://doi.org/10.1179/027249304225013457.

Pal, A., Pari, A. K., Sinha, A., & Dhara, P. C. (2017). Prevalence of undernutrition and associated factors: A cross-sectional study among rural adolescents in West Bengal, India. *International Journal of Pediatrics and Adolescent Medicine, 4*(1), 9–18. https://doi.org/10.1016/j.ijpam.2016.08.009.

Patel, N. B., Toral, D., Bansal, R. K., Thakar, G. (2011). Occupational profile and perceptions of street children in Surat city. *National Journal of Community Medicine, 2*(2), 297–301. Retrieved from http://njcmindia.org/uploads/2-2_297-301.pdf.

Patel, S. (1990). Street children, hotel boys and children of pavement dwellers and construction workers in Bombay-How they meet their daily needs. *Environment and Urbanization, 2*(2).

Patro, B. (1997). India-AIDS: Street children are the most vulnerable. *International Express News Services, September.*

Roy, É. (2004). Mortality in a cohort of street youth in Montreal. *JAMA, 292*(5), 569. https://doi.org/10.1001/jama.292.5.569.

Saini, N. (2013). Child abuse and neglect in India: Time to act. In *The 28th CMAAO General Assembly & 49th Council Meeting* (Vol. 56, pp. 302–309). https://doi.org/10.1007/s12098-014-1620-3.

Savarkar, T. (2018). Psychosocial distress among children living on the street in Mumbai City. *India. Journal of Depression and Anxiety, 07*(02), 5. https://doi.org/10.4172/2167-1044.1000308.

Save the Children. (2012). *Life on the street: The street children survey in 5 cities: Lucknow, Mughalsarai, Hyderabad*. New Delhi: Patna and Kolkata-Howrah.

Save the Children. (2015). *Forgotten voices: The world of urban children in India*. New Delhi.

Scheper, H. N. (2006). Dangerous and endangered youth: Social structures and determinants of violence. *Annals of the New York Academy of Sciences, 1036*(1), 13–46. https://doi.org/10.1196/annals.1330.002.

Seth, R. (2013). Protection of children from abuse and neglect in India. In *The 28th CMAAO General Assembly & 49th Council Meeting Takemi* (pp. 292–297).

Seth, R., Kotwal, A., & Ganguly, K. K. (2005). Street and working children of Delhi, India, Misusing Toluene : An ethnographic exploration. *Substance Use & Misuse, 40*(11), 1659–1679. https://doi.org/10.1080/10826080500222792.

Sharma, N., & Joshi, S. (2013). Preventing substance abuse among street children in India: A literature review. *Health Science Jounral, 7*(2), 137–148.

Sharmila, K., & Kaur, S. (2014). Experiences of abuse among street children: Nature, magnitude and practices. *American Journal of Advanced Drug Delivery, 2*(3), 387–396.

Shaw, M., & Dorling, D. (1998). Mortality among street youth in the UK. *The Lancet, 352*(9129), 743. https://doi.org/10.1016/S0140-6736(05)60868-9.

Srivastava, M., & Shareef, N. (2016). Plight of street children: An explorative study from Varanasi. *India. Indian Journal of Public Health, 60*(4), 290. https://doi.org/10.4103/0019-557X.195856.

Srivastava, R. (2008). Child abuse and neglect: Challenges and opportunities. *CANCEL News*, pp. 3–4.

Teta, D. M. (2002). *Early childhood: Socio-emotional risks*. University of Maryland, Baltimore, USA.

The Hindu. (2019, June 27). Students' body asks for rewriting of draft National Education Policy. *The Hindu*, pp. 1–2.

The Independent. (2017). Care worker who rescued Nigerian 'witch' boy recreates photo for his first week of school. Africa. Retrieved from https://www.independent.co.uk/news/world/africa/nigeria-witch-boy-photo-anja-ringgren-loven-facebook-images-first-day-of-school-a7561581.html.

Thilagaraj, R., & Priyamvadha, M. (2000). Deviance among street children. *Indian Journal of Criminology, 28*(1), 41–44.

Tipple, G., & Speak, S. (2004). Attitudes to and interventions in homelessness : Insights from an international study. In *International Conference on Adequate & Affordable Housing for All* (pp. 1–15). Toronto. Retrieved from http://www.urbancentre.utoronto.ca/pdfs/housingconference/Tipple-Speak_Attitudes-Home.pdf.

UNICEF. (2004). *Street children's experiences in the injustice system.*

UNICEF. (2006). *Excluded and invisible: The state of World's children. The United Nations Children's Fund.* New York, USA. Retrieved from http://www.unicef.org/sowc06/pdfs/sowc06_fullreport.pdf.

UNICEF. (2011). *The United Nations Convention on the Rights of the Child.*

UNICEF. (2013). *Child protection from violence, exploitation and abuse—Thematic Report 2013.*

Veale, A., & Dona, G. (2003). Street children and political violence: A socio-demographic analysis of street children in Rwanda. *Child Abuse & Neglect, 27*(3), 253–269.

Walolkar, D. (2003). Child labour in India. Lecture delivered in the Ist multidisciplinary training programme on child abuse and neglect, jointly organized by the Government Medical College, Nagpur and MIDSW- Metropolitn (Bypass) Institute for Developmental Studies and Welfare, Kolkata during February 3–4, 2003 and sponsored by ISPCAN, USA.

Whitbeck, L. B., Hoyt, D. R., & Bao, W.-N. (2000). Depressive symptoms and co-occurring depressive symptoms, substance abuse, and conduct problems among runaway and homeless adolescents. *Child Development, 71*(3), 721–732. https://doi.org/10.1111/1467-8624.00181.

Chapter 2
Child Trafficking for Prostitution: The Exploitation of Poverty-stricken Situation

Abstract The inhuman act of commoditizing humans for the comforts and pleasures of the powerful is an excruciating diagnosis of the infected society that we live in. Child trafficking is gaining its momentum across the globe every day with millions of innocent children disappearing from their homes. The highly organized nature of such scandals makes it impossible for their families and even the police to rescue the victims from the trap. These trafficked children are used for many purposes such as prostitution, organ harvesting, forced labour, illegal adoption, marriage and begging. Child prostitution, being the third most lucrative trade practice, is widely entertained all over the world along the dynamics of a demand-supply cycle. Latest statistics reveals the painful reality that despite the precautionary measures taken by international and national bodies, the cumulative demand for child prostitutes are increasingly being met. Newer or unknown strategies adopted by the managers of sex markets remain unknown to the outside world, which has to be addressed jointly by all individuals and communities. This chapter aims to understand the various reasons why our children, especially girls, become victims to trafficking for prostitution and has been supplemented by various case studies and first-hand field experiences. Various psychosocial rehabilitation techniques for trafficked children rescued from prostitution are discussed in this attempt to understand the unfortunate consequences of child trafficking for prostitution along personal, relational and societal domains. Taking the nuances of India, a multi-deterministic action plan to prevent child trafficking for prostitution is proposed further. This chapter is also an effort to instigate a sense of responsibility in every member of the society to safeguard the lives of our children.

Keywords Children · Trafficking · Prostitution · Prevention · Rescue · Rehabilitation · Abuse · Exploitation

2.1 Introduction

Trafficking of human beings has turned out to be the most callous trade form ever in human civilization, crossing all the nuances of human rights and justice. As is popularly understood, human trafficking refers to "the process through which individuals

S. Deb et al., *Disadvantaged Children in India*,
https://doi.org/10.1007/978-981-15-1318-3_2

are placed or maintained in an exploitative situation for economic gain" (UN, 2014). It has gained its prominence all over the world, irrespective of the country's development indices. Child trafficking, of all, has sought increasing prevalence in terms of its statistics and threat. "Child prostitution is not only a cause of death and high morbidity in millions of children but also a gross violation of their rights and dignity" (Willis & Levy, 2002). Children are trafficked with various intentions; prostitution, forced marriages, organ harvesting as well as to be used for sports, bonded/unpaid labour and street begging. Trafficking is raising a global concern, its intricate nature making it impossible to draw an estimate on that count. The UN supposes that annually at least 4 million children are abducted and are forced to work as servants or construction labourers across the world. A huge number of them are forced into begging and/prostitution as well. These devastating annual estimates puts into question the dignity and rights of innocent human lives.

Child prostitution is a predominant reason for which millions of children are trafficked. Innocent children who are the future of the nation are trafficked for various purposes for the vested interest of some antisocials and criminals (Deb, 2005). It is really shameful for human civilization that even in the twenty-first century one group of children play on the computer and surf the internet while another group of disadvantaged children are found to end up into prostitution or work as child labourers. The small children of economically disadvantaged families do not know when they are sold to some middlemen and/or for what purpose they are shifted from one place to another. Finally, they land up in some unknown place and grow up in an uncongenial, unhealthy and criminogenic environment, which is far from their home and they accept the deviant life and/or life of bonded labour under compulsion. Since they do not get the opportunity of studying throughout their lives, they are exploited and abused. While these children work as domestic servants, they are badly treated across the social strata. Educated and moneyed people do not treat them as human beings and take them for granted to carry over their orders and take care of all household chores. Even then, if they forget to perform any duty/task by mistake or by accident, they are subjected to physical and mental torture. In India, especially in the middle and upper middle-class families, there is a need for small girl children to work as domestic servants and to look after small babies in absence of parents especially during office hours. In order to meet this need, every year, a large number of rural children are traded to urban areas through some channels for domestic work. This apart, a large number of girls from very poor families are traded to brothels for child prostitution.

The inter-correlation between trafficking and prostitution often takes noteworthy formulations, that one is inseparable from the other. Child prostitution due to debt bondage, child pornography, children prostitution for survival (survival sex) and child prostitution, which is sanctioned by the society through various socio-cultural norms, are all widely practiced. The global market that runs this organized crime has millions of children (particularly girls) involved as commodities being sold and traffickers as benefiters making billions of dollars in return. Reports says that women and girl children from countries like Nepal, Bangladesh, Burma, Laos and Cambodia are found to be sent to cities of Bombay, Karachi and Bangkok as cheap sex workers by foreigners. Talking specifically about India, Andhra Pradesh, West Bengal, Delhi, Tamil Nadu and Karnataka have been found to be trafficking the largest number of children, while Goa, Delhi and a few North-eastern states being the biggest receivers.

Even though their number is less, girls from Pakistan and Thailand are increasingly being reported to be trafficked. These girls, who are less educated and ignorant about the legal systems, are brought to areas whose culture and language are unfamiliar to them, are considered to be far more profitable than localities. They are easier to be persuaded and threatened into this lucrative trade, curbing their physical and psychological health. Another notion works behind recruitment of foreign children from vulnerable background is in line with the popular notion they would not be the carriers of STDs, especially HIV/AIDS. "The new slave trade is related to extreme poverty, lack of access to resources, unemployment and poor education, and because of the marginalization of women in society and the feminization of poverty, it obviously affects especially women and children" (Scarpa, 2006). The UNICEF's East Asia and Pacific Regional Office report (2001) entitled '*Children on the Edge*' notes that those girls who willingly enter into prostitution do so, so as to escape from the physical and mental torture they encounter at their homes/place of stay. "Prevention efforts should be to improve economic opportunities and security for improvised women and girls, educate communities regarding the tactics ad identities of traffickers, as well as promote structural interventions to reduce trafficking" (Silverman, Decker, Gupta, Maheshwari, Patel, Willis, & Raj, 2007).

This chapter concentrates on child trafficking for prostitution. Attempts to understand the causal factors are made by grounding the findings to India's socio-cultural contexts. Preventive measures and intervention strategies are also discussed along with the proposal of a multi-deterministic action plan against child trafficking for prostitution.

2.2 Definition

2.2.1 Trafficking

The UN Protocol to Prevent, Suppress and Punish Trafficking, Especially Women and Children (Palermo Protocol) states that

> Trafficking in persons shall mean the recruitment, transportation, transfer, harboring or receipt of persons, by means of the threat or use of force or other forms of coercion, of abduction, of fraud, of deception, of the abuse of power or of a position of vulnerability or of the giving or receiving of payments or benefits to achieve the consent of a person having control over another person, for the purpose of exploitation; Exploitation shall include, at a minimum, the exploitation of the prostitution of others or other forms of sexual exploitation, forced labour or services, slavery or practices similar to slavery, servitude or the removal of organs

2.2.2 *Child Trafficking*

"The recruitment, transportation, transfer, harboring or receipt of a child for the purpose of exploitation shall be considered 'trafficking in persons" is the definition according to the United Nations Protocol to Prevent, Suppress and Punish Trafficking in Persons, especially Women and Children (2002).

2.2.3 *Definition of Child Prostitution*

'Sexual exploitation' includes trafficking in children for purposes of sexual exploitation, child sex tourism, distribution of pornographic material featuring children, exploitative use of children in prostitution (Source: UNICEF).

2.2.4 *Commercial Sexual Exploitation of Children*

It is defined by the United Nations as "the use of a child for sexual purposes in exchange for cash or in kind favors between the customers, intermediary or agent and others who profit from the trade in children for these purposes (parent, family member, procurer, teacher, etc.)". United Nations had identified sexual exploitation of children for the following three commercial reasons: child prostitution, trafficking and sale of children across borders with or within countries for sexual purposes and pornography.

Over one-third of humans been trafficked are children, as has been estimated by UNICEF on World Trafficking Day of 2018. Heightened vulnerability is found among refugees, migrants and displaced children (UNICEF, 2018); "sexual exploitation is by far the most commonly identified form of human trafficking (79%), followed by forced labour (18%)" (UNODC, 2009). The severity of trafficking for prostitution is increasing at an alarming rates, that "Underlying the global traffic in children are some harsh realities, including the vast and widening gap between the poor of the world and those with greater resources and choices" (Beyrer, 2004). A close watch on the various estimation reports that comes out every year shows that the number of trafficked children are only increasing. Why and how does this happen? The answer to this query is as difficult as it is to accurately estimate the number of children lost to trafficking.

2.3 Factors Responsible Behind Trafficking and Prostitution

Child prostitution is the largest form of commercial sexual exploitation of children. Every year, at least one million children are forced into prostitution (Willis & Levy, 2002) and the business of trafficking and prostitution is the third-largest profitable business with millions of turnovers, and is commonly referred to as the 'dry dollars business'. The unfortunate fact is that more than 85% of prostitutes in Calcutta and Delhi are estimated to have entered into this profession at a very early age, and this number is only rising. Over 10,000 girl prostitutes are found in Bangalore, Delhi, Calcutta and Hyderabad alone (Thappa, Singh, & Kaimal, 2007). The common targets of such exploitation are children from poor families, living in rural or semi-urban areas. They are being told to be taken for a job or to be married with no dowry. (Source: Red Alert: Combat Commercial Sexual Exploitation of Children, produced by Sanlaap-an NGO). Hence, one of the most important causes of child trafficking is poverty; it does not allow curious minds of parents to ask the middlemen and exploiter whether their girl child will be safe in the city and/or in the workplace. Thus, the family circumstances also prove to add to the child's vulnerability to commercial sexual exploitation and this remains valid all over the world. As can be understood, a great proportion of children who get exploited come from marginalized family backgrounds, children of women who are already involved in prostitution are found to have high likelihood of entering into sex industry either voluntarily or forcefully. Unhealthy and malfunctioned home environment such as marital discord, abuse, family pressure, gender discrimination within family and any such non-congenial atmosphere have reportedly increased the vulnerability towards child trafficking and prostitution (Deb, Srivastava, Chatterjee, & Chakraborty, 2005).

Substantiating the above-mentioned understanding, the Human Rights organization, Asia Watch, indicated that children less than 10 years are deceived by promising a better job and living conditions to leave their homes. Families who get convinced by these fake promises also tend to persuade their girl children under the notion that they are being sent to work as domestic help abroad. The family receives an amount as remuneration for which these girls are trapped in the brothels for ages. They are only allowed to leave the brothel upon repayment of this amount. As discussed, these target families are mostly the ones that experiences severe financial burden, that repayment of the amount is not a practical way forward. Young girls taken out of homes in the name of employment would be long absorbed to brothels much before they realize the truth. The money paid to their family would be the basis of the debt on which the pimps/brothel owners would impose control. This is the debt bondage which these girls are forced to repay through prostitution. The interesting reality is that these girls would never be told about the real size of the debt. They are put to work till the time they escape or are found to be unfit for the job in time. Added to this would be the money taken for their clothing, food, accommodations and medicine. Coupled with debt bondage, these additional charges would create a huge burden on these girls when they are left with hardly any opinion. Escape is an impossible dream as they will be frequently sold and transported to areas which are unknown to them. Utilizing their ignorance about the location, culture and language, the brothel owner would easily intimidate the girls with force, abuse and torture and ensure that they entertain their guests well.

In Asia, child prostitution is deeply embedded in many local and national cultures. This could be why Asian countries including Indian and Thailand receive many foreigners who visit the countries in search of cheap sex. The understanding that youngsters will be virgins and also would less likely be prone to HIV would make then the most sought after 'commodity' for sexual gratification. Similarly, there are other distinctive factors pertaining specifically to the Indian culture that has potentially entertained child prostitution. Cultural systems of child prostitution as varied as the Devadasi or the Jogini, as well as several myths and beliefs, reinforce the vicious cycle. For instance, the worshippers of Goddess Yellamma in South India encourage the parents to push their daughters into prostitution with a religious label. Myths like 'sex with virgins can cure sexually transmitted diseases' would only result in heightened proneness to sexually transmitted diseases like HIV/AIDS among sexually victimized girls. Along the same lines, the supposed lesser proneness of young girls to Sexually Transmitted Diseases (STDs) creates great demand for them in the sex market. The conditions of girls in some rural parts of India are so pathetic that there seems to be no escape from the trap. In West Bengal, (India) there are villages like Madhusudanpur and Jyotishpur where each household has at least one girl child who works in the Sonagachi red-light area as a child prostitute. The poor economic background of most of the families aggravates the plight. Hence, it has become a common practice where girls would be sent to the red light area for prostitution by their own families in the name of jobs in Kolkata. An interesting field covering 35 rescued girls in a Rehabilitation Home in Kolkata (West Bengal) found that that the main factors influencing the trafficking of these children include poverty and illiteracy, followed by influence of external agents, promise of job, lack of supervision, immaturity, family crisis, uncongenial family environment, love for adventure, helplessness, kidnapping, addiction, environmental crisis, running away from home, false promise of marriage and mother being a prostitute.

Globalization can be seen as a contributing factor since that has pushed people to "search for better lives in the hands of smugglers/traffickers who promise to get them to their desired destinations" (Engle, 2013). The increasing migration of rural Indians to urban areas has also contributed to the prospects of child trafficking and prostitution. To understand the new demand-supply dynamics, one has to analyze the situation from different perspectives: Urban migration of men is another phenomenon that increased the demand for sexual services massively; encouraging the middlemen and antisocials to look for more supply. Peoples' desire to escape from poverty, or in other words, aspiration for economic and social prosperity and similar secondary benefits meets this demand from time to time. The desire of families to break out of their cycle of poverty as well as the inhibitory role played by social stigma towards local prostitution causes such families to be increasingly receptive of 'opportunities' abroad. The apparent lack of alternative options for women, other than looking after children, domestic services, marriage to a wealthy outsider or prostitution, also makes it easier to convince women to migrate for employment or sell their daughters to brothel for cash.

Ill-effect of migration and its impact on the sex market has an international range as well. A growing concern is the ever hiking number of women and children moved across the borders of Western Europe, Central and Eastern Europe (CEE), the Commonwealth of Independent States (CIS) and the Baltic States. Presence of trafficking systems that moves young Indian girls into urban centers and across South Asia is at a hike that comes to light in popular tourist destinations (Scarpa, 2006). The demand for foreign women in the Indian sex market is also an issue to be informed about. There exists a number of factors that increase the vulnerability of children to exploitation: unemployment, lack of skills suitable for the available employment opportunities, poverty and the pressure on youngsters to earn money for living from the families, discrimination based on gender age, disability and ethnicity are a few among them (Dottridge, 2004). Other causes include increasing income disparity, improved communications and un-kept promises. In addition, adventurous mind of some sections of the people have added momentum in trafficking (Deb, 2004). This may make them more vulnerable to pimps and recruiters or to move within the country or across borders where perceived returns are greater. A notable report by UNICEF (2001) pointed out that over a million children growing up in institutional setup are at high vulnerability when they get exposed to outside world without proper guidance, training and preparedness. "Ill treatment by parents, bad company, family prostitutes, social customs, inability to arrange marriage, lack of sex education, media, prior incest and rape, early marriage and desertion, lack of recreational facilities, ignorance and acceptance of prostitution" are understood to be instigating child prostitution (Thappa et al., 2007).

Lack of education increases the vulnerability of the children to fall into the never-ending loop of child trafficking since literacy and inaccessibility to education comes with a series of consequences. The education profile of victims of child trafficking showed that 50.8% of them had never been to school, the maximum of education attained is the second standard (12.3%) (Sen, 2004). Less qualified children remain unfit for jobs and would remain so even otherwise, due to unfamiliarity and ignorance about other alternative ways of living. They are less informed about exploitation, misleading information and their consequences in turn. The other side of the coin is about how child prostitution in itself deny children of school-going age their right to education, health and life (Mikhail, 2002); which again hinders their potential to earn legitimately even if they are out of prostitution. Added to this are other unmet needs and problems that are unaddressed: most of clinical issues of children into sex slavery correlates to that of children subjected to brutal sexual abuse (Fong & Berger Cardoso, 2010). After-effects of acute physical and sexual trauma, as reported by children who have been rescued includes mental illness, substance abuse, STDs, pregnancy and abortion-related complications (Willis & Levy, 2002). Personal characteristics such as low self-esteem, lack of self-control, indecisiveness and impulsivity lifts the vulnerability towards trafficking (Nair & Sen, 2005). Despite all the news and stories, it is quite unfortunate that there still exist many who are willing to take risks and explore the world outside. Adding to this tendency is the lack of law enforcements and policies against child trafficking for prostitution. (Source: Red Alert: Combat Commercial Sexual Exploitation of Children, produced by Sanlaap-an NGO). A number of factors work together behind child trafficking. Following are the examples of correlation of poverty, wrong promise of job, hard reality and child trafficking/prostitution.

> ***Case Study 1:*** *Rina was born and brought up in a red light area in Rambagan, Kolkata (India) by her mother and grandmother who were working as commercial sex workers. She had five siblings. Suddenly, her mother became physically sick and was unable to run the business. During this crisis, author of this book and his colleagues wanted to include Rina in an action research project as one of the study subjects, which was funded by the Save the Children Fund, U.K. The seven member family of hers was completely relaying on the income earned by her mother and hence it was understood that, she could be drifted into this profession any time. Because of the said reason, the study team wanted to remove her from the locality to a Halfway House. In this regard, the study team members discussed the issue with her, her mother and both of them replied that her grandmother is the decision maker in the family and so the study team members were advised to speak to the grandmother. Next day when the study members discussed the issue with the grandmother, she gave an ambivalent response regarding the replacement of Rina in a Halfway House. The very next day, the study members again visited the area and enquired about Rina to convince her grandmother, but Rina disappeared. Later on, it was found that Rina was sold to a brothel in Mumbai in exchange of money. However, when she was brought back home after 6 months, she has diagnosed to be HIV positive.*

> ***Case Study 2***: *Anima, 17 years, was born with six siblings and brought up in a very poor family in a remote village. Her father was working as a petty businessman while the mother was making 'beedi'. It was very difficult for them to have two meals a day. Anima studied up to class IV in a village school. At the age of 12, a tout offered her a job in Mumbai. Utter poverty encouraged her to visit Mumbai to explore this opportunity. In Mumbai, she landed in a red light area. When she realized it and wanted to come back, the middlemen had disappeared. She was in Mumbai's red light area for two years in this commercial sex trade. She did not receive a single penny and she had to work without money as her contact person has taken the money on behalf of her. After two years of service, Police sent her to Liluah Observation Home through the Juvenile Court. She was soon diagnosed with HIV Aids and is currently rehabilitated in a shelter home. Under the supervision and supported in the shelter home, she could overcome Depression and is leading a productive life.*

> ***Case Study 3:*** *Farida, 20 years of age, was trafficked six years back. She was born in a farmer's family in Bangladesh and had four siblings. She had never been to school. Farida got married and had a daughter. Her husband was mentally ill and she used to stay with her father, mother and her siblings. Farida's family was very supportive regarding her unfortunate marriage but they lived in a very wretched condition and it was becoming difficult for her to run the family and look after her child. A woman from her village promised her work at Kolkata. But instead, she handed Farida over to a dalal who sold her in Bombay at a beer bar. She was there for 1 year. She used to be beaten when unable to dance as expected. She was rescued in a police raid and sent to 'Sanlaap' – an NGO working for the rehabilitation of trafficked children and women. She has been staying in 'Sanlaap' for the past 5–6 months. She wants to go back home as soon as possible to her only daughter. She feels depressed most of the time and is anxious about her daughter's wellbeing. She does not have any apparent physical anomaly but occasionally suffers from headache and insomnia.*

> ***Case Study 4:*** *Dolly, aged 24, was trafficked when she was barely four years old. She was born in U.P but her mother now stays at Khidderpore. She is in touch with her mother. Her father was a magazine vendor and she had four siblings. Dolly's father was a drug addict. He sold her when she was not even four years old. The person to whom he had sold Dolly*

took her to Bombay and sold her to one of the beer bars there. The 'Seth' and 'malkin' of the bar brought her up. When she started growing up she was taught to dance so that she got prepared for the work. Gradually, she became one of the several dancers out there. The moment she stepped into her puberty, she was transferred to the 'bazaar' (red light area). She then became one of the thousands CSW's working in Bombay. She used to take customers out of the city to various states. She continued like this for 5–6 years. Then once when she was in Andhra Pradesh with one of her customers, she was caught in a police raid. Then she was sent to the Liluah Observation Home for female juvenile delinquents in West Bengal where she stayed for one year. For the past 10 years, she has been staying in 'Sanlaap' – an NGO working for trafficked children. Currently, she is getting vocational training in embroidery and stitching in 'Sanlaap'. She is found to be HIV positive.

Case Study 5: *Khushboo is 17 years old. She was born in Bhopal. She was trafficked four years back. She has three siblings. She used to stay with her mother and younger brothers. Her elder sister was married a year before her father had expired. After her father's death, they had severe financial crisis leading to a state of begging. Khushboo was totally fed up with her wretched condition and started looking for an opportunity to get some work. She then came to Kolkata with an unknown person, who promised her job and took her to Sonagachi (Red Light Area) and sexually abused her. He left her over there. There she thought of starting to earn by selling herself for the reason that she considered that she had already been spoilt. She hired a room and started the so-called 'dhanda'. She used to send some money to her home to support her family. After continuing for almost two years, she was caught by the police and sent to Liluah Observation Home for female juvenile delinquents and later to 'Sanlaap' – an NGO working for trafficked children. Here she is the vice head girl and is learning karate, English, dancing and block printing. She wants to stay here forever and earn her livelihood well. She is suffering from a skin problem and has headaches frequently.*

Case Study 6: *Padma comes from Kolkata, is 17 years of age, was trafficked three years back and has no contact with her family. Her parents had died when she was young. Her mashi (Aunti) and mama (Uncle) brought her up. They didn't treat her very well. One day her mama traded her to a pimp of Sonagachi. Within 2 weeks of her stay there she was rescued by the police and was sent to Liluah Observation Home for juvenile delinquents. She stayed there for one year and was then sent to 'Sanlaap'. She is learning embroidery and block printing there. She wants to spend her life there and doesn't want to look back to her past life.*

Case Study 7: *Sister to three other siblings, 17 year old Swapna was trafficked two years ago. She was born to a farmer in Orissa and never got a chance to go to school. Her husband, an alcoholic, left her. Poverty compelled her to look for work. Her uncle assured her a job and brought her to Sonagachi and sold her. The police rescued her from there after 10 days. She is worried about her future and also feels restless. Now her father comes to meet her often in 'Sanlaap'.*

2.4 The Consequences of Trafficking and Child Prostitution

The consequences of trafficking of children and child prostitution on the well-being of the individual create irreparable damage to the society. Ultimately, it is the valuable human resource of the country that is needed in nation-building and that is getting mishandled. Its malingering impact on the lives of victims has not been researched enough, mainly due to its intensive nature. Nonetheless, the understood facts are, this lucrative trade is greatly altering the physical and mental health of the children during their very crucial developmental phase. Health issues are related to injury, resulting from accidents and physical conditions in the working environment, long working hours, lack of sleep and substance use. "The common symptoms of psychosocial disorders manifested by most of the children engaged in commercial sex are severe depressive states including trauma, an attitude of hopelessness and helplessness in relation to future decisions, guilt, powerlessness, deflated self-esteem and self-love, escapism through dissociation, distorted perceptions of sex, inability to trust others, excessive emotional attachment, multiple phobias, loneliness, isolation, impaired ability to learn, poor memory and concentration span, social stigma and discrimination especially if HIV positive, sterility and other terminal physical illness" (Source: ESCAP HRD, United Nations, 2002). Physical pain and injury, if given attention can be completely healed, but "psychological and medical consequences can persist through adulthood" (Johnson, 2004). Repeated physical and sexual abuse, uncertainty and fear and the absence of personal control, poor health care and working conditions and infection from STDs including HIV/AIDS would all continue to curb their physical and mental health throughout the time of forced prostitution.

From the available data, their heightened vulnerability towards HIV infections and other STDs are evident. This is so because of the lack of controllability and the predictive nature they have over the sexual acts they are required to comply with depending upon the clients they get. Unhygienic environment of work, insensitive and selfish customers, poor knowledge and understanding of safe and protected sex are the main contributing factors for this proneness. While many commercial sex clients believe that having sex with the so-called 'virgins' or children with reportedly few sex partners will help protect them from HIV/AIDS, the report says that they are badly mistaken. Surveys show that some girls are forced to serve an average of 5–10 customers a day. In addition, the report notes that child sex workers are themselves often ignorant of HIV/AIDS and how to prevent it, are powerless to insist on condom use with clients, and are extremely vulnerable to not only HIV/AIDS but other sexually transmitted diseases such as syphilis and herpes (UNICEF's East Asia and Pacific Regional Office report, 2001). Even though HIV testing is carried out in many brothels, they are often not told about the results. It is very unlikely that infected women and children are aware of their illness. They continue to work, mostly with reduced prices.

The cases of younger girls are at higher risks of infection due to an immature reproductive system and inadequate immunity. After getting the disease they are unable to bear the expenditure of treatment costs and face the consequences of the diseases. More so, they are subjected to social discrimination owing to their profession and disease. Hence, a majority of them remain untreated. Strong social stigmas discourage trafficked women and child prostitutes to get merged into the family in future. "Compounding the original abuse, a proportion of girls may feel compelled to return to or stay in prostitution because the shame of having worked as a prostitute, regardless of the deception perpetrated against them; their marriage prospects are very low and the likelihood of discrimination is high in cultures where virginity and sexual inexperience is prized" (David, 1998). As a result, later on, they lead a lonely life and nobody is there to take care of their basic needs. Economically, they are in miserable condition in their old age as there is a negative correlation of age with this profession of prostitution. A more disturbing possibility is that most of times, the sexual act they perform would be so severe that it might cross the limits to reach sexual abuse. Regular clients would prefer young girls in fear of infection and would involve into deviant and dangerous acts which can leave these children shattered and devastated.

Child trafficking and child prostitution have significant impact on mental health of children in terms of adjustment, psychological trauma, depression and anxiety and in developing aggression among them towards the larger society (Bhuvaneswari & Deb, 2016; Deb & Mukherjee, 2009; 2011; Deb, Mukherjee, & Mathews, 2011; Deb & Sen, 2005).

Deb and Chatterjee conducted a study in Kolkata covering 35 rescued trafficked children. The problems encountered by the trafficked children may be categorized into four groups like mental, physical, social and economic. HIV/AIDS is the most prevalent physical health problem among the trafficked children. Among the mental problems, depression is most common, followed by loneliness and loss of interest towards life. Finally, social discrimination, i.e. rejection by the family members after rescue from the red light areas, shatter their last hope of living in this world.

In another study Deb, Mukherjee and Mathews (2011) examined the severity of aggression among sexually abused girls who were trafficked and who were then further used for commercial sexual exploitation. Findings disclosed that "16.7% of the girls were first sexually abused between 6 and 9 years of age, 37.5% between 10 and 13 years of age and 45.8% between 14 and 17 years of age. Findings further revealed that 4.2% of the sexually abused trafficked girls demonstrated saturated aggression and 26.7% were highly aggressive, that is, extremely frustrated and rebellious. Across age groups, the sexually abused trafficked girls suffered from more aggression ($p < 0.05$), when compared with the non-victimized girls. Psychological interventions, such as individual and group counseling, were found to have a positive impact on the sexually abused trafficked girls. These findings should motivate counsellors to deal with sexually abused children. It is also hoped that authorities in welfare homes will understand the importance of counseling for sexually abused trafficked children and will appoint more counsellors for this purpose."

By and large, the consequences faced by the victims of child trafficking for prostitution infect all spheres of their lives: they are alienated from personal and public spheres of life, their fundamental rights to live a safe and healthy life, to get educated, to have freedom to access health care facilities, etc. are put under hold. They are highly prone to several health hazards and psychological distress, which leads into leading a downgraded and worthless life. They are constantly subjugated to abuse at multiple levels and are made to remain helpless and obedient to other's commands. Informal interviews facilitated the first author during an action research to capture the mind of these children which is very much shocking. According to some of the trafficked children,

"We are used as sex slave" – a trafficked child

"Perpetrators use us as and when they feel the sexual desire" – a child working as child prostitute

"Sometimes some elderly people force us to take alcohol or drugs" – a child working as a child prostitute

"Clients never care about our mental state before using us" – a trafficked child

"Some of the clients do not behave with us politely" – a child working as a child prostitute

"I wanted to go back to my house. But they confined me forcefully and used me for about six months for earning money" - a trafficked child

"I heard that I have got a disease, but I am not sure what the disease is all about" – a trafficked child from Kolkata who was sent to Mumbai for child prostitution

"I am very much scared. I do not know how to contact my parents" – a trafficked child

The above verbatim responses are clear illustrations of situations and mental state of the trafficked children and the children who are working as child prostitutes.

Following are bright examples of consequences of child trafficking for child prostitution.

2.4.1 Alienation from Personal and Public Spheres

Several studies have cited the cause and effect relationship between dysfunctional families and child trafficking for prostitution. But ironically, the biggest concern of a majority of the survivors is the abandonment they face from their own families. The number of families who have voluntarily sent their children and survive on their income are many; most of the times, these children are tortured at the brothels in the name of the huge debt their family is in with the people who run the prostitution racket. These children succumb to the demands of the prostitution runners to clear their family debt, in the hope of returning home one day. Stigma and labelling follow them everywhere, along with lack of money and the very unlikelihood of getting a job in the future make the families to view these survivors as a burden and also brings ill-repute that they are avoided and in many cases shooed out of their homes.

Case Study 8: *Rani is 18 years old girl from Bongaon, West Bengal. She comes from a poor family and her father is a lorry driver by profession. Her mother does not work and looks after the household. She has a younger brother. Rani had a quarrel at home with her mother. Being fed up with her mother she decided to leave home and find some work for herself. Rani discussed her family problems with a local dada. The dada promised her a domestic job. The dada took Rani to Bombay. There she was kept in a 'jhoprapatti' for 2–3 days. Then Rani was sold to a kothi. Rani was not told about that deal. There were many more girls in the kothi and it is from them, that she got to know, that she had been sold for Rs. 10,000. Rani stayed there for 2 months and she began with prostitution. At the beginning she was not ready to take up the profession but soon she realized that she had no other way out. While the kothi was raided, Rani told the entire story to the police. Rani still hoped for being rescued. The police took Rani to a home in Bombay. From there she was sent to 'Sanlaap' – an NGO working for rehabilitation of trafficked children through Liluah Observation Home for female juvenile delinquents. Rani says,*

> *"I have lost everything from my life, I don't have a family now, and I know nobody at home will accept me. Nobody can marry me ever. Still I want to go home, but I have got HIV positive. A small trust on the dada has taken away everything from my life. I don't know how people can do this type of things to girls. Where ever I go I will be known as a dhandawali only (prostitute) ..."*

The alienation continues to follow them outside their homes as well, making their disadvantage quotient even higher. The society views and calls them as prostitutes till the day of their death or even after that. They find it difficult to find accommodation and job, if their previous history is known to others. Since they were trafficked as children, there wouldn't be educated enough to get a job or be trained in any skills, so they mostly end up being a helper at homes, restaurants, etc. Despite the quality of their work, these women would soon be kicked out of their jobs, once their previous history is known to others. The society targets women who live alone and are always viewed with suspicion; unfortunate incidents in the form of violence, abuse and torture may continue to follow them.

Case Study 9: *Deepa was just 13 years old when she was sent off with a man, who was supposedly a distant relative, to the town for a job by her parents. It took her another 21 years to get out of prostitution with the help of a rescue group. She was not welcomed back to her family and so she settled in a faraway district of Tamil Nadu. She was only educated up to class VI and so finding a job was difficult for her. In a few weeks, she found a job as a domestic helper at a house in the town. In less than 2 months, the owners of that household found out about her life in prostitution from Deepa herself and soon dismissed her from the job.*

> *"I struggle everytime to find a job to soon lose it when they know about my previous life" said Deepa.*

She remembers being convinced by the 'uncle' about how the job he had found for her could solve all the problems at her home. She was taken to Bombay where she was handed over to lady for Rs. 50,000.

2.4.2 Deprivation from Fundamental Rights

Unseen consequences of child trafficking for prostitution are often the denial of basic human rights that the country guarantees its citizens. Basic human rights like right to live a life safely are completely threatened when the children are kidnapped and sold in brothels and later forced to entertain their customers. In the light of this, their basic right to get educated is totally ignored, availability to quality and nutritious food is under question and access to health care facilities is denied. Most of the survivors report about a life totally out of their control where they are threatened and forced to obey the commands of the '*dadas*' or pimps who attack then verbally and physically. Deprived of all these basic rights, they live confined to the walls of the brothel for years, to finally, if given a chance, leave the brothel for the outside world. By then, they would be tormented to a state where bringing back a life of quality would be next to impossible. Following is an example where the struggle of a survivor, who was denied her rights for several years and was abandoned when found as a misfit for the profession.

Case Study 10: *Shilpa is 18 years old girl from Kakdwip, West Bengal. She came out of her home at the age of twelve. She has no siblings. Her father works as fishermen. At present, Shilpa has no attachments to the family. She had received education till class V. Shilpa's mother expired and the father married again. The stepmother treated her very badly. She received thrashing from her. A man from the local village promised to give her a job in the city. She left with that person for good. This man sold her in Bombay for Rs. 1500. She was put into prostitution with several other girls like her. She was doing quite well in the profession. She used to get Rs. 4000–5000 per month. Shilpa became ill suddenly and the 'malkin' found her of no further use. Forcefully, she was put into a train. She landed up in Kolkata. She knew nobody out there. In Howrah station the police caught her. She was sent to Liluah home. There she stayed for 2 years. From there she has been sent to Sanlaap, Narendrapur.*

2.4.3 Health Hazards

Empirical evidence on the life of people involved in prostitution are very scarce but in the light of advent of AIDS awareness and prevention programs, several statistical studies are found, where high prevalence and incidence of HIV AIDS and other STDs are widely seen to be prevalent among these women. The general understanding that their lives are being led in poor standards, in unhygienic environment and contaminated spaces, have been corroborated by the in-hand experience with the survivors. Given the fact that they get inadequate food in terms of quality, their consumption is downgraded in terms of the nutritional content as well. Hence, the victim of child prostitution grows up lacking the needed nutrients for their healthy growth. In order to avoid the prejudice against them, they often avoid visiting hospitals and clinics and tend to treat by themselves, to further alleviate their health status. Various kinds of STDs that intensifies in due course make them unfit for the profession and they are forcefully thrown out the place.

Case Study 11: *Shilpa was 37 years old when she was asked to leave the brothel she was associated with for 12 years. She had been trafficked to Kolkata at the age of 16 by a local villager. She remembers herself to be unhealthy and weak since a very young age. "I have never had enough food to my satisfaction since my childhood. I was sent away from home due to poverty and the situation just worsened for me after that" she commented. She found herself to fall sick very often, but still was forced to entertain her customers. She was very susceptible to illness, so much so that, she was mostly sick from her customers as well and she got infected by HIV from one of them. Soon after been detected by AIDS, she had to leave the place and struggle until she found a space in one of the rescue homes where she lives today.*

2.4.4 Psychological Distress

Constantly under threat and ill-treatment, psychological distress is at its highest prevalence among children who are forced into prostitution at such a young age. Along with dealing with the separation from their homes, they struggle to understand their surroundings and themselves. Forcefully being involved in sexual practices at such a young age often leaves them uncanny. They get subjected to trauma, depression, aggressive behaviours and personality disorders. The state of uncontrollability would adversely affect their sense of self, identity and personality development. They reported to feel low about themselves and found no meaning to their life. For the ones who are fortunate to escape the place are often made to feel worthless by the family and society by abandoning them. Unless otherwise, most of them live a life fighting through these distresses every single day with little or no hope.

> ***Case Study 12:*** *Maya is 23 years old and was hardly 12 when she was taken to a brothel. From the age of 14 she has been forced into prostitution till she was rescued 2 years back. Her adversely brought-up childhood had left lasting impressions on her physically and psychologically. In order to cope with the hardships, she developed the habit of hurting herself and enjoying the pain out of it. She accepted to have had suicidal ideation for quite a long time but never got a right chance to attempt it. She still continues to have vivid and absurd dreams at night which would remind her of her life as a prostitute.*

2.4.5 Victims of Multiple Abuse

Physical, emotional, verbal and sometimes sexual abuse is often used by the runners of the brothels to get these girls under their control. Followed by this would be the misuse and abuse done by the customers, who uses them as commodities to meet their pleasure. They are forced to take client after client and earn income to these pimps. Reports of being abused by policemen have also come out, that even the keepers of the law are keeping double standards. The following example would validate the point.

> ***Case Study 13:*** *Nalini, an 18 years old survivor who is rehabilitated in Kolkata recollected of a day when she was verbally abused and brutally beaten up by her landlord, soon after which she was burned with cigarette butts by a customer. She was not given proper medical care or emotional support and it took her over a week to settle her wounds.*

2.4.6 Poor Quality of Life

All the gradients that add up to one's life of quality are downgraded for children who are trafficked for prostitution. Their physical health and related outcomes are weak due to poor nutritious food intake, illness, inaccessibility to medical care and unhygienic lifestyle. Psychological distress, illness, suicidal thoughts, depression, poor self-esteem and similar thoughts would make them perceive life as meaningless. Social circles around them are unhealthy and accuse that they get subjected to stigma and labelling and that they are alienated from their families as well as other mainstreams in the society. Unhygienic environment and poorly maintained rooms, bathrooms and surroundings with little or no privacy would challenge their feelings of comfort. Thus, if understood closely, these children would grow up in an environment that would curtail their standard of living and deteriorate their quality of life in every possible aspect.

2.4.7 Drainage of Valuable Human Resources

Child trafficking for prostitution is a phenomenon that hinders any country in terms of tormenting its valuable human resources. If one lakh children are trafficked every year, the aggregate lose that it can cause in 30 years would be irreparable. Needless to say, if this social issue has the potential to dormant the lives of many children in ways beyond description, its accumulated impact on a nation would be devastating. The need to review the legislative reforms that support mandatory reporting of child abuse and trafficking is urgent in India so as to consider appropriate reforms in Indian context. Hence, this inhuman practice of commoditizing humans should be tackled by putting in place stringent provisions along with taking multi-dimensional steps to combat the issue.

2.5 Combating the Problem of Child Trafficking and Rescue of Child Prostitutes

Fighting the causal and contributory factors of this ever-worsening social issue requires a continuous and coordinated effort. Considering this extremely complicated undercurrent, prevention, at any level, is undoubtedly the hour's need. For combating child trafficking and prostitution, steps at the local, regional, state, international and bi-lateral levels are required. The progress made in the recent past is commendable; but a lot more is remaining to be done.

2.5.1 At International Level

Appreciably, the United Nations is at its forefront as a responsible international instrument in ensuring human rights protection; The Protocol to Prevent, Suppress and Punish Trafficking in Persons, Especially Women and Children, adopted in 2000 is actively creating all-inclusive antitrafficking strategies, by providing the needed assistance and overseeing the corrective implementation of its various targets. Over 173 parties are in alliance with this Trafficking Protocol at present, which targets to prohibit child trafficking for prostitution, ensure the return of children subjected to cross-border trafficking, provide residence to the rescued children on humanitarian grounds and introduce national trafficking legislations, to name a few. The Blue Heart Campaign—an international antitrafficking program by the United Nations Office on Drugs and Crime, launched in 2009, is another prominent international initiative. The campaign, by using the information and communication technology, was successful in reaching masses by educating people and society on human trafficking and showing solidarity to the victims of the same. The UN Voluntary Trust Fund for Victims of Trafficking in Persons supports the Campaign following the launch of 2010 UN Global Plan of Action to Combat Trafficking in Persons- which was aiming to provide financial, legal and humanitarian aids to the victims. The Hague Convention on Protection of Children and Co-operation in Respect of Inter-country Adoption (dealing with international adoption of trafficked children), the UN Global Initiative to Fight Human Trafficking (a multi-stakeholders body to fight human trafficking), the Council of Europe Convention on Action against Trafficking in Human Beings and the Council of Europe Convention on the Protection of Children against Sexual Exploitation and Sexual Abuse are a few international initiatives launched with fighting against child trafficking with child prostitution as their objective.

> Eliminate forms of violence against all women and children in the public and private spheres, including trafficking and sexual and other types of exploitation (Target 5.2 of SDGs).

The promising Sustainable Development Goals (SDGs) undertaken by the United Nations General Assembly in 2015 also targets to end human trafficking by bringing "accountable and inclusive institutions" for all by 2030. To fight against human trafficking in Asia, the European Union under the ASEAN agreements has provisions to promote human rights. A few cross-regional Memorandums of Understanding signed, such as that with Philippines, Thailand and Sri Lanka, has enabled the development of ties among such countries through effective case investigation and advocacy legal measures for child protection.

2.5.2 At National Level

Nearly twenty countries have now developed National Plans of Action as well as created national focal points for tackling the sexual exploitation of children. The key elements of this National Plan are international cooperation, in order to fight together against a strong global concern. Legislative reforms, such as in Nepal, for example, have created special police units to specifically combat the trafficking of girls, is instrumental in setting examples for other countries to take up child protection as its supreme priority. Several western countries, such as the UK and Sweden, have extra-territorial legislation to ensure that the rights of their children are protected in even internationally. NGOs like the Cambodian Center for the Protection of Child Rights (CPCCR), have been broadly supportive of the National Plans and are willing to assist in the implementation of the Plan, having a strong role to play in the training of national counterparts (for instance; World Vision in Vietnam has been active in training social workers in recognizing families at risk). Most NGOs have tended to concentrate primarily on the provision of services to those who have been trafficked, in preventive activities to vulnerable communities, and, increasingly, in advocacy. While in some cases, NGOs are now getting involved more directly in the rescue of trafficked children, these cases are still rare.

Unfortunately, India is also a breeding ground for this inhuman demand-driven phenomena; that is, child trafficking for prostitution. Research reveals that more than 40 percent of the victims of commercial sexual exploitation in the country are children who are trafficked (MoWCD, 2008). In the light of this upsetting reality, the Government of India and several of its state governments has been trying out means to fight against this organized crime. At the legislative level, institution of Immoral Trafficking (Prevention) Act, 1956, the Protection of Children from Sexual Offences Act, 2012 (POSCO), Juvenile Justice Act, 2015 and several provisions under the IPC such as section 339, 340, 366, 366(A), 370, 372 and 373, and others laws against organized crimes are instituted to ensure the rights of children. The Ministry of Women and Child Development, the Ministry of Home Affairs (MHA) and the judiciary has been putting earnest efforts at prevention, rescue and rehabilitation of the innocent victims of this callous act. The GOI's specialized Anti Human Trafficking Units (AHTUs) at its various nodal centers are actively engaging in addressing the concerns of sexual commercialization of children. Along with this, many other sensitive and responsible governmental and non-governmental organizations and schemes, and voluntary initiatives like the National Commission for Protection of Child Rights (NCPCR), the Integrated Child Protection Scheme (ICPS), Save the Children (*BalRaksha Bharat*), Child Rights and You (CRY), CHILDLINE India Foundations, Prajwal India etc., have been providing support to the children. Despite the efforts, neither the count of children being trafficked for prostitution nor their demand in the viscous sex market is reducing. The government continues to strive for the protection of child's rights by revising the legislations and implementing/revising schemes in order to face issues related to child trafficking.

2.5.3 Local/Community Level

In India too, there has been actions instituted at all levels of government to fight against commercial sexual exploitation of children, but, its spread is mostly observed to be minimal and lack establishment at the community level. Trafficking in children is an explicit symbol of a society that has lost its sensitivity to care for its children. The people of the larger society pretend to be ignorant about this enormous mishap. Hence, check on the cause-effect equations as well as prevention-control calculations are far from predictions that such preventive mechanisms have to be enforced from the grassroots levels onwards. Preventive measures through community mobilization, training and advocacy should be effective in reaching the inner belts of the nation where the victims of child trafficking for prostitution is prominent.

First and foremost, the root causes of trafficking and its complicated methodology of execution has to be identified. Aforementioned factors are the prominent causal and contributory factors of this exacerbated nexus involved in this phenomenon, based on the available data and hands-on experiences. Poverty is found to be the root cause, particularly in backward villages of the country which are found to be the source area of both the victims and a good proposition of traffickers. The brothels, which are the symptoms of this social problem, are also found in the inner corners, which may be exclusively kept and known for prostitution. However, there is a need to look at reasons beyond poverty. Every poverty-stricken community does not find its children dispensable or disposable to violence and discrimination. The perfect example to illustrate this incidence is Purulia in West Bengal. While almost all other states, in some degree, are affected by trafficking, the incidence of trafficking in Purulia is almost negligible. Instances where a poor family grabs the chance of marrying off their teenage daughter to a trader from the city who does not ask for dowry leads us to the broader issues of child marriage, dowry and discrimination against the girl child, which leaves her without an education or a means of supporting herself. Thus, program interventions need to identify the peculiar and crucial factors that lead to trafficking Hence, the hypothesis that prevention should begin from the community stands valid.

To begin with, at the community level, primary prevention can be targeted at the parents, which at large, is targeted for the development of a positive system of living in the society. "Primary prevention programs focus on awareness creation regarding the causes, the exploiters and methods of recruitment, the effect on the children and appropriate ways of intervening" (Source: EASCAP-HRD, United Nations, NY, 2002). Activities targeted to encourage healthy family functioning can be important in eliminating risky behaviours and attitudes that would lead to maltreatments at home. Plans to curb poverty such as educational and vocational training for the parents, employment opportunities, awareness creation of effective family planning and effective health care methods for pregnant women and similar policies to reduce overall violence in the society can all be involved in primary prevention strategies. More specifically, the primary preventive measures, which could be beneficial include:

- Ensuring free and compulsory education for all; specifically, in high-risk areas.
- Arrangement of safe shelter for displaced, homeless orphaned and runaway children.
- Promotion of child rights in family and school education program to curb abuse and maltreatments at homes.
- Advocacy for the effective implementation of existing laws for protection of child trafficking and sexual exploitation of children.
- Mobilization of business/corporate sectors to come forward and to take up programs for child protection activities.

Identification of high-risk populations can be the first step in secondary prevention. Specific approaches can ensure support during crisis and stress like self-help groups, medical aid, social behavioural managements, etc. Providing an opportunity to acknowledge past suffering, teaching effective interpersonal problem solving and planning strategies and offering situations in which abused and neglected children can revive their self-esteem, can serve to reduce the probability of maltreatment in the next generation.

All interventionists—program support, designers and implementers and the target community—need to understand the real reason for a community targeting violence on its children, the girl children in particular. Considering the multi-deterministic and perpetrators- driven vicious cycle of this issue, it is not a feasible objective to set up organizations in each of these areas to work on trafficking; rather, the psyche of the whole society should take up the responsibility to deter this social evil. An intersectional approach to integrate consciousness among all existing NGOs who work with the vulnerable groups of women and children on issues of health and education and sensitizing them to address issues of gender inequity, violence against women, discrimination against the girl child and role of Panchayat and Police in ensuring protection to all children vulnerable to trafficking is a better approach (Sen & Sinha, 2003). There is a need to integrate all these initiatives and link it up with an advocacy network to lobby with the police and Panchayat to ensure prosecution of traffickers as well as those who perpetrate violence against women and children. To reiterate, one has to focus on the continuing practice of child marriage and the deprivation of education to girl children, preventing them to grow into self-reliant individuals who have the option of living a dignified life.

2.6 The Multi-deterministic Action Plan to Prevent Child Trafficking for Prostitution

Taking cognizance of the situation, single-handed tackling methodology would only remain few and far between. Rather, a multifaceted approach by effectively incorporating the existing systems of governance of the nation could be helpful in deterring child trafficking. The number of precautionary, preventive and rescue missions initiated at the international, national and regional levels have to be allied into action-based service delivery. Through proactive planning and working-out, these cooperative alliances should be intensified to provide a platform to learn, support and collaborate (Model 2.1).

Given the fact that India has made available various regulatory measures as well as policies and plans to safeguard the nation's children from such evil acts, the reachability of these provisions to the people in need are questioned. Apart from the available legislative and constitutional provisions as discussed earlier, there also exist specific monitoring initiatives by independent ministries such as Ministry of Women and Child Development, Ministry of Social Justice and Empowerment and

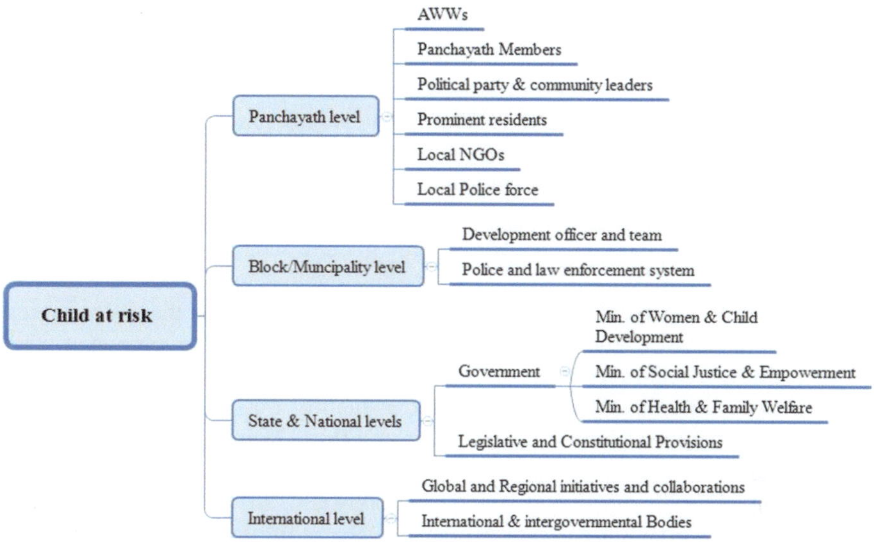

Model 2.1 The multi-deterministic action plan to prevent child trafficking for prostitution

Health and Family Welfare. Regulatory measures as well as law enforcement are taken care of by the Police force under the Ministry of Home Affairs. Nevertheless, the demand-supply chain of child prostitution is only getting thicker. This drives home the point that the system in place requires restructuring and evidence-based methodology building.

Monitoring of the implementation of these existing provisions as well as course-correction in law enforcements have to be taken up as a joint responsibility at all levels of the country. In order to ensure the protection of every child of the nation, a multi-agency partnership can be envisioned that would ultimately guarantee his/her right to live with dignity and free will.

The cleansing process should undoubtedly begin at the grassroots level, in the rural part of India, where the vulnerability index is seemingly high. As discussed earlier, the prevention as well as intervention should begin at households for various reasons. Therefore, the local-level service delivery system can be involved into the mission of child protection from trafficking by equipping and sensitizing the Anganwadi Asha Workers (AWWs) and Panchayat members to form a structure of observation and identification of children and their households who are at risk. This could be rightly done by AWWs since they are informed about the economic conditions of the families and vulnerability status as well as the perpetrators and agents of the locality. They can be trained to be watchful about the presence of outsiders, susceptible family relatives and acquaintances that approach with marriage and job offers. Educating the families and the whole locality about the potential risks and complexities around this issue can be helpful in heightening the sensitivity and alertness towards child trafficking for prostitution in the region. The involvement of MLAs and community leaders would attract the contributions of prominent residents of the area such as teachers, doctors, lawyers and so on, which would, in turn, boost up the security system in the locality. The police can be assisted in spotting the local agents, pimps and customers to enforce legal action by punishing the culprits. This would also ensure reliable reporting and effective management of information systems and record keeping. Involvement of local NGOs is detrimental to ensure the best interest of the children through action plans, research and funding.

Due commitment should be shown towards matters such as ensuring education, nutrition and health of the children. By remaining attentive and responsible towards such needs of the children, these agents of change can ensure that the children grow up in a nurtured and fertile ground, equipped to face the challenges as and when it comes. Similarly, entrepreneurship through self-help groups (SHGs) should be promoted among families that face economic instability. Financial assistance can be sorted through National Bank for Agriculture and Rural Development (NBARD) as well through numerous wavering offered by nationalized banks and micro-finances. This has helped rural women to grow independently (Bh, 2018), curbing the tendencies to fall prey to the inhuman trade practice. Therefore, by imparting a sense of reassurance and security in the children and their families, as well as by discouraging the potential perpetrators of the area, this system instigates collective responsibility and protection to the children in danger. The Development Officers at the Block Panchayat and Municipalities can enhance measures to broaden the scope of the preventive measures. These can be overseen by the aforementioned multi-ministerial convergence at national and state levels along with the active participation of the country's law and order bodies. Hence, through systematic check and timely intervention, this multi-agency partnership targets reachability to every child at risk to keep their rights non-negotiable.

2.7 Intervention

Hardly any studies have been undertaken with a view to understanding the phenomenon and evolving strategies to prevent and combat sexual exploitation of children. Moreover, caregivers have not received adequate training to enable them to address the needs of the victims of sexual exploitation and their families. This means that care is often provided on a trial and error basis (Source: EASCAP-HRD, United Nations, NY, 2002). Hence, there is a need to carry out systematic studies to understand the efficacy of various preventive measures/strategies. Residential rehabilitation continues to remain as a new concept in our country with very few organizations that has successfully rehabilitated sexually misused children. Despite the scenario, there do exist various models have been developed by various agencies for intervention, taking into account the overall trafficking scenario in the country. However, by and large, most of the models cover the following aspects for intervention.

- Psychosocial re-integration of trafficked children and children rescued from prostitution.
- Child Protection Program.

In particular, the victim and the family require the following support services:

(i) **Immediate Medical Care**: Child victim of sexual abuse needs immediate medical care followed by reporting of the incident to police and integration of the child with family or guardian.

(ii) **Psychological Support Services to Victim**: Child sexual abuse is both physically painful as well as psychologically traumatic. They develop fear, guilt and blame themselves for the incident. Therefore, the psychologist's role is very important to give them a feel that they should not feel ashamed for the incident and they are not at fault. In addition, psychological support services in terms of individual and group counselling give a lot of mental support to the victim to overcome the traumatic experiences and resume their daily activities, which is attending schools and playing with other children as they used to do earlier. In case of severe psychological trauma, psychologists may think of applying cognitive behaviour therapy since this therapy has been found to be beneficial.

(iii) **Support to the Family Members**: When the victim's family members come to know about the incident, they become very upset and angry. Sometimes, they blame their own child for the incident. During this phase, they need support from the psychologist to cope with the situation and to take appropriate medical, social and legal measures in addition to accepting the child unconditionally and giving him/her full support so that the child feels safe and secured.

(iv) **Follow-up**: Some of the child victims of sexual abuse may experience social adjustment problem, disinterest in studies and/or suicidal ideation. Some may also feel likely to meet the same victim for further sexual abuse. Therefore, there is a need to follow-up the case for some time and help the child to deal with the situation accordingly.

2.8 Psychosocial Rehabilitation of Trafficked Children Rescued from Prostitution

Equally important are the rescue and re-integration of trafficked children back to the society, in the hope of them regaining their composure and leading a quality life. Predominately, issues related to stigma and labelling, financial insecurity and physical and mental illness, rejoining with their family members or the society, in general, are often impossible. A mixture of factors wraps around the individual, who in most cases would have been a child when trafficked, to get back to a mainstream living condition (Baker, Dalla, & Williamson, 2010).

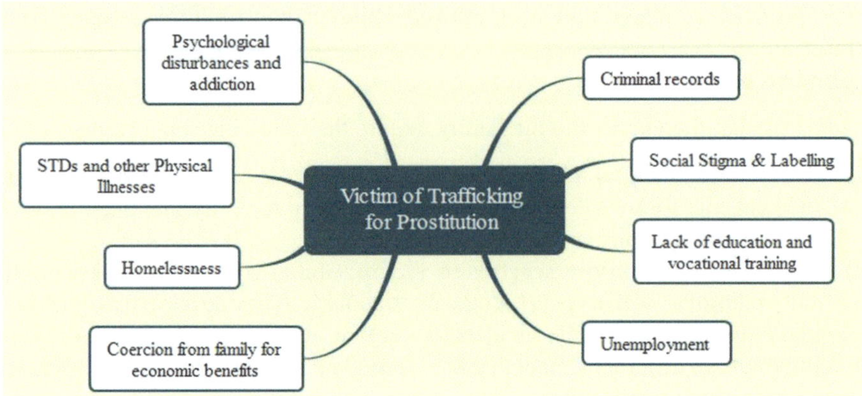

Model 2.2 Challenges faced by trafficked children

Coercion from the part of the family has been observed since the individual would be an important source of income. Ironically, their return back home is not encouraged and they are often seen as a burden if they return. Fear of social stigma and labelling, as well as their unemployment would make them unwanted and homeless after rescue. Along with this, continuous stay in the brothels would have high correlations on the addiction and substance misuse; prevalence of physical ailments, STDs and associated illness, as well as psychological disturbances. Moreover, due to lack of education and training, they would hardly be left with any option for finding the means of daily living. Criminal records, imbibed aggressive behaviours, learned helplessness, debt would all aggravate the situation. These individual, relational, financial and societal barriers encircle the individual from coming out of prostitution. Despite all these concerns, there are appreciable efforts made by the police as well as several NGOs working for this cause for rescuing this population and bring them back to normal life. The multi-staged re-integration process is highly demanding in terms of planning and execution and requires great caution, knowledge and sensitivity (Model 2.2).

2.8.1 Rescue

First, it is important to rescue a trafficked child for re-integration. Rescue operation, of minors in prostitution, is primarily a State responsibility, which is to be carried out by the State Police. NGOs which play a more active role in the identification and rescue of minors using their own strategies in obtaining the information can be identified to work in partnership with the police. The risk of such informants, who helps Police in rescue missions, being later attacked is an issue that cannot be unseen. Such incidents, where identified people being injured, or killed, might have been demoralizing to other people and scare them off. One must be aware of the

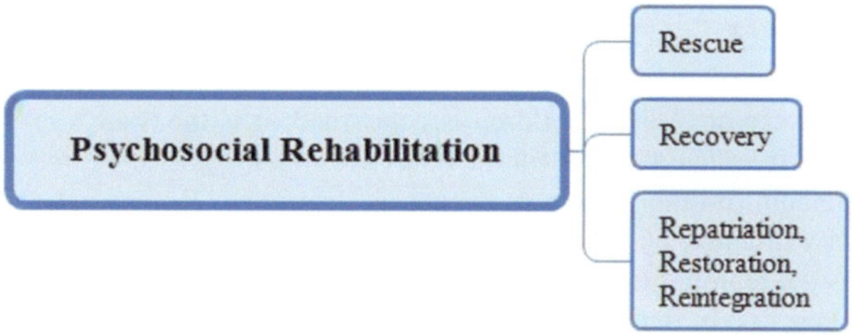

Model 2.3 Psychosocial rehabilitation of trafficked children

fact that the Mafia controls all forms of institutionalized and street prostitution. It is this Mafia that extorts the women and coordinates the balance between supply and demand of prostitution—madams, brothel owners, pimps and brothel keepers among others. There are organizations that work in the red light areas providing services to the children of women in prostitution as well as the women themselves. It is not possible for them to take such a direct role in rescue operations. There are models (Sanlaap, Prerana) in which organizations have facilitated a process whereby the youth and the women in prostitution have organized to resist sale of children and women into the red light areas. There are examples set where the youth groups or the women have reported a case to the police or the 'link NGO' as soon as a new girl or woman is brought to the area by a trafficker for sale. These have been met with varying degrees of success. There have been instances where the reporting has resulted in the rescue of the girl or the woman by the police through an immediate raid. In other cases, where the liaising with the police has not been as successful, the raid has not achieved the rescue of the girl. The nexus of corrupt officials and the people who control the movement of the trafficked girl have been the prime hindrance to the process (Model 2.3).

Some rescue operations carried out in the past have been often ill-planned and hasty. There had been no planning or coordination between the police and the shelter homes or NGOs who run shelter homes to ensure sensitive handing of the rescued children. Unfortunately, there are first-hand reports which testify that children go through victimization at the hands of the State when rescued without adequate arrangements of their shelter and custody. Thus, there needs to be a constant process of sensitization of the law enforcing agents who carry out the rescue operations. Agencies that initiate rescue operations need to network with Government remand homes or shelter homes run by NGOs recognized by the Juvenile Justice Board under the J.J. Act authorized to take custody of the child. Such collaborations and partnerships ensure sensitive handling of the rescued child and minimize the trauma that the child is subjected to during the operation.

2.8.2 Recovery

So far as recovery of rescued children is concerned, it is the State's responsibility to keep a child in remand homes till the court files against the identified criminal—trafficker, madam, brothel owner or keeper, is dismissed. Bureaucratic red tapism and slack investigation and judicial processes keep the cases running for years at the end. It is the classic example of lack of State accountability and irresponsibility where children live in the remand home for years. There are Model Interventions that include the State Remand Home in Liluah (West Bengal) where NGOs work inside the remand home with programs for the children—on education, mental health recovery and vocational training programs. The NGO interventions inside the shelter home also aids in indirect monitoring of the staff inside the remand home. The NGO staff also assists in sensitization of the government staff who can be ignorant in handling children and are, thereby, insensitive. Certain changes in the structure and processes in preparation, which are insensitive to children and violate their rights, can also be changed through advocacy. Such examples can be found in changes that have been brought in the State Remand Home, at Liluah, with regard to forced HIV testing and breach of confidentiality and of sero-positive children rescued from prostitution.

Very few systematic studies have been conducted on problems of trafficked children and that too most of the study findings are not reported in the standard journals. Hence, there is an urgent need to carry out a study to understand the psychological as well as physical health problems encountered by the trafficked children engaged in different professions. However, personal experience of the author and other NGOs in dealing with trafficked children engaged in domestic work and in prostitution reveal that these children mostly suffer from severe stress disorder and behavioural problems like poor self-esteem, poor self-concept and disturbance in sleep, depression, anxiety, frustration and so on. Apart from this, they also suffer from adjustment problems owing to loss of trust and prolonged isolation. Substance abuse is very common among a good number of such children. The individual counselling of such children is found to be very much effective in helping them to overcome psychological problems like depression, inferiority complex, adjustment problems and to regain confidence in developing a positive outlook towards life. Practical experience of the author's recent visit to an NGO in West Bengal called 'Sanlaap' is a bright example of how a group of motivated and dedicated people can bring smiles to the faces of helpless/rescued trafficked children.

2.8.3 Repatriation, Restoration and Re-integration

With the intention of speeding up the procedures, the NGO Sanlaap set up the best repatriation practices in Nepal (1997) and Bangladesh (1998). This was particularly important with regard to Bangladeshi victims who were, until then, 'pushed back', which put the victims in grave danger during and after the push back. The Repatriation

Process that involved the Consulate/High Commission of both countries along with the NGOs who facilitates the process (especially from the sending country) and takes custody and initiates restoration (receiving country). The model has, since then, been replicated by other NGOs dealing with the same target group as well as other groups, like Prajaak, an NGO dealing with destitute boys, some of whom have been trafficked from Bangladesh and Nepal, has since January '2001', repatriated 16 boys to Bangladesh following that set process (Sen & Sinha, 2003).

The following are the needed concerns to be addressed by the host in order to ensure effective restoration.

- Consent and participation of the child.
- Sensitization of the family of the survivor.
- Sensitization of the community, especially community leaders like the Panchayat members, school teachers and the Police, who are likely to be responsible for the child and his/her welfare and safety.
- Identification of the dimensions of the situations that prompted trafficking.
- Recognition of local agents/agencies that can be involved in monitoring and follow-up of restored children.
- Assessment of the viability and exploring options of the child to be restored if s/he is sero-positive and taking possible safeguards without the breach of confidentiality of the status of the child.
- Ensuring that the child has a contact to turn for help in crises.
- Effective case management, information sharing, outreach and drop-in services, counselling, education, training and employment opportunities.

Restoration processes that address all the concerns are very few. This can be achieved if collaborations can be made between more rural and urban NGOs. Currently, those NGOs which work on trafficking issues have to extend to rural areas as well by building networks with agencies/organizations in rural districts of the country. Another relevant plan of action can be the identification of children's aptitude and interest to train them vocationally, which would also be based on their future prospects. Hence, the child can grow up to be economically independent and support his/her families a well. In addition, NGOs in association with Government and other international agencies should identify the pockets or areas from where children are mostly trafficked and they should concentrate on those areas and sensitize people about the negative consequences of trafficking. It is also necessary to address the basic problems which lead trafficking (Model 2.4).

2.9 Mandatory Reporting: Global Scenario

In a study, Dora found that "out of 72 responding countries to ISPCAN survey, 49 indicated the presence of policy-based reporting duties of child abuse in law or policy, and 12 respondents indicated the presence of voluntary reporting by professionals." In this regard, Mathews and Kenny (2008) stated that "among all the nations adopted

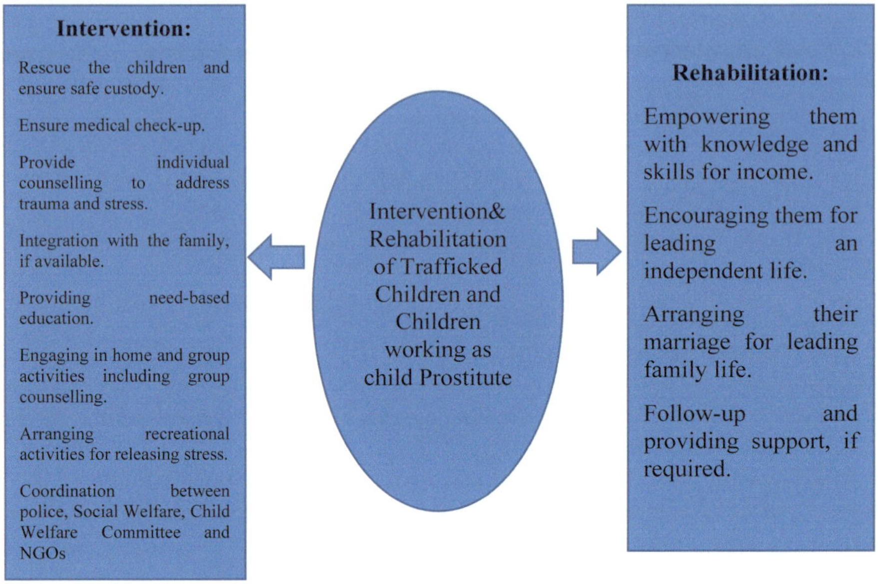

Model 2.4 A conceptual model for intervention and rehabilitation

legislation concerning mandatory reporting, it is worth referring legislation of US, Australia and Canada for the developing countries who are yet to adopt legislation." In addition, legislative measure toward this end adopted by Ghana especially for prevention of Human Trafficking Act (2005) is worth mentioning here.

2.10 Reporting of Child Sexual Abuse Cases in India

As compared to reporting and recognition of various forms of child abuse and neglect in the industrial countries such as the United States and Australia, reporting of child abuse and neglect is very low in India because of a number of reasons like social stigma, perceived harassment, unwillingness of parents, disbelief of parents and threat by perpetrators (Modak, 2009). In a study in Kolkata, India, only 1.7% of sexually abused cases were reported to the police (Deb & Mukherjee, 2009) while in case of another study carried out in Agartala, Tripura (India), 15.5% of the sexually abused cases were reported to the police (Modak, 2009).

2.11 Legislative and Social Measures for Prevention of Child Trafficking and Child Prostitution

Child trafficking for commercial sexual exploitation has become a serious concern for national and international policymakers. Reporting of such cases to the appropriate authority on time could arrest the problem to some extent. However, evidence suggests that reporting is very poor across the countries and it is worse in developing countries like India. One of the main reasons for poor reporting is the non-mandating any social agent by the law except media professionals in one legislation, that is the Protection of Children from Sexual Offences Act, 2012 (POCSO Act, 2012).

It is relevant to mention here that the government of India has taken various legislative measures for the protection of child rights in addition to a number of articles for child protection in the Indian Constitution (1949). However, no legislation clearly mandated any social agent for mandatory reporting except two. They include the Indian Penal Code (IPC, 1860), and the Protection of Children from Sexual Offences Act, 2012 (POCSO Act, 2012). Even the Immoral Traffic (Prevention) Act (ITPA), 1956 did not specify anything about mandatory reporting. In the IPC sections like 176 (Omission to give notice or information to public servant by person legally bound to give it), 177 (Furnishing false information), 197 (Issuing or signing false certificate) and 201 (Causing disappearance of evidence of offence, or giving false information to screen the offender) talked about reporting of any offences without specifying the category of professionals and/or social agents.

In the given situation, it is very important to examine legislation of other countries' concerning mandatory reporting of child sexual abuse with a view to taking appropriate legislative measures in India for prevention of child trafficking and child prostitution.

A number of policies, The National Policy for Children, 1974, The Integrated Child Protection Scheme, 2012 are in place for the protection of child rights in India. In addition, the National Charter for Children (2003) has a provision to protect the rights of the children against neglect, maltreatment, injury, trafficking, sexual and physical abuse of all kinds, corporal punishment, torture, violence and degrading treatment (article 9).

So far as legislation is concerned for prevention of child trafficking and child sexual abuse, a number of Indian legislations have provision towards this end. For example, The Indian Penal Code (IPC), 1860 provides for criminal liability and prosecution of offenders for simple and grievous hurt (sections 319 to 329); wrongful restraint and wrongful confinement (sections 339, 340–346); criminal force and criminal assault (sections 350 and 351); and dealings such as buying and selling of any person as a slave (section 370).

Section 372 and 373 of the IPC set punishments for selling and buying of minors for purposes of prostitution while section 376-2C spells out the punishment for rape and so on. However, there are no provisions which require individuals to be named to report known or suspected cases of abuse or trafficking.

In order to address this issue of child trafficking and commercial sexual exploitation of children and women, the Immoral Traffic (Prevention) Act (ITPA), 1956 was passed by the Indian Parliament. This act clearly specified the punishment for various acts against children and women which include:

- Section 3: Punishment for keeping a brothel or allowing premises to be used as a brothel
- Section 4: Punishment for living on earnings of prostitution
- Section 5: Procuring, inducing, or taking individuals for the sake of prostitution
- Section 6: Detaining individuals in premises where prostitution is carried on
- Section 7: Prostitution in or in the vicinity of public places.

However, ITPA did not mandate any specific category of professional or social agent to report the incident of child trafficking to the police or any appropriate authority or any person with information about trafficking to inform the issue to the police.

(i) **The Juvenile Justice (Care and Protection of Children) Act, 2015**: This law also recognizes certain offences against children as special offences and provides for punishment. However, there is no provision for mandatory reporting of sexual abuse and child trafficking in this law.

(ii) **The Child Marriage Restraint Act, 1929**: This law prohibits marriage of a male child below twenty-one years of age and for female child, it is 18 years. Further, The Prohibition of Child Marriage Act, 2006 prohibits a male adult above eighteen years from contracting a child marriage. Section 10 of the same law says that whoever performs, conducts, directs or abets any child marriage shall be punishable with rigorous imprisonment which may extend to two years. At the same time, section 11 of the same act punishes a person for promoting or permitting solemnization of child marriages. Had this law been implemented in the truest sense, child marriage, which is rampant in rural areas, could be tackled.

(iii) **Protection of Children from Sexual Offences Act, 2012 (POCSO Act, 2012)**: This law intends to check child sexual abuse in India. It has a provision for mandatory reporting without clearly specifying the category of social agent for reporting of such incidents. For example, section 19 of POCSO Act, 2012 defines reporting of offences

> Any person (including the child), who has apprehension that an offence under this Act is likely to be committed or has knowledge that such an offence has been committed, he shall provide such information to (a) the Special Juvenile Police Unit; or (b) the local police.

The section 19 has given sufficient importance on proper recording of complaints and gets it checked by the informant to avoid any discrepancy. Further, section 19 has mandated the Special Juvenile Police Unit or local police to make immediate arrangements for care and protection of the child informant into safe shelter within 24 h and report the matter to the Child Welfare Committee and/or the Special Court within 24 h.

The POCSO Act, 2012, however, mandated that the media, studio and photographic profession related persons to report sexual exploitation of the child to the police. For example, section 20 of POCSO Act, 2012 states the obligation of media, studio and photographic facilities to report cases.

> Any personnel of the media or hotel or lodge or hospital or club or studio or photographic facilities, by whatever name called, irrespective of the number of persons employed therein, shall, on coming across any material or object which is sexually exploitative of the child (including pornographic, sexually-related or making obscene representation of a child or children) through the use of any medium, shall provide such information to the Special Juvenile Police Unit, or to the local police, as the case may be.

Section 21 of POCSO Act, 2012 clearly states the punishment for failure to report or record a case. As per sub-section (2) of section 19, a person shall be punished with imprisonment of either description which may extend to six months or with fine or with both.

This act has been implemented since 2012. Now the time has come to evaluate the efficacy of the law in improving the situation and the shortcomings in the law.

It is very important to introduce mandatory reporting for prevention of child trafficking and child prostitution and the category of social agents, professionals and law enforcement personnel need to be specified in the law for mandatory reporting. Since child trafficking is more of a rural phenomenon in India, Gram Panchayat Members (elected by the villagers) at the village level, health workers, Anganwadi workers, doctors, nurses, teachers and social workers in addition to parents are the potential agents for reporting the incident to local police, child protection officer and/or child welfare committee members as they have close contact with the village people (Deb, 2018).

In general, in the Indian society, sexual intercourse with a minor is considered to be sexually abusive and other forms like stimulation, showing pornographic picture, touching private parts of a child and so on are not generally recognized as sexual abuse and are ignored. Other types of sexual abuse cases should be treated with equal seriousness for defining child sexual abuse in developing countries like India and the perpetrators should be penalized.

Training for Reporters and Professionals

There is an urgent need to organize orientation programs for all stakeholders on latest legislations of child sexual abuse for understanding the issues from the right perspectives and applying the law for delivering justice on time. First track courts need to be introduced in every part of the country for a speedy disposal of child sexual abuse cases.

Need for Appointment of Female Juvenile Officers in Police Stations

Non-availability of Female Juvenile Officer in most of the police stations across India is discouraging for the reporting of sexual abuse cases. On and above, insensitivity on the part of male investigating officers in questioning and collecting information about the incident is sometimes highly traumatic and humiliating. Therefore, every police station should appoint at least one female juvenile officer for taking first information report about child sexual abuse. Second, every police station should have a room with some privacy for such purposes as mentioned in the Juvenile Justice (Care and Protection) Act 2015.

2.12 Conclusion and Implications

Child trafficking and child prostitution for commercial sexual exploitation is a serious social problem in India owing to a number of factors like poor financial conditions, lack of education, gender discrimination, migration, overpopulation and so on.

Nevertheless, attempts to answer the question made at the beginning of this chapter: 'how and why does children, at larger numbers, are lost to prostitution' would take one through the intense and awful dynamics of the society. Child trafficking for prostitution remains a heated up global concern and demands intergovernmental collaborations. Individual countries have to tailor their own regulatory mechanisms within the country using the smart application of the existing system of governance. Taking the Indian scenario, the multi-deterministic action plan to prevent child trafficking as well as the psychosocial rehabilitation after the rescue of trafficking victims are discussed here. Prevention efforts should be to "improve economic opportunities and security for impoverished women and girls, educate communities regarding the tactics and identities of traffickers, as well as promote structural interventions to reduce trafficking" (Silverman et al., 2007). However, the prominent understanding that pertained is the commitment and sense of responsibility each individual in the society should develop in order to tackle the issue.

For prevention of child trafficking, government officials, NGO personnel and Panchayat members, especially in the rural areas, should work together by strengthening their network with rural poor people and ensuring income-generating programs for them through loan facilities and formation of self-help group. Reporting of child trafficking and child sexual abuse is very low because of a range of factors and they include threat from the perpetrators, social stigma and perceived harassment. One of the most important factors is threat from the perpetrators. Therefore, police should ensure security for the victim. In a number of cases, the victim parties experienced further victimization because of reporting the incident to the police.

So far as intervention is concerned, in reality, in a country like India there exist no psychological support services for the sexual abuse victim and his/her family, except a few places. Hence, it is important for the government and the NGOs involved in child protection to have trained psychologists for addressing the issue in an urgent manner and give a feel to the victim that he/she is not responsible for the incident and guide the family members for reporting the incident to the police and ensure the security with intervention from the Police. There should be special orientation for all concerned people involved in child protection for understanding the sensitivity of the issue involved in the incident and for dealing with them accordingly.

In a number of cases, ongoing supportive psychological services are required because of the severity of psychological trauma and poor social network. In this regard, if concepts like '*One Stop Abuse/Rape Crisis Centre*' could be introduced for addressing all related issues like reporting, medical care and examination, investigation, psychological support services, safety and justice, under one roof, it could be beneficial for the victim and her family.

In developing countries like India, policymakers and bureaucrats hardly consider the potency of psychological rehabilitation for which there are no sanctioned posts of psychologists in the educational institutions and in the health centres. Of late, some State governments have started recruiting psychologists in the psychiatry unit. People feel the need of a psychologist when they go through serious crisis in their life. Therefore, like other professions, posts for psychologists should be created in all institutions like other industrial countries and their services should be utilized in "child protection system, law enforcement agency, industry, educational, NGOs and/or health institutes" (Deb, 2015).

Lack of trained psychologists for extending psychological support services to the victim is another challenge. Sexually abused children hardly receive any mental health support services. They live with the lifelong psychological trauma of the abuse, affecting their interpersonal relationships, personality and career development (Deb & Sen, 2005).

Although there are a number of legislations for the prevention of child sexual abuse, lack of trained manpower, not mandating social agents for reporting and causal outlook of the service providers and law enforcement authorities concerning the issue are partially responsible for ineffective implementation of laws. Prevention of child trafficking would not only protect the rights of girl children, it would also ensure quality of life girl children and healthy society.

References

Baker, L. M., Dalla, R. L., & Williamson, C. (2010). Exiting prostitution: An integrated model. *Violence Against Women, 16*(5), 579–600. https://doi.org/10.1177/1077801210367643.

Beyrer, C. (2004). Global child trafficking. *The Lancet, 364*(Suppl. 1), 16–17. https://doi.org/10.1016/S0140-6736(04)17624-1.

Bh, S. (2018). Self-help groups and rural women enterpreneurship development. *International Journal of Engineering Technology Science and Research*, *5*(1), 1–5. Retrieved from http://ror.isrj.org/UploadedData/1123.pdf.

Bhuvaneswari, K., & Deb, S. (2016). Child sexual abuse: A progressive social disorder. *Indian Journal of Health and Wellbeing, 7*(6), 651.

David, W. (1998). *Child trafficking in Asia*—child rights and The UK promoting the convention on the rights of the child world-wide, Briefing Paper No. 4, November 1998.

Deb, S. (2015). Legalisation concerning reporting of child sexual abuse and child trafficking in india: A closer look. In B. Mathews & D. C. Bross (Eds.), *Mandatory Reporting Laws and Identification of Severe Child Abuse and Neglect* (pp. 541–564). Berlin: Springer Science.

Deb, S. (2004). Dynamics, causes and consequences of child trafficking in south Asia with special reference to prevention and intervention. Lecture delivered in the ISPCAN Global Institute in San Diego, California, USA on January 25, 2004 as Visiting Faculty of ISPCAN Global Institute.
Deb, S. (2005). Child trafficking in South Asia: Dimensions, roots, facets & interventions. *Social Change, 35*(2), 143–155.
Deb, S. (2018). *An empirical investigation into child abuse and neglect in India: Burden, impact and protective measures*. Springer.
Deb, S., & Mukherjee, A. (2009). *Impact of sexual abuse on mental health of children*. Delhi: Concept Publishing Company.
Deb, S., & Mukherjee, A. (2011). Background and adjustment capacity of sexually abused girls and their perceptions of intervention. *Child Abuse Review, 20*(3), 213–230.
Deb, S., Mukherjee, A., & Mathews, B. (2011). Aggression in sexually abused trafficked girls and efficacy of intervention. *Journal of Interpersonal Violence, 26*(4), 745–768.
Deb, S., & Sen, P. (2005). A study on psychological trauma of young trafficked women. *The 6th Asian Conference on Child Abuse and Neglect* held in Singapore during November 16–18, 2005.
Deb, S., Srivastava, N., Chatterjee, P., & Chakraborty, T. (2005). Processes of child trafficking in West Bengal: A qualitative study. *Social Change, 35*(2), 112–123.
Dottridge, M. (2004). *Kids as Commodities? Child trafficking and what to do about it.*
EASCAP—HRD, United Nations, NY. (2002). *Training manual on psychosocial and medical services for sexually abused and sexually exploited children and youth.*
Engle, L. (2013). *The world in motion: short essays on migration and gender. International Organisation for Migration* (Vol. 6). https://doi.org/10.13005/bpj/397.
Fong, R., & Berger Cardoso, J. (2010). Child human trafficking victims: Challenges for the child welfare system. *Evaluation and Program Planning, 33*(3), 311–316. https://doi.org/10.1016/j.evalprogplan.2009.06.018.
Johnson, C. F. (2004). Child sexual abuse. *The Lancet, 364*(9432), 462–470. https://doi.org/10.1007/978-1-4757-9777-0_15.
Mathews, B., & Kenny, M. C. (2008). Mandatory reporting legislation in the United States, Canada, and Australia: A cross-jurisdictional review of key features, differences, and issues. *In Child Maltreatment* (vol. 13). https://doi.org/10.1177/1077559507310613.
Mikhail, S. L. B. (2002). Child marriage and child prostitution: Two forms of sexual exploitation. *Gender & Development, 10*(1), 43–49. https://doi.org/10.1080/13552070215896.
Ministry of Law and Justice. (2012). *The Protection of Children from Sexua Offences Act*, 2012.
Ministry of Women and Child Development. (2008). *India Country Report to Prevent and Combat Trafficking and Commercial Sexual Exploitation of Children and Women*. World Congress III. Rio de Janeiro.
Modak, S. (2009). *Violence against children in Tripura and its impact*. An Unpublished Doctoral Dissertation, University of Calcutta.
Nair, P., & Sen, S. (2005). *Trafficking in women and children in India*.
Scarpa, S. (2006). Child trafficking: International instruments to protect the most vulnerable victims. *Family Court Review, 44*(3), 429–447. https://doi.org/10.1111/j.1744-1617.2006.00098.x.
Sen, S. (Coord). (2004). *A report on trafficking in women an children in India 2002–2003. Volume I*. Retrieved from http://www.nhrc.nic.in/Documents/ReportonTrafficking.pdf.
Sen, R., & Sinha, I. (2003). *Trafficking in children: An overview*. Lecture delivered in the Multi-disciplinary Training Programme on Child Abuse and Neglect for NGO and Police Personnel in Kolkata, Conducted by MIDSW in association with the Government Medical College and sponsored by the ISPCAN, USA, held in February and June, 2003.
Silverman, J. G., Decker, M. R., Gupta, J., Maheshwari, A., Patel, V., Willis, B. M., & Raj, A. (2007). Experiences of sex trafficking victims in Mumbai, India. *International Journal of Gynecology & Obstetrics, 97*(3), 221–226. https://doi.org/10.1016/j.ijgo.2006.12.003.
Thappa, D., Singh, N., & Kaimal, S. (2007). Prostitution in India and its role in the spread of HIV infection. *Indian Journal of Sexually Transmitted Diseases and AIDS, 28*(2), 69. https://doi.org/10.4103/0253-7184.39007.

The Indian Penal Code. (1860). Human Trafficking Prevention Under Section 370 of IPC, 1860.
UN. (2014). Human rights and human trafficking. In A. Nollkaemper & I. Plakokefalos (Eds.), *The practice of shared responsibility in international law* (Vol. Fact Sheet, pp. 556–582). Cambridge: Cambridge University Press. https://doi.org/10.1017/9781316227480.023.
UNODC. (2009). Factsheet on human trafficking. In *United Nations Voluntary Trust Fund.*
UNICEF. (2001). *Children on the Edge: Protecting children from sexual exploitation and trafficking in East Asia and the Pacific.*
UNICEF. (2018). Children make up almost one-third of all human trafficking victims worldwide. Retrieved from UNICEF website: https://www.unicef.org/stories/children-make-almost-one-third-allhuman-trafficking-victims-worldwide.
Willis, B. M., & Levy, B. S. (2002). Child prostitution: Global health burden, research needs, and interventions. *The Lancet, 359*(9315), 1417–1422. https://doi.org/10.1016/S0140-6736(02)08355-1.

Chapter 3
Slum Children: Innocent Victims of the Social Reality

Abstract Child Labour happens to be one of the most debilitating concerns affecting children around the world, more so in the developing countries, where resources are scarce. It denies children the necessary foundation of education, health and recreation, affecting their physical and mental well-being and potential to lead quality lives as adults. With child labour forming a staggering 13% of the total workforce as per the 2011 census, India has been one of the major victims of this issue. While in recent times, rural child labour has shown a downward trend, it is on the rise in urban areas. Further, in many cases, it remains invisible, as legal vigilance has shifted their focus of child labour from registered factories and establishments to unorganized sectors, such as small shops and eateries, unregistered small-scale industries, street vending, domestic labour and family trade. The Indian scenario has witnessed several policy and legal interventions to deal with the problem, including preventive legislations and making Right to Education for children aged between six and fourteen years a fundamental right. Despite these measures, child labour remains a reality, owing to an ecosystem of poverty, lack of education, inadequate enforcement of law and increasing pressure on resources due to a growing population. This chapter investigates the past and ongoing issues concerning child labour in India, theoretical positions of its dynamics, and the underlying socio-economic issues that helps child labour sustain. Based on the review and analysis, the chapter discusses the effect of various interventions and proposes need-based interventions and policy solutions.

Keywords Child labour · India · Right to education · Policy

3.1 Introduction

> Child labor is coming down, especially for younger children and for the most harmful areas of work… But the decline in child laborers is happening unevenly and at too slow a pace.
>
> —Gordon Brown, UN Special Envoy for Global Education (2012)

Rising interconnectedness of the global order has interesting implications upon the socio-economic environment of countries across the world. While the world is witnessing unprecedented growth in quality of life, prosperity, health and education, on an average, the positive impact is often not spread out uniformly. This exposes

S. Deb et al., *Disadvantaged Children in India*,
https://doi.org/10.1007/978-981-15-1318-3_3

many sections of the society, who are vulnerable to maladies of poverty, displacement, ill-health and war, as they were a century ago. Technological revolutions have also multiplied global complexities. Wars are fewer but far more devastating than before, markets are interconnected but far more price-competitive than what they used to be, and rising quality of life is continuously failing to cater to an ever-expanding population size. Key victims of this unpredictable world order are the vulnerable sections of the society, particularly children, who are denied their basic rights and are exploited for monetary gains. As the world economy expands exponentially, it is becoming increasingly clear that a scary proportion of it rests prematurely on the shoulders of the children, a portion of whom are involved in child labour.

In 2012, the United Nations Conference on Sustainable Development witnessed the genesis of the Sustainable Development Goals (SDGs), targeted to 'meet the urgent environmental, political and economic challenges' that assail the world (United Nations Development Program [UNDP], 2019). The SDGs, which came about as a replacement of the Millennium Development Goals (Department of Economic and Social Affairs, 2015), were significant for their focus on the economic exploitation of the most vulnerable segments of the world's population, the children. Two of the SDGs that particularly stood out in this regard are: (i) the Goal for Decent Work and Economic Growth—aimed at the complete eradication of child labour by 2025 and an immediate eradication of its worst forms, and (ii) the Goal for Peace and Justice—that envisaged the end of torture, abuse, trafficking and exploitation of children (International Labour Organization [ILO], 2018). Close to 170 nations of the world accepted the SDGs as a road map for the coming decades, and many took active efforts to implement them. However, in November 2017, the ILO cautioned that the Sustainable Goal for eradication of labour by children looks unachievable in the next decade. Further, such is the scale of the problem, that is 'dramatically' enhanced efforts are needed to bring about a difference (Wahlén, 2017). In 2013, data showed the number of child labourers worldwide to be at 168 million (The International Program on the Elimination of Child Labour [IPEC], 2013). As of 2017, more than 85 million children were engaged in hazardous work, with over 51% of them aged between 5 and 14 (O'Driscoll, 2017).

Child labour tends to be a major menace in the developing parts of the world, owing to its close and complex association with poverty, illiteracy and failure of legal systems. At the same time, the largest economies of the world are not free from this issue either and the statistics are far from optimistic. An important case in question is India, a prominent participant of the crusade against child labour, and a major victim of this phenomenon. India as of 2019, with 29.7% of the population aged less than 15 (India Population, 2019). A long legacy of employing children as an easy alternative to adult workforce, population boom and poverty have made the Indian situation conducive to child labour, in both hazardous and non-hazardous occupations. Such recruitment mostly happens for insufficient compensation and in denial of the child's access to education, nutrition and safety. The Indian scenario is also interesting for the sheer volume of interventions against child labour—governmental, non-governmental, legal and advocacy-based. Moreover, with time, the nature, incidence and drivers of child labour has also altered dramatically, leaving policymakers to deal with new challenges and roadblocks. This chapter offers a contemporary perspective relevant to the issue of child labour in India, recent trends, insights into its catalysts and ways to combat it in the future.

3.2 Definition

Labour is defined as work done by individuals of either sex to produce goods and services (International Labour Organization, 2003). However, when it comes to child labour, the issue is further nuanced, as many activities that are considered appropriate for adults may be physically and psychologically hazardous for children. Again, child labour often includes activities that are unpaid, particularly those that occur within domestic boundaries.

Case Study 1: The child workers in Kathmandu, Nepal

"While travelling within the city [Kathmandu], you go to office in a micro-bus with a child conductor; you go to the canteen for lunch with a child waiter serving you water and cleaning the table; you go to a shop to buy fish where an 11-year-old boy cleans the fish for you. The rag pickers moving around in your locality are usually children under 15 years. You are invited to a friend's house for dinner, they have school-going children as domestic help.

The causes of child labour are many. From poverty to abandoned children to orphans to children chasing city dreams, all those innocent little ones end up in a place where they do not belong. One major concern has been the hazardous environment in which children work, but another big concern is their commercial sexual abuse, certainly one of the most brutal forms of violence against children. Though prostitution is illegal in Nepal, it is prevalent in the urban areas, and many young girls are trafficked to for commercial sex work within the country and in India."

Pratistha Koirala, In *Ending child labour: Whose concern is it?* (Koirala, 2019)

It is interesting that while the outrage against child labour is relatively recent, children have been a part of the workforce since the earliest days of human civilization. Owing to the low population size, it made sense for the early human inhabitants of the world to bring into use every resource available. Children have been known to be a part of the relatively less hazardous food gathering and farming activities, and later, of hunting expeditions, in ancient hunter–gatherer and farming tribes. Involving children into occupational trades was also a way to give them a head start into professional lives and make them equipped to look after themselves when the time comes. Education in its modern sense was relatively unknown, and hence, professional endeavours were ways to keep children industrious, productive and remained as ways to acculturate them into the norms of the prevailing social order, which more often than not were divided into occupational ranks. Ancient history illustrates children to be a part of light farming activities, such as chaffing, weeding and planting; apprenticing for trades such as blacksmiths, carpentry, cooking, or masonry, or even as helps for soldiers in war. Child labour became widespread in Europe and later in the USA, as the Industrial Revolution happened (Basu, 1999; Van den Anker, 2003).

Children were attractive as labourers, as they could be hired with little pay and compensation can be ordered about easily. They were relatively less likely to turn rogue or disobey the master. Children were particularly attractive as slaves, owing to their easy trainability and relatively lower demand on resources.

It was not until the beginning of the twentieth century that a growing discontent against child labour became noticeable. The biggest complaint against child labour was that, despite the immediate gains, it heavily stunts the developmental possibilities of children—both physically and in terms of their mental growth. Concerted efforts against child labour began in the early nineteenth century, the earliest documented effort being that of keeping children out of hazardous professions, such as chimney sweeping in England. Subsequent efforts to address child labour has led to numerous legislations in many countries, which tend to range from being selectively restrictive to universally prohibitive in nature. In 1979, the world celebrated the International Year of the Child, which led to a renewal of attention of scholarly workers, activists and policymakers to the issues of children at work.

While child labour has been in the spotlight across nations of the world for quite some time now, there are significant differences in how child labour is defined. Countries differ on what constitutes childhood, with the age of consent and maturity varying drastically across nations (Anker & Melkas, 1996). Again, there are differences on what constitutes labour, and whether some forms of non-hazardous labour should be viewed as detrimental to children. The Child and Adolescent Labour (Prohibition & Regulation) Act, 1986 (The Ministry of Labour & Employment [MLE], 1986) prohibits and regulates child labour in the following areas: (i) shop, (ii) commercial establishment, (iii) workshop (for industrial processes), (iv) farm, (v) hotel, (vi) restaurant, (vii) eating house, (ix) theatre, or other places of public amusement or entertainment.

According to Van den Anker (2003), there needs to be a distinction between work performed by children and child labour, to appreciate that 'not all child work is harmful'. Child labour differs from child work in that, the former is non-domestic in nature and is harmful to the child, while the latter takes place within the home and is not harmful. Child labour is further distinguished from child slavery in that, the former is paid, while the latter is unpaid and is usually under duress. Anker and Melkas (1996) defined child labour as:

> *'(i) work by very young children; (ii) long hours of work on a regular full-time basis; (iii) hazardous working conditions (physically or mentally); (iv) no or insufficient access, attendance or progress in school; (v) abusive treatment by the employer; and (vi) work in slave-like arrangements (bonded labour).'*

One or more of the above conditions is sufficient to label an engagement as child labour.

IPEC (2019) states that to be identified as child labour, a work needs to be '**mentally, physically, socially or morally dangerous and harmful to children** and interfering with the schooling of a child.' It further broadens the definition by including labour put in family firms for production or consumption (Faraz, 2019).

3.3 Extent and Dimensions of Child Labour in India

India, currently one of the world leaders in terms of growth rate of the economy ('India to Remain', 2019) is of considerable interest in the child labour context because it is also the nation with one of the largest young workforces (TNN, 2016, March 12). With a declining number of youths in the developed nations in North America and Europe, it is likely that a large percentage of the jobs generated globally, not to mention the jobs in India, will be filled by Indian workers in the years to come (Sharma, 2017). Child labour in India thus directly affects the quality of the workforce globally, as it affects the employability of youths for generations to come and reduces the number of new entries in the workforce who are suitably educated and vocationally trained.

Case Study 2: Migrant child workers at brick kilns of Odisha, India

"Although Indian law is against child labour, in this part of the country, a child is as important as an adult worker in brick kilns, because the child is part of a work unit called pathuria that constitutes (sic) three members of a family...kiln workers find the children's small hands good for piling mud and flipping bricks for drying. "The labour contractor also prefers children and agrees to pay an advance if the unit consists of a child or two, he said." ...From travelling in unreserved train compartments to working in exploitative conditions, the children face many risks. "There are incidences of children facing abuse at worksites and girls exposed to physical and sexual abuse.""

—*Rakhi Ghosh, In Migrant Children gets a Shot at Education* (Ghosh, 2019)

From what scriptures and historical evidences tell us, the ancient Indian society placed importance on education and training of young children, something that is likely to have delayed their entry into the vocational world. However, at the same time, India has been a land of close-knit family structures and generational trades, making the children's early participation and apprenticeship in the family trade common (Bajpai, 2017; Rhodes, 1990). Post colonization, degrading economic situations made children from the backward sections of the society particularly vulnerable to child labour. The National Sample Survey Organization (NSSO) estimated that, in 1979, India had 16.6 million child workers, of which 10.4 million were boys and 6.2 million were girls (Ministry of Labour and Employment, 2018). To tackle the problem, the Government of India formed the Gurupadswamy Committee in 1979. The Committee recommended gradual removal of child labour, with an immediate ban on hazardous activities and strict regulation for engagement in other areas. In 1986 came the Child Labour (Prohibition & Regulation) Act, which listed the potentially hazardous activities where children cannot be employed (MLE, 1986). In 1987, the National Policy on Child Labour came, which laid down the path for the rehabilitation of former child workers (Ministry of Labour & Employment, 1987). Owing to a series of legal and social-economic reforms, the incidence of child labour saw an impressive drop among children aged between 5 and 14 years, between 2001 and 2011 (Ministry of Labour & Employment, 2015). From 12.67 million as per the 2001 census, the 2011 census projected the incidence of child labour in India at 4.35 million, with the largest concentration being in the 4 largest states of Andhra Pradesh, Bihar, Tamil Nadu and Uttar Pradesh.

While official records are available till as late as 2011, there have been several subsequent surveys by global organizations on child labour, in the subcontinent. According to UNICEF (2017b) figures, around 11.8% of Indian children of 5–17 years are engaged in child labour. Although India contributes to about 6% of the child labourers of the world, India's child labour percentage is the lowest in South Asia, the highest being that of Nepal, at 42% (Devulapalli, 2019). The situation is slightly optimistic in the urban areas. Child labour in urban areas in India, which used to be as high as 20% in 1993–94, now form only 1.6% of the total Indian workforce, as against the Asian trend of 9.3% (Panda, Chakraborty, & Misra, 2016). The Child Labour Index 2019 identifies India, along with its neighbour China, as high-risk nations, with industries such as 'agriculture, manufacturing, apparel, construction, mining and hospitality' as well as 'trafficking and commercial sexual exploitation' being particularly notorious in this regard (Maplecroft, 2019).

3.4 Extent and Dimensions of Child Labour Worldwide

As a socio-economic problem, child labour is not limited to only the developing nations. Countries across the world are subject to this issue, in varying degrees of seriousness. While economic affluence and legal protection ensures a healthy environment for the development of the children in the western world in general, the problem continues to persist for migrant children, children in other marginalized sections of the population, and children involved in family trades.

Case Study 3: Children working in family firms in United States of America

Like children across America's two million family-run farms, Cullen had grown up around farm equipment. He watched his grade-school-age brothers drive the diesel-powered loader, carrying corn and doing chores to help keep their family's struggling Wisconsin dairy afloat. The work was woven into their childhood. But one evening last October, as Cullen's father was using the loader—called a skid steer—to feed the cows, Cullen [6 years old] clambered aboard, and his foot slipped. The machine's hydraulic bucket bit into Cullen's left leg and tore it from knee to ankle, ripping off his tissue as easily as someone slipping off a glove. Two years earlier, Cullen's brother Kholer, 8, had driven the steer into his older brother, Maric, sending him to the hospital. Now another child was hurt.

On family-operated farms, children as young as 5 grow up in the driver's seat of machines many times their size, doing work that is deeply embedded in rural traditions but that also contributes to injuring thousands of children and teenagers every year and killing an estimated 100 more… "I've seen too many children killed," said LuAnne Ujazdowski, a counselor at Cullen's elementary school in central Wisconsin…A 3-year-old in Loyal, Wis., crushed last May by a loader being driven by his 5-year-old brother. A 6-year-old boy in Dowagiac, Mich., run over and killed last July when he fell from the bucket at the front of a skid steer. A 10-year-old boy in Kansas, who had been clearing bush when run over by a tractor driven by his 9-year-old sister.

—**Jack Healy**, ***In 5-Year-Olds Work Farm Machinery, and Injuries Follow*** (Healy, 2018)

According to an ILO estimate, child labourers formed 27.6% of the world's working population in 1950 (Kambhampati & Rajan, 2006). Since then, there have been concentrated efforts to improve overall quality of life, access to natural rights and justice and legal and policy measures to ensure resources for all. As a result, at the start of the new millennium, ILO reported that the share of child labourers in the total workforce around the world has come down to 11.3% (Kambhampati & Rajan, 2006), whereas, in a 2013 press release, the United Nations International Children's Emergency Fund (UNICEF) pegged the incidence of child labour at 150 million (UNICEF, 2013). Since then, there is a declining trend in child labour, going as low as 0.04% in Europe. According to the 2018 End of Childhood Report (Save the Children, 2018), child labour has declined by 40% worldwide since 2000. Although around 2 million child labourers are still present in the high-income countries, no more than 1% of the children are found engaged in child labour in these parts of the world. Further, the situation on child labour has been showing improvement in 95 out of 175 countries of the world (Save the Children, 2018).

Despite the dramatic improvement in child labour statistics in the developed nations, the final picture is far from rosy. In 2013, the number of child labourers was estimated at 152 million, with more than half of them engaged in hazardous activities (IPEC, 2013). The situation is critical in the developing parts of the worlds, where children are far more likely to be denied their rights for economic benefits, than their counterparts in the developed nations. The United States Department of Labour (2014) reported that one in five children in the sub-Saharan Africa are labourers, amounting to over 59 million children in child labour. This region also showed a rise in child labour from 21 to 22% between 2012 and 2016, in contrast to a declining trend across the rest of the world (International Labour Organization [ILO], 2017). In the least developed countries, every fourth child is a labourer (UNICEF, 2017a). Despite an improvement in the average statistics, there is a rise in child labour in as many as 40 countries, with the incidence being the highest in Africa at 72 million, followed by Asia and the Pacific countries at 62 million (Save the Children, 2018).

The Child Labour Index 2019 brought out by the global risk consultancy firm Verisk Maplecroft, in May 2019, also presents a bleak picture (Maplecroft, 2019). The Index reports a 'flat lining of the progress on child labour' in the world's biggest manufacturing centres and 'no tangible improvement since 2016' among the Asian manufacturing giants, such as China and India. North Korea has been identified to have the worst indices in the world in terms of child labour. Twenty-seven countries have been identified to be at 'extreme risk', when it comes to child labour and, 7 of the 10 worst-performing countries are from Africa (The Tribune, 2019). In South Asia, the country that fares the worst is Nepal, where 42% of children are suspected to be child labourers.

3.5 The Shape of the Problem

Despite numerous social, legal and economic efforts to eradicate it, child labour continues to be a debilitating issue for nations. The incentives for child labour outweigh the deterrents, and it continues to be a major issue in the developing nations.

Case Study 4: Mass Gymnastic Displays in North Korea

"Thai Yong-ho, the former deputy ambassador from North Korea to the UK, who defected in 2016, said travel companies and tourists should boycott the cultural displays, which attract large numbers of visitors and social media viewings. He said North Korean children already faced appalling rates of malnutrition; brainwashing and forced labour and the displays were yet another act of cruelty.

"Every year North Korea gives this mass gymnastic display. You should know that it means the children, aged from six to nine, cannot go to school for six months – it's a forced exercise. And who are the audience for this? Europeans, and there are many European tour companies who organise trips. We should argue this with the European companies – these are inhumane displays.""

—**Tracy Macveigh**, ***In Boycott North Korea's 'inhumane' mass gymnastic displays, says ex-diplomat*** (Macveigh, 2019)

Policies have been made to incentivize sending children to school, while laws have been formulated to discourage employing children for work with punitive measures. There have also been initiatives to provide financial aid to needy families, so that child labour is not encouraged. However, despite everything, challenges persist. Some of the major roadblocks in the eradication of child labour are as follows:

3.5.1 Lack of Data

One major problem in formulating effective policies against child labour is the absence of reliable data on the incidence and spread of child labour. In India lacks an updated statistic on spread of child workers in different industrial sectors and in different hazardous and non-hazardous activities. According to the Ministry of Statistics and Program Implementation, Government of India (2019), the two sources of data through which the Government of India collects information on child labour are, the National Sample Survey and the Census. They have wide disparities in their figures when it comes to child workers. Further, many activities, such as bonded labour for children, are underreported, being either difficult to gather or intentionally suppressed, as the activities are illegal (Avis, 2017).

3.5.2 Unorganized Sector

Numerous studies show that laws relating to child labour are primarily enforced within the organized sector, leaving the vast unorganized section of the economy open for the child workers. Diwan (2017) report that although there is about 90% compliance to the child labour prevention laws in the industrial units in Haryana, India, the roadside eateries and construction sites continue to use child labour widely. Children in unorganized sectors are often subjected to hazardous working conditions, leading to permanent health damages. Goel and Chowgule (2019) report cases of lead neurotoxicity in children working in artificial jewelry cottage industry.

3.5.3 Transfer

One of the most potent instruments to fight child labour is crackdown by the legal machinery. However, if it is not supplemented with an attempt to remove the causes of the children landing in the workforce in the first place, the rescued children soon return to the workforce, transferred to a different profession. Anker and Melkas (1996) report that after being thrown out of the garment industry of Bangladesh, owing to international pressure, most children employed previously in these sweatshops went back to the workforce—either in different garment factories, or as domestic workers, or in self-employment. Similar findings have been reported by Bain (2016) in his analysis of children working in the garment industry of Bangladesh. Large factories in Bangladesh, who sign deals with famous Western brands, tend to be supported by numerous satellite subcontractor factories. Such subcontracting often tends to be invisible, absolving the primary contractor, or the purchasing brand, of any illegal activities that go on in the premises of the subcontractors, including hazardous work conditions, economic exploitation and child labour (Avins, 2015).

Prostitution is another common destination for children, who are displaced from the original workplace owing to legal crackdown (Anker, 2000; Narayan, 1999). Thus, attempts to rescue children from child labour through crackdown or boycott of goods often backfire, as they tend to land up the children in far more hazardous, unregulated and exploitative trades than before (Alam, 1999).

3.6 Classification of Child Labour

Rodgers and Standing (1981) proposed that the engagements of children may be divided into nine different kinds of activities: '(i) domestic work; (ii) non-domestic, non-monetary work; (iii) tied or bonded labour; (iv) wage labour; (v) marginal economic activities; (vi) schooling; (vii) idleness and unemployment; (viii) recreation and leisure; (ix) reproductive activities' (Anker & Melkas, 1996; pp. 3). Excess of the first five activities constitute child labour and may be detrimental for children by taking away their opportunity for schooling, rest and leisure.

Based on Burra (2009), the following categories of child labour may be identified:

i. Labourers: Children engaged in paid or unpaid labour in factories, mines, workshops, farms or other commercial establishments.
ii. Bonded labour: Children pledged for unpaid labour in commercial or domestic establishments to pay off inherited debts.
iii. Children in Family Business: Children working in family business or family-owned farms/agricultural fields.

iv. Street Children: Homeless children engaged as hawkers, beggars, or rag pickers.
v. Children in sex trade: Children, of either sex, forced into prostitution, sex trafficking, or pornography.
vi. Children in Household Activities: Children running the domestic activities in absence of their parents.
vii. Migrant Children: Children travelling with migrant caregivers and engaged in labour where the caregivers are employed.

Since the definition of childhood and the definition of labour is different for different nations, International Labour Organization and the Inter-Parliamentary Committee (International Labour Organization, 2002) proposed the ILO Convention No. 182, where the Article 3 describes the worst forms of child labour:

i. Slavery, trafficking, serfdom, bondage, or compulsory labour, such as forced recruitment in war.
ii. Pornography and prostitution.
iii. Illegal acts, such as producing and selling drugs.
iv. Hazardous activities that are 'likely to harm the health, safety, or morals of children' (ILO, 2002). These are further classified as physical, mental or sexual abuse; dangerous working conditions, such as high temperature or noise, confined spaces, or with dangerous equipment; or working for unreasonably long hours or at night.

3.7 Causes of Child Labour

Despite concerted efforts to combat it, the rising trends in many countries indicate that child labour is a complex problem to solve. This happens because child labour stems from an ecosystem that benefit from the process significantly. The result is a zero-sum game where one side must win at the cost of the other.

Case Study 5: Children as Soldiers around the World

"The use of child soldiers is a recognized form of modern-day slavery. The numbers of victims of this form of modern-day slavery are difficult to assess because of the nature of the crime. The UN assessed that in 2016 that there were at least "4,000 instances of children recruited and used in armed conflict by government forces and more than 11,500 such instances by non-state armed groups" including in Afghanistan, the Central African Republic, Colombia, Democratic Republic of Congo (DRC), Iraq, Lebanon, Libya, Mali, Myanmar, Nigeria, Somalia, Sudan, Syria and the Philippines.

The use of child soldiers by non-state actors is especially challenging to address. Groups like Daesh have abducted thousands of children to turn them into fighters in Syria and Iraq. Because of the fragility of these states (and the ongoing Syrian Civil War) addressing the issue and ensuring safe return of the children has turned to be an extremely difficult task - despite international involvement."

—Ewelina U. Ochab, In *the Transatlantic Slave Trade and the Modern Day Slavery* (Ochab, 2019)

The vicious cycle that feeds child labour often ensures that any attempt to uproot it falls short. In other words, the inconvenience (whether threat of legal action or long-term deterioration of quality of life) often do not appear terrifying enough to upstage the immediate perks available from the system. Understanding the ecosystem of child labour is crucial to address the situations that make child labour rewarding for the stakeholders.

3.7.1 Poverty and Child Labour

Poverty relates to child labour in several intricate ways. About 43% of all child labourers are in the low-income countries. Even within a country, the poorest children are 3.7 times as likely to be engaged in child labour as their wealthiest counterparts, with the likelihood being 8 or 9 times as high in low-income countries such as Vietnam or Mongolia (Save the Children, 2018).

The correlation between child labour and poverty stems from the lifestyle and economic choices of poor families. Poor parents tend to have more children, owing to lack of education about healthy life choices, lack of access to and knowledge about contraceptives and birth control measures (e.g. Jacobson, 2018), and lower life expectancy of a child in a low-income household (Spencer, 2018). Child labour, ironically, itself is a motivator, as poor households tend to look upon children, early on, as additional sources of income rather than as cost centers for education and nutrition, which, in turn, incentivizes childbearing (Ali, 2019; Bowen & Finegan, 2015). Anker and Melkas (1996) reported that child labour form 20–25% of the family income and children get to spend only 10–15% of their income as pocket money. High fertility rates add to the vicious cycle, making it impossible for the parents to feed their children. Child labour thus becomes a necessity for survival for children in poor families.

A major way poverty leads to child labour is by depriving families of social security. Poor families are usually not eligible for loans and are not able to avail government grants and schemes owing to their lack of awareness. Often, such families depend on informal moneylenders for their dire financial needs and borrow money at exorbitant rates. The burden of debt subsequently makes them put their young children at work (Human Rights Watch, 1996). Diwan (2017) reported that poverty leads families to put children to work in family trades or as bonded labour, to pay off ancestral debts.

Poverty also pushes children to child labour by denying them the opportunity of being gainfully employed elsewhere. Poverty leads to malnutrition, illnesses and stunted mental development, causes children to drop out from mainstream education. Research shows that children of poor families are highly likely to drop out of school early, being unable to pay fees, or work to pay school costs (Blank, 2018; Chaudry & Wimer, 2016).

3.7.2 Nature of the Family

Closely related to poverty is the issue of the family as a prime instigator of child labour. Statistics show that certain family structures make children particularly vulnerable to child labour. According to Diwan (2017), 58% of child labourers come from families with size ranging between 5 and 10 members. Large families make it difficult for parents to spend quality time with the children, or even provide the basic minimum resources to them, making children fall prey to child labour for survival. Adegbenro, Opasina, Fehintola, and Olowookere (2017) reported that families having more than three children are strong predictors of child labour in Nigeria.

Absence of parents due to death or broken homes has also pushed children to enter workforce early. According to Singh and Parihar (2016), domestic violence predicts 34.6% of the likelihood of child labour in the automobile service sector. Khatab, Raheem, Sartorius, and Ismail (2019), in their study on children in Egypt, found that child labourers across job areas are significantly more likely to report physical and psychological abuse at home than ordinary children. Violent homes thus deprive children of the safety needed for a sheltered childhood. It makes them adopt desperate measures to escape their daily trauma. Polygamy and remarriage have also been found to be closely linked with child labour in Bihar, India, as stepchildren are often compelled to leave their homes and fend for themselves (Singh & Parihar, 2016). Similar trends have been seen in homes with alcoholic or drug addict parents (Habib, 2017; Laing, McWhirter, Templeton, & Hannah-Russell, 2019).

Educated parents appear to lower the risk of child labour considerably. Mothers without any formal education were 52.9% more likely to have their children engaged in child labour than mothers with any level of formal education (Khatab, Raheem, Sartorius, & Ismail, 2019). Similar findings have been reported by Adergbendo and others from their research on Nigerian mothers (Adegbenro, Opasina, Fehintola, & Olowookere, 2017).

3.7.3 Involvement in Family Trade

Ironically, one of the prime employers of children tends to be the people responsible for their safekeeping, the caregivers themselves. Surveys reported that family businesses tend to lead the charts when it comes to hiring child workers, even in the developed nations, and are also one of the toughest to eradicate (Ballet & Bhukuth, 2019; Janzen, 2018). According to the US Wage and Hour Division 2016, the incidence of children as farm labourers is particularly common in the United States and may involve children 'of any age' (Healy, 2018). The National Institute for Occupational Safety and Health (NIOSH, 2016) reported that every day, about 33 children are injured in agriculture-related accidents, and children belonging to the family are at higher risks to accidents than hired youths.

Diwan (2017) reported that most child workers in rural areas of India are involved in their family trade. A seasonal pattern is common in case of agriculture, where children quit schools during the harvesting seasons to help as farmhands in the family fields or work with parents as labourers. There are even instances of children working with parents as bonded labourers to repay family debt.

3.7.4 Migration

Migration of people in search of livelihood, whether within the country or across national borders, have been found to have significant implications on the well-being of children, particularly in the context of child labour. Migrant labour refers to casual, unskilled, or semi-skilled workers, who move across geographic locations to avail temporary or contractual jobs (Cohen, 2016). Migration of labour within the country occur when resources tend to stay limited to urban areas, causing the rural population to move to urban locations in search of jobs and superior living conditions. Urban migration is also common in economies that are heavily dependent on agriculture, such as India. Such economies witness, what is called, the seasonal migration, where peasants and landless farm labourers migrate to urban locations in search of jobs during off-seasons (Panda & Mishra, 2018). Migration is also likely to happen in response to wars or national conflicts, with people moving away from conflict zones in search of stable life conditions (Papastergiadis, 2018; Schwartz, 2018). ILO (2015), reported that there were over 150.3 million migrant labourers in the world in 2013.

Migration, whether seasonal or lasting, has considerable impact on the migrants, particularly children. Migrant families typically have poor living conditions and lack of access to amenities such as healthcare, education, security or other life resources. Children of migrant workers drop out of schools owing to displacement and academic facilities may not be easily available in the areas where they relocate (Fellmeth et al. 2018). Further, as both parents are typically working, children must run households and engage in cooking, cleaning and childrearing (Roy, Singh, & Roy, 2015). In cases where children do not migrate with parents, they are often engaged completely, carrying on minor work in the family farm or with livestock, in the absence of the parents (Bhattacharyya & Vauquline, 2013; PROBE, 1999).

India, with over 4–6 million children migrating seasonally (International Labour Organization and Understanding Children's Work, 2010), is an interesting case study in this regard. As per the 2011 census, India has around 139 million internal migrants every year (Wanchuk, 2019). Migrant families typically do not have access to the social security measures at their place of migration. Further, they tend to be economically exploited, live in unhealthy conditions and are under the threat of physical and sexual harassment. Dyson (2014) reported that migrant child construction workers are typically denied the basic amenities of childhood and many of them assist their parents in the construction sites. Such children are often absorbed in the workforce along with their parents at minimal payment and are subsequently exploited.

3.7.5 Conflict

Children tend to be among the most vulnerable population, who are exposed to the negative effects of conflict across the world. Child labour rates tend to be significantly higher in locations affected by conflict than in peaceful areas and tend to spike, once conflict starts (Aptel, 2019; Prasad & Prasad, 2009). Conflicts destabilize economies, leading to loss of jobs for adults, which force children to drop out of schools and start earning to supplement the family income. Again, orphans and homeless children in war-ravaged areas are deprived of their safety and are sucked into the labour force, as paid or unpaid workers. Finally, the legal barriers break down in war zones, making children vulnerable to major human rights violations, including sex trafficking, recruitment as child soldiers, or recruitment in hazardous occupations (Kadir, Shenoda, & Goldhagen, 2019). The End of Childhood Report (Save the Children, 2018) states that 7 of the nine nations with 40% or higher child labour rates are presently in conflict zones or have been ravaged by armed conflicts (Save the Children, 2018). Research reports almost a doubling of the child labour rates in Jordan after the Syrian crisis (University of Jordan, 2016). Similar trends have been reported in the war-ravaged regions of Syria (Brussels Conference Education Report, 2017), Pakistan, Tajikistan and Columbia (Justino, 2014).

3.7.6 Shortcomings of the Education System

While the previous factors suggest that children's entry in the workforce is primarily forced by circumstances and is driven by the need for survival, an alternative perspective argues that child labour is an outcome of an unsatisfactory education system that fails to engage and meet the needs of the children (Spaull, 2015). Children located in war zones, poor nations, or in remote areas, often do not have access to schools or even the means for distance education (Keeley & Little, 2017; Maadad & Matthews, 2018). Such children tend to drift into the workforce or into domestic labour early, owing to the lack of productive engagement. School curricula might pose debilitating costs for economically backward families, causing children, particularly girls, to be denied education and be employed elsewhere (Anker & Melkas, 1996; Tilak, 2018). While many countries, including India, promote Right to Education for all children, and provide free or subsidized primary and secondary education, the benefits often do not reach the targeted masses adequately (Brar, 2018).

School dropout and subsequent engagement in child labour also arise from a perceived lack of connection between the ongoing school curricula and the vocational courses. Many parents perceive school education as an opportunity cost, when the child could be trained as an apprentice in the family trade or could already be earning (e.g. Adonteng-Kissi, 2018; Kielland & Tovo, 2006). Another challenge is the lack of assistance from home for first-generation learners, making it difficult for them to keep up with the system (Guio, Choi, & Escardíbul, 2018; McGregor, 2017; Reddy &

Sinha, 2010). This encourages them to drift towards paid labour, where the immediate gains outweigh the long-term setbacks.

3.7.7 Gender

Child labour, in general, tends to be gender-neutral in its impact as children of either sex are equally likely to be its victims. In fact, boys tend to have a higher likelihood than girls to end up in hazardous professions, while, for the latter, domestic labour is more common (Carter & Roelen, 2017; Kar, 2018). Some research indicates that girls are more likely to be denied education and put into labour, while boys are slightly more likely to continue education and receive formal vocational skilling. Research in India and Ethiopia show that girls are highly likely to drop out of schools to take care of siblings (Save the Children, 2016). National Sample Survey data from India indicated that boys in urban areas tend to have significantly greater wage incentives for continuing education than their female counterparts (Diwan, 2017). Again, girls are more likely than boys to put in a double shift, which is, work outside the home for money as well undertake domestic labour (Gamlin, Camacho, Ong, & Hesketh, 2015). According to one survey, girls tend to put 1.5 h extra in housework than boys do in Andhra Pradesh, India (Save the Children, 2016).

3.8 Social Aspects of Child Labour

What sets apart child labour from most other social problems is the complex nature of child labour, which makes it a difficult problem to solve. Despite decades of legal and societal interventions, child labour persists and even shows a growing trend in certain contexts.

> ***Case Study 6: Slum children in Adabar Thana, Dhaka, Bangladesh***
>
> *"Amina reports working 12 hours a day (with two short breaks) as a domestic help, earning Tk 2500 a month ($32). 'I have lost a lot by not going to school. But my family is poor and my father is sick.'*
>
> *Shilpa, also aged 14, completed two years of schooling in a rural area before coming to Dhaka. She completed Grade 5 in Adabar but now works in a garment factory, operating a sewing machine. When asked about her hopes for the future she comments: 'I'm happy to help my family, but I don't have dreams – and I will not be returning to school'. She had a very positive experience of education, did well at school, and wishes she could resume her education. 'If I studied I could learn things, find a better job and earn more', she says"*
>
> —**Maria Quattri and Kevin Watkins, In *Child labour and education: a survey of slum settlements in Dhaka*** (Quattri & Watkins, 2016, p. 42)

Scholars have been increasingly interested in the dynamics of the supply and demand side when it comes to child workers. It is apparent that the phenomenon persists because of the benefits (short-term or long-term) they draw from the process.

3.8.1 Demand Side of Child Labour: Why Children Are Preferred as Workers?

According to Anker and Melkas (1996), a significant impetus to child labour comes from the long-lasting tradition to hire children for certain kinds of work, for instance, waiting tables in small eateries. Also, young children accompany parents to their workshops, owing to lack of creches or caregivers at home and they are gradually drawn into work through assisting the parents (Lancy, 2018).

One of the most commonly mentioned argument in favour of child labour is that of irreplaceability. This perspective states that in some industries, child labour remains in demand despite inhospitable conditions (e.g. legal deterrence) because children bring in skills that cannot be found in adults. One well-cited example is that of the carpet industry. It is said that children's fingers, being small and nimble, are particularly suited for sewing the intricate designs of handmade carpets (Kiranmayi & Joseph, 2018; Srivastava, 2018). Similar arguments have also been forwarded for glass bangles (Thomson Reuters Foundation, 2017) and the fireworks industry (Kiranmayi & Joseph, 2018; Kuriakose & Iyer, 2018; Mehraj, 2019). However, studies conducted by the ILO and Centre for Operations Research and Training (CORT) showed that the benefits of child labour is highly overestimated in these industries, with the real difference in gain between using child labour and using an adult being less than 5% (Anker & Melkas, 1996). Thus, child labour does not lead to any substantial improvement in the quality of manufacture and consequent profitability (e.g. Pinto, 2016).

The advantage of child labour for business primarily arises from their desirability as non-fussy workers. According to Anker and Melkas (1996), children tend to be docile, obedient, energetic, trustworthy and easy to control and are unlikely to form labour unions to demand for their rights. Children also have far less bargaining power than adults and could be paid a paltry sum of money to work for the same hours (Reddy, 2019). The legal barriers against child labour end up harming children. Since child labour is illegal, children have little right to bargain hard and are often forced to work for dismal terms and conditions (Ronzoni, 2016).

3.8.2 Supply Side of Child Labour: Why Parents Would Let Their Children Work?

According to Imoh, Bourdillon, and Meichsner (2018), one needs to understand the perceived benefits of child labour to appreciate the dynamics that encourage and maintain it. Given that child labour turns out to be often exploitative, it may appear counter-intuitive that families with children and even the children themselves, actively seek opportunities to earn through child labour. Scholars argue that it arises from a cost-benefit analysis, where the benefits accrued from child labour outweigh the real and opportunity costs of the activities to which a child's time may be devoted

(Bourdillon, 2019; Chakraborty & Das, 2005; Pham & Nguyen, 2019). In their study on children in mining, Maconachie and Hilson (2016) reported that families prefer to send children to mining as means of earning money to run the household and to expand family businesses. Further, children look upon labour as opportunities to learn and practice occupational skills and socialize with children of their age (O'Driscoll, 2017). Saludes (2015) reported that earning money through labour is preferred over attend school and improving one's quality of life. Thus, banning child labour completely is likely to fail as it does not address the needs that child labour meets and they end up damaging children's lives, instead of protecting them (Diwan, 2017; Imoh et al. 2018).

3.8.3 The Paradox of Economic Growth and Child Labour

Child workers across the world are typically from the poor families, where child labour is seen as a means of subsistence or a compensation for an extra hand in the family trade, where labour is unaffordable (Abdu & Delamonica, 2018; Jones, 2018). Poverty also prevents children from being gainfully employed in schools and hence makes them drift towards economic activities (Cockburn, 2001). This makes it logical to assume that, if poverty is addressed, there will be less incentives for children and their caregivers for considering child labour as a necessity or as an engagement. In his study on Bangladesh, Chakrabarty (2015) reported that microcredit and micro health insurance is significantly related to reduced child labour. Following Pham and Nguyen (2019), this happens owing to multiple reasons:

i. **Risk Management Effect**: Baland and Robinson (2000) argued that families under debt often have to engage their children for paid work and prioritize present flow of money over potential future earnings of the child as an educated adult. When such families receive loans and credits, their need for immediate financial support is reduced, allowing them to put their children back to school for long-term gains
ii. **Welfare Effect**: Scholars, such as Ranjan (2001), propose that poor households put their children to work, not because they seek to gain from the immediate benefits of greater family income, but because they cannot afford an alternative future for their children through formal education. Economic assistance provides households the resources to ensure their children's welfare, and thus lowers child labour.
iii. **Family-Labour-Substitution Effect**: A significant proportion of children are employed in their own family trades across the world, as poor families are unable to afford hiring real labourers. Wydick (1999) proposed that when such families have access to microcredit, they can hire real labourers to substitute the work done by the children. Thus, the credit frees up children from menial work and makes it possible for them to return to schools.

The argument of economic growth has led to numerous policy interventions that seek to enhance the economic well-being of households, such as small-scale loans for family business and entrepreneurial ventures, agricultural loans and farm subsidies. However, the ripple effect of the economic boost tends to manifest itself in interesting ways. Flow of capital in an area leads to an increase in economic activities, which in turn, leads to an increased demand for labour and hike in their wages. This ironically incentivizes children to quit school and start earning (Kambhampati & Rajan, 2006). Similar findings have been reported by Pham and Nguyen (2019), who pointed out that households in Vietnam, who receive microcredit, are more likely to discourage schooling and encourage child labour. Hazarika and Sarangi (2008), on the other hand, pointed out that, far from lowering child labour and increasing school attendance, microcredit increases the burden of domestic work for children, as the adults at home are now engaged in economic activities. Similar findings have been reported by Islam and Choe (2013). Thus, whether microcredit opportunities and economic growth reduces child labour on not, depends on how the money is used. When the credit amount is utilized to substitute child labour, then the resulting prosperity is inclusive of the children's well-being. However, when the loans and subsidies received is used for capital generation, the effect might be detrimental for children, as they are drawn into serve as domestic or industry workers in the growing economy (Dammert, de Hoop, Mvukiyehe, & Rosati, 2018).

Industrial growth, ironically, can be a trigger for child labour. For instance, the state of Telangana, India, ranked first among Indian states in the Ease of Doing Business (EODD) Index in 2018, however, this rise in EODD is correlated with an alarming dip in the monitoring for child labour in Telangana ("Convictions Continue to Plunge", 2019). Jose (2019) reports that labour inspectors in Telangana have carried out only 244 inspections to identify child labour in 2018 in various construction sites, factories and other possible locations, as compared to 702 inspections in 2017. The count of rescued child workers has fallen from 960 in 2017 to a mere 235 in 2018. Further, conviction happened in only 27% of the cases where violations were seen. All these issues raise the concern about whether the urge to encourage entrepreneurship and industrial growth may make government authorities overlook violations of labour and child rights in manufacturing setups.

3.9 Consequences of Child Labour

The obvious immediate and short-term economic benefits associated with child labour for both the supply and the demand sides often takes away the attention from the significant long-term impact of the phenomenon on the economy and the human capital of the country. However, the fact that quality of life and development indices differ in countries that rank high in child labour and in countries that rank low, alerted policymakers and researchers to the different outcomes of child labour, both for the immediate players and for the stakeholders in the larger context.

Case Study 7: Child workers in mica mines of Jharkhand and Bihar, India

"We came upon mines in Jharkhand with children working who were as young as 5 years old. Most reported that they didn't go to school and had been working in mines for as long as they could remember...Breathing in the dust in mica mines can cause infections, disease and permanent damage to lungs, but there's a much more catastrophic risk that worries locals most — and one the Kumari family suffered first hand. SurmaKumari, 11, and her sister Lakmi, 14, was working in a mine when it began to crumble. When they tried to run, Surma got stuck under a rock and Lakmi was buried under a mountain of debris. Their mother and father were in the village when they heard there had been an accident, but by the time they got to the mine, Lakmi had died... Over a year later, Surma is still dealing with the aftermath of two broken feet, a fractured leg and damage to her spine...

Surma's father, Kishar Kumari, told us that deaths are so common that the traders who control this particular cluster of mines have a set rate they give to families who lose loved ones while mining. "For each person who dies, they give 30,000 rupees [or about £330]," Kishar says. "That was it; they don't do anything for safety."

—**Lexy Lesback,** ***In the Makeup Industry's Darkest Secret Is Hiding in Your Makeup Bag*** (Lesback, 2019)

Some thinkers have argued that the apparent negative effects of child labour would persist even in its absence. Child labour is commonly found in low-income countries with poor quality of life and therefore, they may be erroneously taken to be the predecessor of these conditions. However, data shows that child labour, even when practiced in affluent nations, serve to lower the quality of living in those pockets in more ways than one (Lopez-Calva, 2001). In the developing nations' context, child labour provides only short-term relief from poverty, but by eating into resources that might have been invested into more effective and permanent solutions, it feeds into the vicious cycle of strengthening the very conditions from which it was intended to provide a relief (Ballet & Bhukuth, 2019).

3.9.1 Impact on Schooling

When children enter the workforce, full-time or part-time, they essentially trade off the time for leisure and schooling to earn money. Child labour has been named as the primary reason for school dropouts in Latin America (Stromquist, 2015), Syria (UNIGME, 2017) and many other parts of the world (e.g. Asfaw, 2018; Srivastava, 2015). The immediate impact of this is the arrested mental and intellectual growth of the child, as he/she is denied opportunities of education and skilling and learning social skills and human values. Further, bereft of schooling, children miss out on the opportunities of developing human capital and preparing themselves for white-collared or skilled jobs, certifications and degrees (Dinkelman & Mariotti, 2016). This limits them lifelong to the same low-paying and low-skill exploitative career options that had kept them out of school in the first place (Pham & Nguyen, 2019).

In his study on child workers in rural and urban India, Diwan (2017) reported that child workers are often themselves willing to go to school but are forced to drop out by their family (Tumino & Taylor, 2015). In rural areas, many children attend school for the mid-day meal, and go away from school, for work, once lunch is over. Child labour also affects the child's ability to rejoin education at a later age, even if the opportunity arises (Pawar, 2016). Anker (2000) states that children rescued from child labour are often not able to join or benefit from formal education, as schools often reject them as over-aged for the educational level for which they are suitable.

3.9.2 Impact on Economy

Denial of opportunities for skilling to the child affects the economy (Baland & Robinson, 2000). Anker and Melkas (1996) opine that a high percentage of child workers translate into a future workforce that is majorly unskilled, and therefore not ready to cater to the labour needs of an industrialized and smart economy and its white-collar jobs. It has been further found to arrest the innovation potential of a country by limiting a significant part of its workforce to uninspired vocations and thereby not having enough affordable skilled labour to run startups and small businesses. Anker (2000) had pointed out a link between child labour and foreign direct investment in a country. Low quality of workforce due to high incidences of child labour lowers the attractiveness of an economy and often repels investors (Galli, 2001; Neumayer & De Soysa, 2005).

3.9.3 Deviation from the Mainstream of the Society

The children who are involved in economic activities at an early age are deprived from basic minimal education and as a result, in their later life, they do not find good jobs (Bhalotra & Heady, 2003). After some years of work, if they lose their job or the company where they used to work is shut down, no option is left to them to survive, following honest and/or normal means. As a result, during the unemployment period, a good number of them involve themselves in antisocial activities under the slightest provocation and gradually, many of them deviate from the mainstream of the society (Cullen, Williams, & Wright, 1997). The long-term effects of child labour are considerable. Children born of parents who have been child labourers are more likely to end up as child workers themselves than children born of parents who have had a childhood free from the need to earn a living (Basu & Tzannatos, 2003).

3.9.4 Impact on the Mainstream Workforce

Child labour has significant implications for the adult workforce. Children are willing to work at low pay, have little bargaining power and can be easily coerced into working in hazardous conditions or with exploitative terms. Thus, hiring child workers makes economic sense where the work does not require any adult expertise.

When industries depend on child labour, it lowers the bargaining power of adult workers, whose jobs are taken away by illegal means. High incidence of child labour reduce wage rate for all workers (Anker, 1995; Basu & Tzannatos, 2003; Emerson & Souza, 2011), and force adult workers to settle for poor work conditions and exploitative terms. Child workers are denied basic employment amenities such as medical aid, security, holiday, or sick leaves (Diwan, 2017). The readiness of children workers to work in such conditions affects the adult workers who no longer have the bargaining power to fight for healthy and equitable work conditions. Child labour is also associated with adult unemployment and the eradication of child labour is expected to generate real jobs in the economy (Anker & Melkas, 1996; Dessy, 2000).

3.9.5 Denial of the Rights of the Child

Although the United Nations Organization has, from time to time, issued various guidelines and directives with respect to the well-being of children, it was only in 1989 that the UN Convention on the Rights of the Child was adopted as a legally binding set of guidelines to the member states. The Child Rights Convention (CRC) specifies child rights like the right to survival (i.e. adequate living conditions and nutrition), the right to protection (i.e. absence of abuse or exploitation), the right to development (i.e. education, nurture, social security and cultural practices) and the right to participation (i.e. right to receive information and to express one's thoughts and identity). (United Nations Organization, 1989).

Involvement of children in economic activities at an early age amounts to the denial of the CRC in multiple ways (Invernizzi, 2016; Sloth-Nielsen, 2016). Child labour has immediate consequences for the right to protection and the right to survival, by forcing the child to work in unhealthy or dangerous working conditions. Further, child workers tend to be routinely abused by their employers or supervisors and are denied basic nutrition and health facilities. Kara (2014), for instance, reports the appalling conditions prevalent in India's handmade carpet industry in Uttar Pradesh, which exports to leading brands in the West such as Target, Macy's and IKEA. Children are put to work at carpet factories at miniscule wages or are even sold off to factory owners to pay family debts. Over 400,000 children work round the year inside rural shacks, for long hours, devoid of education or recreation, rarely going out and suffering verbal and physical abuse in case of errors (Bahree, 2014; Kara, 2014).

Child labourers have little scope for self-development. They are often denied mainstream education and training for skilled jobs. Deprived of their control over their own lives, child workers are rarely empowered to make knowledgeable choices about their lives and future, making the downward spiral of deprivation and abuse to continue for a lifetime.

3.10 Working Conditions and Health Hazards

A child goes through the process of physical development and, in many cases, his or her body nowhere nears the strength and durability of an adult body. Therefore, while children tend to be energetic and may easily recover from fatigue in the short-run, the strain of work designed for adults create irrecoverable damages to the physical and psychological health of the child (Nicolella & Kassouf, 2018; Parker, 2016). Tasks such as lifting heavy loads, working in poorly lit rooms, or breathing polluted air, has been found to lead to issues in child labourers, such as cuts, burns, bone deformity, poor eyesight, breathing disorders, lung diseases, kidney dysfunctions and tuberculosis (e.g. Abugre, 2017; Goel, 2015). Kujur (2019), in his study on brick kilns, report that child workers in brick kilns work for over 14 h a day, for as low as Rs. 250. Children tend to be preferred for hazardous labour because adult workers are far more likely to protest the working conditions, demand safety measures, or demand a hike in pay. However, this exposes children to significant risks to their lives and health (Larmar et al. 2017). Farm accidents are one of the topmost killers of young children in the USA (NIOSH, 2016), where poorly enforced regulations with respect to family businesses lead children, as young as five, to run tractors, mowing machines, or other hazardous mechanized farm utilities (Healy, 2018). In the words of Clark (1999, p. 11),

> The dangers of child labor are not always apparent to the employers and parents who encourage it. "Pound for pound, children breathe more air, eat more food and drink more water than adults," says Philip J. Landrigan, a pediatrician at New York City's Mount Sinai Medical Center. "So, if there are chemical contaminants in the workplace, children will be exposed to more of them. Children are also less biologically mature and physically weak. Child Labor and physically strong, which makes them more susceptible to injury. They're more likely to trip or get caught in machinery, and their bodies have more trouble breaking down chemical toxins and excreting them. Finally, children may be said to 'have a longer shelf-life,' which means that after exposure to, say, dangerous benzine or asbestos, they have more years ahead of them in which to develop diseases."

Nutritional deficiencies are common in child workers, owing to premature exposure to stress and poverty, leading to ill-health, weaknesses and death (Jones, 2018; Kuimi, Oppong-Nkrumah, Kaufman, Nazif-Munoz, & Nandi, 2018). Devoid of a healthy environment with peers and under benevolent adult supervision, child workers have an early exposure to drugs, unprotected sex and sexually transmitted diseases (Foroughi et al., 2017; Kamruzzaman & Hakim, 2015). Also, the normalization of abuse ensure that children do not develop a capacity for informed consent or a distinction between the hazardous and the non-hazardous, leading to a lifelong exposure to further abuse. Child workers tend to have higher child mortality than non-working children (Roggero, Mangiaterra, Bustreo, & Rosati, 2007), and suffer from chronic occupational illnesses such as asthma, deformed bones, poor eyesight and arrested mental development (Quinlan, 2016; Ramos, 2018).

3.11 Prevention of Child Labour

The magnitude of the problem of child labour necessitates efforts from multiple ends to address the phenomenon. The UNICEF and the ILO recommend a three-pronged strategy of 'better enforcement of laws, increasing awareness and strengthening education systems (Devulapalli, 2019).

Case Study 8: Child abuse in cocoa plantations in Ghana

"It's the crack of dawn in Obuasi, Ghana, and Kwame Twumasi's work has just begun on the farm owned by his uncle in the forest. Like every day, what lies ahead is hard manual labour. He begins by using a chainsaw to clear a wooded area. This done, Twumasi climbs a cocoa tree and with a large machete, expertly cuts down cocoa bean pods. Five young boys wait patiently below ready to stuff the pods into large sacks that sometimes weigh as much as 90 kg. They slowly haul the sacks – at least three times their individual weight – on to their bare backs and lug them through the forest to the depot... One day, the bag was so heavy that it broke and we were beaten badly," says Twumasi.

Twumasi is 13 years old and has been working as a slave since the age of nine, when his mother passed away and he was sent to live with his uncle in the Ashanti Region...

"We barely make enough to survive. I am making about GHS200 ($41) a month as a cocoa farmer and there is a lot of competition out there as these international brands have no loyalty to us. We have to do what we can to keep costs low, and children help make that possible," says Kofi (real name withheld), Twumasi's uncle."

—**Peace Hyde, In *The Scourge of Child Slavery Persists Despite Laws*** (Hyde, 2018)

Several interventions have been identified as useful towards eradicating child labour.

3.11.1 Social Awareness

Social or community awareness is by far the most important intervention to address child labour, so that the long-term concerns outweigh the short-term benefits. Anker and Melkas (1996) found in their survey that community awareness and involvement was seen by organizations as crucial for the development and implementation of programs to eradicate child labour. A bottom-up approach is likely to translate to fewer hiccups when the program is implemented and greater compliance with the laws. The UNO, as well as various national and international institutions working with child labourers, invest a significant portion of their budget in awareness drives across communities. Community involvement is required for a holistic and effective design of the policies, owing to the realistic appraisal of the ground situation and its nuances. This aids in the needed rectifications of measures and customization of programs to suit local needs (Boateng, 2017; Chanda & Dutta, 2019).

Along with community awareness, adult education is also an important intervention to address ongoing child labour practices. Adults who have spent their childhood as part of the workforce and thus have been denied education and empowerment, often experience, what is called, normalization of abuse, which is, seeing child labour as an acceptable way of life. Such adults are likely to continue the cycle of abuse, by pushing their children to the same life situations for temporary benefits. Adult education helps improve life conditions of people from disadvantaged backgrounds, thus reducing the need for them to push their children into the workforce (Das, 2012; Iannelli, 2002). Further, education is likely to make them aware of the long-term disadvantages of child labour and the legal issues surrounding it, making them less likely to opt for it as a life choice (Mukherjee & Das, 2008; Mukherjee & Pal, 2016).

Communities can also help eradicate child labour by not encouraging the conveniences gained through it. This includes creating awareness about demanding ethically sourced goods, selecting products that are free from child labour over cheap alternatives and creating pressure on policymakers through voting to have effective policies on child labour in place (Peled, 2019).

3.11.2 Constitutional Safeguards Against Child Labour

India has had a long tradition of child labour, both in family enterprises and as waged labourers. Therefore, it became one of the prime concerns of policymakers in independent India. Articles 24 and 39 of the Constitution of India provided for eradication of child labour (Bhakhry, 2006; NCPCR, n.d.). In 2009, the Right of Children to Free and Compulsory Education Act was passed. This Act provides for compulsory free school education to children who are 6–14 years old, and reservation of 25% of seats in private schools for differently-abled and socially disadvantaged children.

3.11.3 Legal Measures Adopted by the Government of India

The Factories Act of 1948 is arguably the earliest legislation in independent India on child labour. This law prohibits children below 14 years from working in factories or manufacturing units and prohibits hazardous working conditions for children below 18 years of age. The Mines Act of 1952 specifically banned children below 18 years from being employed in mines (Bajpai, 2017).

In 1976, the Bonded Labour Act was passed, which provided for complete eradication of bonded labour, including exploitation of children as labour without pay. In 1986, the he Child Labour (Prohibition and Regulation) Act came, which sought to eliminate hazardous child labour and regulate the non-hazardous forms. This act provided a list of hazardous occupations where child labour is banned, which was expanded further in 2006 and 2008 (Bag, 2015). The list includes occupations such as beedi making, carpet weaving, foundries, slaughterhouses, handloom and power loom, tanning, brick kilns and lime kilns. The 2016 Child Labour (Prohibition and Regulation) Amendment Act, which puts a blanket ban on all child labour below the age of 14. Between ages 14 and 18, the age of legal adulthood in India, children may not be employed in hazardous activities and may be employed in non-hazardous activities, only under restricted conditions (Ministry of Law and Justice, 2016b). The Juvenile Justice (Care and Protection) of Children Act of 2000 made hiring of children in hazardous occupation a punishable offence (The Ministry of Law and Justice, 2016a). In addition to these punitive legislations, there are laws to restore children rescued from child labour into the mainstream life.

3.11.4 Government of India's Policies and Actions

In 1986, The National Policy on Education was announced, which aimed to bring school dropouts and part-time child workers within the folds of formal education (Goel, 2015). India became one of the first 150 signatories to ratify the Rights of the Child in 1989, presently ratified by 195 countries (UN News, 2015), which laid down the child's right to freedom from exploitation and right to education.

Recognizing the fact that the child workers may find it difficult to rejoin mainstream education, the National Child Labour Project (NCLP) was adopted in 1988. Under this scheme, the Government identifies children engaged in hazardous vocations and rescues them. As a further impetus to this mission, in 2017, the Ministry of Home Affairs, Government of India, launched Operation Smile or Muskaan, which is focused on rescuing and rehabilitating missing children. Once rescued, these children are put into special schools for rehabilitation, where they are put through a curriculum of vocational training and bridge education, to help makeup for the lost years. In addition, the children are provided mid-day meals and a stipend to compensate for their loss of livelihood (Ministry of Labour and Employment, Government of India, 2016). Till date, about 6000 schools have been set up under the scheme, providing rehabilitation to over 10 lakh children (Ministry of Labour and Employment, 2018). To connect all the stakeholders working to eradicate child labour, the Government has also started PENCIL (Platform for Effective Enforcement for No Child Labour).[1] PENCIL is a web portal that is endowed with a forum to lodge complaints, child tracking system and information on government policies and projects under the NCLP (PTI, 2017a). To quicken the process of investigation and rehabilitation, the NCPCR has proposed, in 2019, that a single statement recorded before the Child Welfare Commission may be used as evidence under multiple laws, thus sparing the survivors the trouble of elaborate processes and legal red tapes (Pandit, 2019).

Legal interventions against child labour in India are many, and their impact in making a significant difference in the situation in the subcontinent. However, several critical misgivings have been pointed out in this regard by researchers (e.g. Goel, 2015). The relevant laws in India are often criticized internationally as the legal age of working in India is 14 years, which is lower than ILO's legal working age of 15 (Maplecroft, 2019). This creates disparities in protection available to children in India and their counterparts across the world. The Child Labour (Prohibition

[1] https://pencil.gov.in/.

and Regulation) Amendment Act, 2016 lays down hazardous vocations where child labour is prohibited and others where it needs to be regulated. However, the law places no restriction on children, aged below 14 years, to assist in family enterprises, post-school or during vacations, provided such business activities do not affect a child's education and are non-hazardous in nature. While this has its advantages in providing a child valuable exposure to the family trade, there is little provision of regulation for the kind of activities or the amount of work a child performs in the family trade. Devulapalli (2019) points out that the law leaves scope for employers to hire child labourers under the pretext of being related to them or working with their family. Further, monitoring on whether the activity affects the school education of the child or not, also appears to be a difficult task, requiring the deployment of many more personnel than currently available (Srivastava, 2017). This leaves loopholes where exploitation may take place. In the words of Gupta (2016),

> The clause is also dangerous as it does not define the hours of work; it simply states that children may work after school hours or during vacations. Think of the plight of a 12-year old coming home from school and then helping her mother sow (sic) umpteen collars on shirts to meet the production deadline of a contractor. When will she do her homework? How will she have the stamina to get up the next morning for school?

The Child Labour Amendment Act has been in question for allowing similar engagements of child labour found in family businesses in the audio–visual entertainment industry and in sports. While these industries tend to be more regulated than small-scale family enterprises, the entertainment industry has been under the scanner for rampant exploitation of child artists (Srivastava, 2011). In 2018, an adult singer kissed a minor girl contestant in a reality TV show, which led to considerable furore. Children's reality TV shows have been flagged for age-inappropriate content and stress-inducing situations for the participants, marked by crying and abusing on live television, all which threaten the dignity and innocence of children (Arya, 2018; Thirumurthy, 2017). The Guidelines to Regulate Child Participation in TV Serials, Reality Shows and Advertisements was proposed by the National Commission for Protection of Child Rights (NCPCR) in 2011. However, there is need for clear legal provisions and deterrents on the treatment of children in such industries, and the prevention of any adverse impact on the minds of the child workers. In the words of film director Amol Gupte,

> There should be a model so that kids are not misused in the industry and media. I shoot during holidays. The kids come on reality shows, be there for three weeks, become champions, and then they are forgotten, just think how it affects the children?
>
> Press Trust of India (PTI, 2017b)

Gupta (2016) and Srivastava (2017) points out two major issues with the Child Labour Amendment Act of 2016. One, the latest Act has marked several trades, earlier seen as hazardous and therefore forbidden for children, as non-hazardous (Srivastava, 2017). Thus, the amended list allows the employment of children in risky activities such 'chemical mixing units, cotton farms, battery recycling units and brick kilns.' Second, it indicates that the list of hazardous activities may be amended even at the discretion of government authorities without any parliamentary action. This leaves open possibilities of misuse of the legal provisions to exploit vulnerable children.

Another gap that experts have pointed out concerns child labour in domestic activities. The 2016 Act is silent on domestic labour, which merits a mention, since it is a reason for a clear majority of Indian children from poor socio-economic backgrounds, particularly girls, to drop out of schools. School dropouts for girls have been found to correlate with mother's employment status, farming seasons and MGNREGS schedules, suggesting that it is a form of child work that requires regulation and prevention (Das & Mukherjee, 2019).

3.12 Global Approach to Combat This Social Problem

Child labour is a much-legislated issue, with multiple national and international laws restraining, moderating and eradicating practices of hiring children at work. The need for child labour laws way back in 1786 (Charnovitz, 1996). The first child labour law is said to have been passed in 1836, in Massachusetts, USA, that made it mandatory for working children under 15 years of age to go to school for a minimum of 3 h daily (IPEC, 2019). In 1839, to expand work opportunities for adults, Prussia restricted child labour in factories and restricted working hours for children (O'Sullivan, 2006). Around the same time, Britain restricted child labour in factories through the Factories Act. Subsequently, laws restricting child labour have been passed in several European and American countries.

Laws against Child labour received a major impetus following the establishment of the International Labour Organization in 1919. The ILO aimed to ensure healthy working conditions for all adults and eradicate child labour worldwide. The issue received further impetus with the establishment of UNICEF in 1946, focused primarily on child welfare. The 1973 Minimum Age Convention of the ILO banned employment of people aged below 18 in hazardous activities, and allowed only light work for children aged between 13 and 17 without harming their education, and complete eradication of child labour below the age of 13 (ILO, 1976). In 1992, ILO launched the International Program on the Elimination of Child Labour (IPEC). In 1999, ILO announced the Worst Forms of Child Labour Convention, targeting pornography, trafficking and bonded labour. ILO regulations are considered as binding on its 186 member states (ILO, 1999).

One of the most recent developments in international child labour prevention regulations are the core principles laid down by the World Fair Trade Organization, which are binding upon its 78-member countries. Goods purchased and sold through the WFTO cannot be produced using forced child labour or any child labour that ILO conventions prohibit (WFTO, 2017).

3.12.1 Statistics and Research

Reliable and exhaustive statistical databases on the incidence, spread and dynamics of child labour are crucial for combating the problem. In the absence of accurate data on the incidence of child labour, the problem is often perceived as trivial. This makes it difficult to create effective policy interventions or design sector-specific interventions to address particularly problematic areas (Avis, 2017). The Statistical Information and Monitoring Program on Child Labour (SIMPOC) was set up by the ILO in 1998, for generating and recording accurate and comparable data on child labour worldwide (Janzen, 2018). The Ministry of Statistics and Program Implementation, Government of India (2019) opines that, in order to meet the growing demand for Labour Statistics, nations such as India should increasingly focus on Labour Statistics and set up specialized departments in the Ministry of Child Welfare and the labour department at the state and the district levels.

3.12.2 Safety Net

Child labour is often seen as a consequence of ongoing poverty that forces households to depend on income of children for subsistence. This has led scholars to propose that availability of safety nets, such as minimum income, guarantees on the protection against fluctuations in the economy (e.g. Grootaert & Kanbur, 1995). Many developed nations of the world, such as Canada, offer free healthcare to their citizens, which relieve the strain of additional expenditure on families and also spare them of significant fluctuations in family incomes (Naylor, 2018). Developed nations also provide doles or unemployment support—in the form of cash or food coupons which ensures that children from economically challenged households in such nations do not have to enter the workforce prematurely for subsistence (Marsh, 2018; Patterson, 2018). The steadily declining and even negative rate of child labour in these areas reveal, to an extent, the usefulness of such schemes to eradicate child labour.

India presently runs the largest public distribution system in the world, which ensures heavily subsidized food grains or cash in lieu of food grains to the disadvantaged population, as well as guarantees a Minimum Support Price to farmers for their produce (Chakraborty & Sarmah, 2019; Department of Food and Public Distribution, 2018). The MGNREGS of the Government of India is another such safety net that assures a minimum of one hundred days of wage employment to people living in the rural areas (Ministry of Law and Justice, 2017). Other such programs practiced across the world are crop insurances and buyback guarantees to farmers (Van Kooten, Orden, & Schmitz, 2018; Shields, 2015), and health insurance plans. The Ayushman Bharat program or the Pradhan Mantri Jan Arogya Yojana (PM-JAY) has been launched by the Government of India. The Ayushman Bharat provides economically disadvantaged families in rural and urban areas medical and hospitalization expenses at nominal rates (Chatterjee, 2018; Lahariya, 2018). There are other schemes that provide housing (Gopalan & Venkataraman, 2015) and pension ('Brief on APY', 2019) at affordable rates to the poor living in rural and urban areas. Such schemes are expected to provide economically challenged families with the safety net required to combat income fluctuations, burden of building assets and sudden calamities, thus reducing the need for their children to enter the workforce before they turn into adults. Human Rights Watch 2015 reports that a government scheme of paying USD 7 per child to a family has cut down child labour rates by 33% in Morocco (Koirala, 2019). Similar financial incentives by World Vision Canada in Philippines have cut down child worker participation in sugarcane factories by 74% (Subcommittee on International Human Rights, 2017).

While safety nets appear to be crucial to combat the menace of child labour, there needs to be some additional structures in place to ensure that they are effective to this specific end. For instance, efforts need to be taken to ensure that safety nets are comprehensive in their coverage, such that they reach almost the entirety of the intended population (Patterson, 2018). Second, it is important to ensure that the benefits reach in their entirety to the targeted people, rather than being wasted through leakages, corruption, or middlemen (Meyer & Mittag, 2019). A major criticism of the PDS in India had been the leakages, due to which it is suspected that only a percentage of the intended recipients benefit from the scheme (e.g. Gulati & Saini, 2015). One of the steps taken in this regard is Direct Benefit Transfer, where, instead of the benefit in kind, the commensurate cash is transferred directly to the bank accounts of the intended recipients (Deuss & Adenauer, 2017; Singh & Singh, 2016).

Safety Nets, like microcredit, may have interesting ripple effects in unintended directions. The MGNREGS of India is an interesting case study in this regard. The MGNREGS is targeted at providing assured employment, for at least one hundred days, to people living below the poverty line. While this is expected to lead to lessen the economic pressure on families for survival, Shah and Steinberg (2015) reported that MGNREGS is associated significantly with school dropouts, with boys dropping out to cater to the demand of labour and girls dropping out to take charge of the household while their mothers work (Das & Mukherjee, 2019). Free schooling, subsidized food rations, housing and other amenities and unemployment allowances might also encourage a spurt in the population as they reduce the burden on parents of supporting large families (Geyer, Ngidi, & Mans, 2018). A growing population puts increasing strain on the safety nets, causing people to slip out of them, in turn making them ineffective for the very purpose of their creation. Further, safety nets make children less serious about education and vocational training, because the bare minimum is assured, thus creating generations who are dependent on doles for their survival (Filges, Jonassen, & Jørgensen, 2018). Thus, safety nets need to be accompanied by stringent and clear policies and community awareness programs, encouraging and incentivizing family planning, productive employment of adults, schooling and vocational training, asset creation and entrepreneurial ventures (e.g. Alderman & Hoddinott, 2007). It is recognized that to remain sustainable and effective, safety nets need to be supplemented with efforts to make people empowered enough to opt out of them in the long run, rather than depending on them indefinitely.

3.12.3 Schooling

School education tends to be one of the first amenities to be sacrificed towards child labour. But it may also help prevent child labour. Children absorbed into a meaningful and high involvement formal education system early on, are likely to appreciate the benefits of schooling. Such children are less likely to give into the temptation of easy money through underage economic activities (Mauras, Mendez, & Himes, 2018; Rahikainen, 2017). Further, children who join schooling at age-appropriate levels are more capable of coping with the academic pressure of secondary education and are less likely to drop out, than children who start school late, after spending their initial years in economic activities (Adam, 2017). Schooling also provides a child a productive peer group and opportunities for socialization with teachers and keeps them away from illegal pastime activities, such as drugs, one of the chief spurs for earning money through child labour. Finally, owing to legislations such as the Mid-day Meal Scheme (Chakraborty & Jayaraman, 2019; Ramachandran, 2019) in India, schools are a source of valuable nutrition for children, which discourage them from drifting into hazardous labour for subsistence.

According to Quattri and Watkins (2016), schooling has the advantage of monitoring and vigilance in the context of child labour and child abuse. As the unorganized sector is the biggest employer of child workers, particularly in the illegal sweatshops of South Asia, tracking such establishments becomes difficult. The authors opine that it is easier to monitor children in schools through interventions, such as compulsory education till the age of 14, than through crackdown on illegal establishments across a country (Bain, 2016). Similarly, Ferguson (2018) reported that in Yemen, the likelihood of a child to be recruited as a labourer or a soldier increases when the child is not enrolled in a school.

To ensure that compulsory and continued schooling reaches every child, several steps need to be taken. Governments need to have in place the infrastructure needed to school every child, even those in the remotest corners of the country. Research shows that the long distance between homes and schools and associated safety hazards are a major reason for school dropouts, as are the lack of toilets, particularly for adolescent girls (FAAE, 2018). High dropout rates and fictitious enrolments (Sinha, 2015) are other problems that require vigilance by local governments and executive bodies. The curriculum too needs to be made relevant for vocational skilling, so that schooling is seen as an alternative to apprenticeship (Chanda & Datta, 2019). Schooling needs to be free, or at least low cost, for the economically backward sections of the society, by subsidizing books, uniforms and other school accessories. Monetary and non-monetary incentives for the school-going children, such as scholarships, cash grants and awards also need to be promoted. Anker and Melkas (1996) found that respondents perceived cash grants to be effective when they matched the child's previous income levels, or when they matched the needs of the child and the family. In India, states have practiced similar models, such as giving out bicycles, solar lamps, subsidized tablets, to school children from disadvantageous backgrounds, with significant success against dropouts (India CSR Network, 2018; TNN 2016, August 23).

Scholars have also emphasized on the importance of promoting non-formal education for children and young adults. Most children rescued from the workforce are over-aged for their educational level and are not able to keep pace with the learning in formal classrooms. To address this, the Non-formal Education (NFE) and the National Institute of Open Schooling (NIOS) were adopted in India, which let the children and adults of any age, study and complete secondary education at their own pace, from home (Gaba, 1997; Singal, 2006). Encouragement of open schooling is likely to encourage the dropouts to come back to education and benefit from it, without facing the time-bound restrictions and full-time commitment of formal educational systems.

3.12.4 Child Day Care

Domestic duties form a major component of child labour across the world. Data shows that many children drop out of school to look after their younger siblings and to run the house, when the adults in the family are gone for work. Anker and Melkas (1996) opine that a major step to prevent children's involvement in domestic activities is having child daycare at offices, industrial and construction sites and shops and establishments. If mothers and fathers can take infants with them to the work, then there shall be no need to keep back older siblings at home in order to take care of them (Egyed, McIntosh, & Bull, 1998; Putnick & Bornstein, 2016). Child daycare also has the advantage of keeping young children, who accompany their parents to work, away from the hazardous conditions of the shop floor or work site. The time spent at the parent's place of work may be utilized to provide the child, basic education and training in life skills at the daycare, which will prepare him/her for formal schooling (Bajaj & Sharma, 2016; Sharma & Chadha, 2018). This is likely to keep the child away from joining the parent's occupation prematurely out of idleness or curiosity. In India, The Factories Act 1948 provides for creches for factories employing more than 30 women, and the Maternity Benefit Amendment Act 2017 provides for creche and child daycare at any establishment that has 50 workers or more (Sharma, 2017). Similar measures have been recommended and adopted in corporate offices. However, these laws cover only a fraction of the workplaces in the country and tend to be poorly enforced (Mishra & Joshi, 2016; Rangeela & Anil, 2018).

3.12.5 Involving Corporate Houses and Non-governmental Organizations

The incidence of child labour intimidating, particularly when it comes to the most populous countries. This often renders the funds and the efforts that are allocated to the eradication of child labour inadequate. Governments often tend to have priorities, such as boosting the GDP, which go against the greater cause of eliminating the exploitation of children (e.g. Jose, 2019). Second, punitive legal provisions or acts of separation of children from families during rehabilitation, although necessary, often alienate labour law inspectors from the numerous stakeholders at the ground level, such as small business owners, parents of child workers and the children themselves (Deshingkar, 2009; Malhotra, 2015).

Researchers opine that a significant portion of this gap may be bridged through the involvement of non-governmental organizations, philanthropic bodies and corporate houses. NGOs and philanthropic bodies, particularly those specializing in child rights, have the strength of a workforce of individuals, motivated by the cause and having subject-matter expertise and long-term experience in the area. Further, their informal network aids them in reaching stakeholders in the remotest locations, without threat of persecution of legal crackdown. Finally, NGOs are effective in crowdsourcing funds from philanthropists worldwide, which is of crucial importance for many resource-starved developing nations. Some leading NGOs working for child rights are Child Rights and You (CRY), Aide et Action, SOS Children's Village, ChildLine India Foundation, Bachpan Bachao Andolan, Goodweave and Uday Foundation.

Aide et Action is an interesting case study on private-public partnership when it comes to child rights for migrant workers. Famous for their worksite schools that provide bridge education and food to children of construction workers, Aide et Action has cooperated with Odisha Police in India to execute Operation Smile (also called Operation Muskaan), launched by the Ministry of Home Affairs, Government of India, in 2017. Together, this drive provides rehabilitation and education to child workers in brick kilns of Odisha and has graduated more than 2000 students from the worksite schools between 2017 and 2019 (PTI, 2017a; Wangchuk, 2019).

Corporate organizations have been a major stakeholder in social endeavours worldwide. Philanthropic ventures have emerged as a prime vehicle for businesses to give back to the society. It has also been a critical mode for brand building and advertising, through social marketing strategies. In India, the Companies Act 2013 mandates that businesses valued over 100 crores, or with annual net profits of at least INR 5 crores, should spend 2% of their net profit on Corporate Social Responsibility (CSR). This has led to a significant participation by businesses, such as the Tata Group, Microsoft, Mahindra and others in India, in social causes through corporate foundations, in collaboration with NGOs, or in collaboration with the government. Similarly, under the Responsible Cobalt Initiative in China, firms such as Apple, HP and Sony are taking measures to avoid raw materials generated through child labour and to train the rescued children in less hazardous vocations (Conca, 2018). Other examples include that of chocolate manufacturers such as Tony's Chocolonely, which has undertaken to sell products free of slave labour (Rushe, 2019). Businesses can thus contribute to the cause of child rights by creating supply chains free of child labour, creating awareness about child rights and investing their profits in initiatives to protect the children (Webb 2019).

3.12.6 Economic Incentives and Economic Growth

Pham and Nguyen (2019) pointed out that rather than deterring child labour, microcredits for the economically challenged families exacerbated child labour, by boosting family business activities where the children of the family are drawn into save wages. This indicates that, to ensure that the benefits of economic assistance percolate down to the last child, microcredit's need to be accompanied by strict vigilance on how the fund is used, labour hired for the business, and the subsequent social and economic activities of the children of the recipient family. This might, to some extent, ensure that children are not victimized owing to the revival and growth of the family trade. Second, continued education of the children may be made a criterion for doling out microcredit or for partial loan or interest waiver, thus incentivizing the parents in kind for not involving the children in the family business.

Kambhapati and Rajan (2006) proposed the child labour Kuznets curve to describe how growth of the economy affects child workers. According to this model, when economy grows, it will initially provide a boost to child labour, by increasing the number of low-skill jobs in the economy. However, as the economy grows further, it will become more and more sophisticated, mechanized and knowledge-driven. This will cause the menial jobs to dry up and be replaced by skilled jobs of the knowledge economy, for which only adults are suitable. Hence, sustained economic growth will bring down child labour. Moreover, when the economy becomes more prosperous, parents shall increasingly have the wherewithal to send their children to schools and also receive incentives to get them educated to become knowledge workers of the future. As Worstall (2016) puts it,

> As those absolutely poor get richer then they become free of that absolute income constraint and child labour quite naturally disappears all on its own some. Parents do rather have an interest in their children doing well and parents around the world do, as soon as they are able to, withdraw their children from earning pennies and send them to school instead.

Law enforcement is also likely to be more effective in a prosperous society, thus discouraging child labour (Grootaert & Patrinos, 1999). Thus, economic growth is likely to lead to a short-term spurt in child work activities, but once it is sustained, economic growth is likely to be a major deterrent to child labour.

3.12.7 Legal Enforcement and Customization of Policies

Strict and consistent implementation of law is crucial for combating child labour. While most nations of the world have elaborate legal provisions, many are sadly lacking when it comes to implementation of these laws (FAAE, 2018). According to O'Driscoll (2017), many of the legislations and policy interventions relating to child labour fail to consider the ground realities of an area. For instance, children working in trades as apprentices are part of long-standing traditions among many indigenous people (Chakraborty & Chakraborty, 2016). Montgomery (2009), in her study on child prostitutes in Thailand, reported that the subjects did not look upon prostitution as work or abuse, but rather as a moral obligation to their own families. Again, non-hazardous child labour is seen as acceptable and even beneficial in many societies. So, it is important to frame policies to aim at a gradual weaning out of this practice, rather than sudden prohibitions (Maconachie & Hilson, 2016).

Child labour is also contextual, in that, the drivers to the problem differ in intensity and seriousness in different areas. In poverty-stricken zones, it is difficult to remove children from the workforce if the income is not replaced. Thus, a blanket ban only makes child labour go undercover, further jeopardizing the fates of the children (Bain, 2016). Again, in war zones and conflict-laden areas, such as in African nations with child soldiers, families have little discretion in whether to send their children to the force or not (Klasen, Reissmann, Voss, & Okello, 2015; Rikhof, 2019). Thus, the target for the awareness campaigns and the policy interventions need to be redesigned accordingly.

Worstall (2016) proposes the radical solution that child labour need to be legalized rather than banned. He mentions the case of India, where employment surveys show that child labour had showed a declining trend when no ban was in place and had spiked after an age-specific ban was implemented (Bharadwaj, Lakdawala, & Li, 2013). This is because bans only reduce the bargaining power of child workers, by increasing the risks for the employers, thus lowering their wages. This makes them spend more hours at work to earn at the same level as before, thus spiking child labour rates (Worstall, 2014). Further, once banned, child labour happens behind closed doors, where it is far less likely to be monitored for safety standards than when it is practiced in the open.

3.13 Conclusion and Implications

The declining trend in child labour statistics in recent times, particularly in the developed corners of the world, makes one optimistic about the eradication of child labour soon. However, the spike in the trends in the poorest of the poor nations indicates that a lot needs to be done to address the issue satisfactorily.

Case Study 9: Adolescents in cobalt mines of Kolwezi, Congo'

"Most of his neighbors are still sound asleep at 5 a.m., when Lukasa rises to begin his 12-hour workday. The slender 15-year-old, with an oval face and piercing stare, slips out of his family's mud-brick home before dawn six days a week. Then he makes the two-hour walk from his tiny village in the southern region of the Democratic Republic of the Congo to a government-owned mining site…Once at the mine, Lukasa spends eight hours hacking away in a hole to accumulate chunks of a mineral that is crucial to keeping our modern lives moving: cobalt.

By about 3 p.m., Lukasa has filled a sack with his day's haul. He hoists the load, which can weigh up to 22 lb, on his back and lugs it for an hour by foot to a trading depot. "I sell it to Chinese people," … he says, "On good days I can earn 15,000 francs." That adds up to about $9. Lukasa has, he says, recently begun to grasp that his cobalt mining earnings are a pittance compared with the sums that traders make selling it on the world market…It's *more difficult still for diggers living in poverty, like Lukasa, to understand a surge in demand for the mineral that has sent the price of cobalt on commodities markets rocketing up some 400%, from about $10 a pound in 2016 to a peak of about $44 in April...The metal is a key component in the lithium-ion batteries that power countless millions of smart phones, computers, and tablets."*

—**Vivienne Walt and Sebastian Meyer, In *Blood, Sweat, and Batteries: Inside Congo's Cobalt Mines*** (Walt & Meyer, 2018)

All said and done, the core impetus against child labour is not economic incentives or compensations, but a core conviction that childhood is a phase of development and growth, where an individual need to be built and equipped. It is not a phase of exploitation, where one may extract whatever economic value one can from the vulnerable child. Hence, policies and interventions need to appeal at the deeper understanding of the purpose of having progeny and of the role of a child in building the future of the world. Ensuring education for all children by preventing child labour will ensure producing more skilled labour for nation-building. On the other hand, this approach will protect the right of an individual to lead a life with self-respect and dignity and enjoy equity and equality.

3.14 Recommendations

Keeping the overall socio-economic scenario of India, the following steps are recommended to address child labour:

- There is a need to improve the economic condition of people living below the poverty line, by ensuring income-generating activities for all the families. Parents with disposable income are likely to be open towards education of children.
- Migration of families from rural to urban areas needs to be prevented by improving the rural economy and/or creating industry-friendly environment. More industries in rural areas mean more job opportunities and automatically, the rate of rural to urban migration will go down.
- Compulsory admission of children in school is another solution. Children coming from poor families need special attention of the school authorities in terms of support for academic learning so that they do not discontinue education. Continuation of education means remaining in the mainstream and becoming a skilled manpower.
- In a country like India, total prevention of child labour is very difficult for government for several reasons like lack of labour inspectors and economic condition of the family and/or situational affairs of the family. In that case, government should ensure that all safety measures are taken in all the hazardous industries and owner of an industry provides non-formal education to the child labour, so that they do not exploit them and also allow the child to visit the family and/or enjoy holidays.
- Sensitization of the larger society about child rights is the need of the hour and in turn, it would help to improve the status of the children.

References

Abdu, M., & Delamonica, E. (2018). Multidimensional child poverty: From complex weighting to simple representation. *Social Indicators Research, 136*(3), 881–905.

Abugre, J. A. (2017). *Child labour, poverty and health outcomes: The Ghanaian experience* (Doctoral dissertation, University Of Ghana). Retrieved from http://ugspace.ug.edu.gh/bitstream/handle/123456789/23470/Child%20Labour%2C%20Poverty%20And%20Health%20Outcomes%20The%20Ghanaian%20Experience.pdf?sequence=1&isAllowed=y.

Adam, I. S. S. A. H. (2017). *The perceived causes and effects of child labour on children's education: A case study of shea butter industry in Sagnerigu district of Northern Ghana* (Doctoral dissertation). Retrieved from http://udsspace.uds.edu.gh/bitstream/123456789/1790/1/the%20perceived%20causes%20and%20effects%20of%20child%20labour%20on%20children%e2%80%99s%20education%20a%20case%20study%20of%20shea%20butter%20industry%20in%20sagnerigu%20district%20of%20northern%2c%20ghana.pdf.

Adegbenro, C. A., Opasina, O. F., Fehintola, F. O., & Olowookere, S. A. (2017). Predictors of child labour among in-school adolescents in a rural local government area in Oyo state, Nigeria. *European Scientific Journal, ESJ, 13*(23), 193.

Adonteng-Kissi, O. (2018). Causes of child labour: Perceptions of rural and urban parents in Ghana. *Children and Youth Services Review, 91,* 55–65.

Alam, S. (1999). Efforts to ban goods made by children are counterproductive. In M. E. Williams (Ed.) *Child labor and sweatshops* (pp. 43–47). San Diego: Greenhaven Press. Retrieved from http://www.dikseo.teimes.gr/spoudastirio/E-NOTES/C/Child_Labor_and_Sweatshops_Viewpoints.pdf.

Alderman, H., & Hoddinott, J. (2007). Growth-promoting social safety nets. In *2020 focus brief on the world's poor and hungry people.* International Food Policy Research Institute (IFPRI). Retrieved from https://idl-bnc-idrc.dspacedirect.org/bitstream/handle/10625/37176/127826.pdf?sequence=1.

Ali, F. R. M. (2019). In the same boat, but not equals: The heterogeneous effects of parental income on child labour. *The Journal of Development Studies, 55*(5), 845–858.

Anker, R. (1995). Labour market policies, vulnerable groups and poverty. In J. B. Figueiredo & Z. Shaheed (Eds.) *New approaches to poverty analysis and policy—II: Reducing poverty through labour market policies* (pp. 49–88). Geneva: International Institute for Labour Studies.

Anker, R. (2000). The economics of child labour: A framework for easurement. *International Labour Review, 139*(3), 257.

Anker, R., & Melkas, H. (1996). *Economic incentives for children and families to eliminate or reduce child labour*. Geneva: International Labour Office.

Aptel, C. (2019). The protection of children in armed conflicts. *International Human Rights of Children*, 515–536.

Arya, U. R. (2018, March 19). Children's shows: Entertainment or exploitation? *Entertainment Times*. Retrieved from https://timesofindia.indiatimes.com/tv/news/malayalam/childrens-shows-entertainment-or-exploitation/articleshow/63354036.cms.

Asfaw, A. A. (2018). The effect of coffee price shock on school dropout: New evidence from the 2008 global financial crisis. *Applied Economics Letters, 25*(7), 482–486.

Avins, J. (2015). The way to start a real fashion revolution: put Bangladesh's invisible garment factories on a map. *Quartz*. Retrieved from https://qz.com/390238/to-avoid-another-rana-plaza-lets-start-mapping-bangladeshs-invisible-garment-factories/.

Avis, W. (2017). *Data on the prevalence of the worst forms of child labour: KD4 Helpdesk Report*. Retrieved fromhttps://opendocs.ids.ac.uk/opendocs/bitstream/handle/123456789/13067/101%20Worst%20forms%20of%20child%20labour.pdf?sequence=1&isAllowed=y.

Bag, A. (2015). *What are the laws related to child labour in India*. Retrieved from https://blog.ipleaders.in/laws-related-child-labour-india/.

Bahree, M. (2014, February 5). Your beautiful Indian rug was probably made by child labor. *Forbes*. Retrieved from https://www.forbes.com/sites/meghabahree/2014/02/05/your-beautiful-indian-rug-was-probably-made-by-child-labor/#61cb375b74a0.

Bain., M. (2016). Researchers have identified a very simple, universal solution to child labor's vicious cycle of poverty. *Quartz*. Retrieved from https://qz.com/858374/child-labor-is-a-global-epidemic-but-researchers-in-bangladesh-have-one-blueprint-for-a-solution/.

Bajaj, M., & Sharma, S. (2016). Scaling-up early childhood centres for migrant construction workers' children in India. *Early Childhood Matters, 125,* 74–79.

Bajpai, A. (2017). *Child rights in India: Law, policy, and practice*. New Delhi: Oxford University Press.

Baland, J., & Robinson, J. A. (2000). Is child labor inefficient? *Journal of Political Economy, 108*(4), 663–679.

Ballet, J., & Bhukuth, A. (2019). Fighting against child exploitation: Policy implications. In *Child exploitation in the global South* (pp. 205–217). Palgrave Macmillan, Cham.

Basu, K., & Tzannatos, Z. (2003). The global child labor problem: What do we know and what can we do? *The World Bank Economic Review, 17*(2), 147–173.

Basu, K. (1999). Child labor: Cause, consequence, and cure, with remarks on international labor standards. *Journal of Economic Literature, 37*(3), 1083–1119.

Bhakhry, S. (2006). Children in India and their rights. *National Human Rights Commission*. Retrieved from http://14.139.60.153/bitstream/123456789/1945/1/Children%20in%20India%20and%20their%20Rights.pdf.

Bhalotra, S., & Heady, C. (2003). Child farm labor: The wealth paradox. *The World Bank Economic Review, 17*(2), 197–227.

Bharadwaj, P., Lakdawala, L. K., & Li, N. (2013). *Perverse consequences of well intentioned regulation: evidence from India's child labor ban* (No. w19602). National Bureau of Economic Research. Retrieved from https://www.nber.org/papers/w19602.

Bhattacharyya, R., & Vauquline, P. (2013). A mirage or a rural life line? Analyzing the impact of Mahatma Gandhi Rural Employment Guarantee Act on women beneficiaries of Assam. *Journal Space and Culture, India, 1*(1), 83–101.

Blank, R. M. (2018). *It takes a nation: A new agenda for fighting poverty-updated edition*. Princeton: Princeton University Press.

Boateng, P. (2017). *Interventions on child labour in South Asia*. K4D helpdesk report. Retrieved from https://opendocs.ids.ac.uk/opendocs/bitstream/handle/123456789/13071/105%20Interventions%20on%20Child%20Labour%20in%20South%20Asia.pdf?sequence=206.

Bourdillo n, M. (2019). "Child labour" and children's lives. In *Global childhoods beyond the North-South Divide* (pp. 35–55). Palgrave Macmillan, Cham.

Bowen, W. G., & Finegan, T. A. (2015). *The economics of labor force participation* (Vol. 2054). Princeton: Princeton University Press.

Brar, N. K. (2018). A comparative study of the exclusion of girl child in school education in India And Punjab. *MIER Journal of Educational Studies, Trends and Practices*, *8*(2).

Brown, G. (2012). Child labor & educational disadvantage—Breaking the link, building opportunity. *The Office of the UN Special Envoy for Global Education*. Retrieved from http://www.ungei.org/child_labor_and_education_US.pdf.

Brief on Atal Pension Yojana. (2019). Retrieved from http://www.jansuraksha.gov.in/Files/APY/English/About-APY.pdf.

Brussels Conference Education Report. (2017). *Preparing for the future of children and youth in Syria and the region through education: London one year on*. Retrieved from http://wos-education.org/uploads/reports/170331_Brussels_paper.pdf.

Burra, N. (2009). Child labour in rural areas with a special focus on migration, agriculture, mining and brick kilns. *National commission for protection of child rights*. Retrieved from http://www.ncpcr.gov.in/Reports/Child_Labour_in_Rural_areas_with_special_focus_on_Migration_Agriculture_%20Mining_by_Neera_Burra.pdf.

Carter, B. & Roelen, K. (2017). *Prevalence and impacts of child labour in agriculture*. Retrieved from https://opendocs.ids.ac.uk/opendocs/bitstream/handle/123456789/13345/95%2696%20child%20labour%20in%20agri%20%28revised%2020.10.17%29.pdf?sequence=1&isAllowed=y.

Chakraborty, K., & Chakraborty, B. (2016). Child labour ban versus Education subsidy in a model with learning by doing effect in unskilled work.

Chakraborty, S., & Das, M. (2005). Mortality, fertility, and child labor. *Economics Letters, 86*(2), 273–278.

Chakraborty, S., & Sarmah, S. P. (2019). India 2025: The public distribution system and National Food Security Act 2013. *Development in Practice, 29*(2), 230–249.

Chakraborty, T., & Jayaraman, R. (2019). School feeding and learning achievement: Evidence from India's midday meal program. *Journal of Development Economics, 139,* 249–265.

Chakrabarty, S. (2015). A nexus between child labour and microfinance: an empirical investigation. *Economic Papers: A Journal of Applied Economics and Policy, 34*(1–2), 76–91.

Chanda, R., & Datta, R. (2019). Policies and strategies of international organizations in combating child labor in India: A win-win analysis. In *Handbook of global economic policy* (pp. 217–232). Abingdon: Routledge.

Charnovitz, S, (1996). Child labour: What to do? *Journal of Commerce*.

Chatterjee, P. (2018). India launches Ayushman Bharat's secondary care component. *The Lancet, 392*(10152), 997.

Chaudry, A., & Wimer, C. (2016). Poverty is not just an indicator: The relationship between income, poverty, and child well-being. *Academic Pediatrics, 16*(3), S23–S29.

Clark, C. S. (1999). Child labor and sweatshops: An overview. In M. E. Williams (Ed.), *Child labor and sweatshops* (pp. 10–20). San Diego: Greenhaven Press.

Cockburn, J. (2001). Child labour versus education: Poverty constraints or income opportunities. *Center for the Study of African Economies, Oxford University, 17*(1), 1–32.

Cohen, R. (2016). *Migration and its enemies: Global capital, migrant labour and the nation-state*. Abingdon: Routledge.

Conca, J. (2018, September 28). Blood batteries—Cobalt and the Congo. *Forbes*. Retrieved from https://www.forbes.com/sites/jamesconca/2018/09/26/blood-batteries-cobalt-and-the-congo/#63fd1d0acc6e.

"Convictions continue to plunge in Telangana's child labour cases" (2019, May 18). *The New Indian Express*. Retrieved from http://www.newindianexpress.com/cities/hyderabad/2019/may/18/convictions-continue-to-plunge-in-states-child-labour-cases-1978460.html.

Cullen, F. T., Williams, N., & Wright, J. P. (1997). Work conditions and juvenile delinquency: is youth employment criminogenic? *Criminal Justice Policy Review, 8*(2–3), 119–143.

Dammert, A. C., de Hoop, J., Mvukiyehe, E., & Rosati, F. C. (2018). Effects of public policy on child labor: Current knowledge, gaps, and implications for program design. *World Development, 110,* 104–123.

Das, S. (2012). Incidence of child labour and child schooling in India: Pattern and determinants. *ISRN Economics*.

Das, S., & Mukherjee, D. (2019). The impact of MGNREGS on child labour and child education: An empirical analysis. *Development in Practice, 29*(3), 384–394.

Department of Economic and Social Affairs. (2015). *The Millennium development goals 2015*. Retrieved from https://www.undp.org/content/dam/undp/library/MDG/english/UNDP_MDG_Report_2015.pdf.

Department of Food and Public Distribution. (2018). *Annual Report 2017–18*. Retrieved from https://dfpd.gov.in/E-Book/examples/pdf/AnnualReport.html?PTH=/1sGbO2W68mUlunCgKmpnLF5WHm/pdf/fdhindi17-18-min.pdf#book/.

Deshingkar, P. (2009). Extending labour inspections to the informal sector and agriculture. *Chronic Poverty Research Centre Working Paper*, (154).

Dessy, S. E. (2000). A defense of compulsive measures against child labor. *Journal of Development Economics, 62*(1), 261–275.

Deuss, A., & Adenauer, M. (2017). *Food subsidies in India: Comparing the medium term impacts of physical grain transfers and different types of cash transfers* (No. 2060-2018-333).
Devulapalli, S. (2019). Where is child labour most common in India? *Livemint*. Retrieved from https://www.livemint.com/politics/news/where-is-child-labour-most-common-in-india-1549906952167.html.
Dinkelman, T., & Mariotti, M. (2016). The long-run effects of labor migration on human capital formation in communities of origin. *American Economic Journal: Applied Economics, 8*(4), 1–35.
Diwan, V. (2017). Child Labour: A Chronic Problem. *Social Science and Humanities Journal*, 250–255.
Dyson, J. (2014). *Working childhoods: Youth, agency and the environment in India*. Cambridge University Press.
Egyed, C. J., McIntosh, D. E., & Bull, K. S. (1998). School psychologists' perceptions of priorities for dealing with the dropout problem. *Psychology in the Schools, 35*(2), 153–162.
Emerson, P. M., & Souza, A. P. (2011). Is child labor harmful? The impact of working earlier in life on adult earnings. *Economic Development and Cultural Change, 59*(2), 345–385.
FAAE. (2018). *A call to action: Ending the use of all forms of child labour in supply chains*. FAAE Committee Report. Retrieved from https://www.ourcommons.ca/DocumentViewer/en/42-1/FAAE/report-19/page-5.
Faraz, M. A. (2019). Economics of child labor: A multidimensional approach. *Journal of Social Science Research, 14,* 2979–2996.
Fellmeth, G., Rose-Clarke, K., Zhao, C., Busert, L. K., Zheng, Y., Massazza, A., … & Orcutt, M. (2018). Health impacts of parental migration on left-behind children and adolescents: A systematic review and meta-analysis. *The Lancet, 392*(10164), 2567–2582.
Ferguson, S. (2018, December 6). To build a better future, Yemen's children must be educated. *Forbes*. Retrieved from https://www.forbes.com/sites/unicefusa/2018/12/06/to-build-a-better-future-yemens-children-must-be-educated/#62b8f0411fc3.
Filges, T., Jonassen, A. B., & Jørgensen, A. M. K. (2018). Reducing unemployment benefit duration to increase job-finding rates. *Campbell Systematic Reviews, 14*.
Foroughi, M., Moayedi-Nia, S., Shoghli, A., Bayanolhagh, S., Sedaghat, A., Mohajeri, M., … & Mohraz, M. (2017). Prevalence of HIV, HBV and HCV among street and labour children in Tehran, Iran. *Sex Transm Infect, 93*(6), 421–423.
Gaba, A. K. (1997). Open schooling in India: Development and effectiveness. *Open Learning: The Journal of Open, Distance and e-Learning, 12*(3), 43–49.
Galli, R. (2001). *The economic impact of child labour* (Vol. 128). Geneva: International Institute for Labour Studies.
Gamlin, J., Camacho, A. Z., Ong, M., & Hesketh, T. (2015). Is domestic work a worst form of child labour? The findings of a six-country study of the psychosocial effects of child domestic work. *Children's Geographies, 13*(2), 212–225.
Geyer, H., Ngidi, M., & Mans, G. (2018). Do social grants contribute to the jobless population growth in the former South African homelands? *Town and regional planning, 72*(1), 58–69.
Ghosh, R. (2019). Migrant children get a shot at education. *The Quint*. Retrieved from https://www.thequint.com/news/india/migrant-children-get-a-shot-at-education.
Goel, A. D., & Chowgule, R. V. (2019). Outbreak investigation of lead neurotoxicity in children from artificial jewelry cottage industry. *Environmental Health and Preventive Medicine, 24*(1), 30.
Goel, S. (2015, May 3). *Gujarat's diamond industry and child labour: the legal scenario*. Retrieved from https://www.lawctopus.com/academike/child-labour/.
Grootaert, C., & Kanbur, R. (1995). Child labour: An economic perspective. *International Labour Review, 134*(2), 187.
Grootaert, C., & Patrinos, H. A. (Eds.). (1999). *The policy analysis of child labor: A comparative study*. Macmillan.
Gopalan, K., & Venkataraman, M. (2015). Affordable housing: Policy and practice in India. *IIMB Management Review, 27*(2), 129–140.

Guio, J., Choi, Á., & Escardíbul, J. O. (2018). Labor markets, academic performance and school dropout risk: evidence for Spain. *International Journal of Manpower, 39*(2), 301–318.
Gulati, A., & Saini, S. (2015). *Leakages from public distribution system (PDS) and the way forward* (No. 294). Working paper.
Gupta, R. (2016, August 10). A law that allows child labour. *The Hindu*. Retrieved from https://www.thehindu.com/opinion/columns/A-law-that-allows-child-labour/article14560563.ece.
Habib, F. (2017). Causes of homelessness among children. *Biomedica, 26*(2), 109–113.
Hazarika, G., & Sarangi, S. (2008). Household access to microcredit and child work in rural Malawi. *World Development, 36*(5), 843–859.
Healy, J. (2018, January 29). 5-Year-Olds Work Farm Machinery, and Injuries Follow. *New York Times*. Retrieved from https://www.nytimes.com/2018/01/29/us/family-farms-child-workers.html.
Human Rights Watch. (1996). *The small hands of slavery: Bonded child labor in India*. Retrieved from https://www.hrw.org/legacy/reports/1996/India3.htm.
Hyde, P. (2018, December 19). The scourge of child slavery persists despite laws. *Forbes Africa*. Retrieved from https://www.forbesafrica.com/featured/2018/12/19/the-scourge-of-child-slavery-persists-despite-laws/.
Iannelli, C. (2002). Parental education and young people's educational and labour market outcomes: A comparison across Europe.
Imoh, A. T. D., Bourdillon, M. F. C., & Meichsner, S. (Eds.). (2018). *Global childhoods beyond the North-South Divide*. Berlin: Springer.
India Population. (2019). Retrieved from https://countrymeters.info/en/India#Child_dependency_ratio.
'India to remain the fastest-growing economy, widen lead against China: OECD'. (2019, May 29). *Business Today*. Retrieved from https://www.businesstoday.in/current/economy-politics/india-to-remain-fastest-growing-economy-oecd/story/351765.html.
International Labour Organization. (2018). *Decent work and the sustainable development goals: A guidebook on SDG labour market indicators*. Retrieved from https://www.ilo.org/ilostat-files/Documents/Guidebook-SDG-En.pdf.
International Labour Organization. (2017). *Global estimates of child labour: Results and trends, 2012–2016*. Geneva: International Labour Office. Retrieved from https://www.ilo.org/wcmsp5/groups/public/—dgreports/—dcomm/documents/publication/wcms_575499.pdf.
International Labour Organization. (2015). *ILO global estimates on migrant workers Results and methodology Special focus on migrant domestic workers*. Geneva: International Labour Office. Retrieved from https://www.ilo.org/wcmsp5/groups/public/—dgreports/—dcomm/documents/publication/wcms_436343.pdf.
International Labour Organization. (2003). *International training compendium on labour statistics—Statistics of employment, unemployment, underemployment: Economically active population*. Geneva: International Labour Office. Retrieved from https://www.ilo.org/public/english/bureau/stat/download/module.pdf.
International Labour Organization. (2002). *Eliminating the worst forms of child labour A practical guide to ILO Convention No. 182*. Geneva: International Labour Office. http://www.ilo.org/ipecinfo/product/download.do?type=document&id=1200 .
ILO. (1999). *C182—Worst forms of child labour convention, 1999 (No. 182)*. Retrieved from https://www.ilo.org/dyn/normlex/en/f?p=NORMLEXPUB:12100:0::NO::P12100_ILO_CODE:C182.
ILO. (1976). *C138—minimum age convention, 1973 (No. 138)*. Retrieved from https://www.ilo.org/dyn/normlex/en/f?p=NORMLEXPUB:12100:0::NO::P12100_ILO_CODE:C138.
India CSR Network. (2018). *Educational tablets for schools in rural India*. Retrieved from https://indiacsr.in/educational-tablets-for-schools-in-rural-india/.
International Labour Organization and Understanding Children's Work. (2010). *Joining forces against child labour Inter-agency report for The Hague Global Child Labour Conference of 2010*. Retrieved from www.ilo.org/ipecinfo/product/download.do?type=document&id=13333.

Invernizzi, A. (2016). Has research improved the human rights of children? Or have the information needs of the CRC improved data about children?. In *The human rights of children* (pp. 151–176). Abingdon: Routledge.

IPEC. (2013). *Marking progress against child labour: Global estimates and trends 2000–2012*. Retrieved from https://www.ilo.org/wcmsp5/groups/public/—ed_norm/—ipec/documents/publication/wcms_221513.pdf.

IPEC. (2019). *What is child labour*. Retrieved from https://www.ilo.org/ipec/facts/lang–en/index.htm.

Islam, A., & Choe, C. (2013). Child labor and schooling responses to access to microcredit in rural Bangladesh. *Economic Inquiry, 51*(1), 46–61.

Jacobson, J. L. (2018). Women's health: The price of poverty. In *The health of women* (pp. 3–32). Abingdon: Routledge.

Janzen, S. A. (2018). Child labour measurement: Whom should we ask? *International Labour Review, 157*(2), 169–191.

Jones, A. (2018). Malnutrition, poverty, and climate change are also human rights issues in child labor. *Health and Human Rights, 20*(2), 249.

Jose, D. (2019, May 18). Ease of doing business reforms affecting scrutiny of child labour? *The New Indian Express*. Retrieved from http://www.newindianexpress.com/cities/hyderabad/2019/may/18/eodb-reforms-affecting-scrutiny-of-child-labour-1978458.html.

Justino, P. (2014). Barriers to education in conflict-affected countries and policy opportunities. *Paper commissioned for fixing the broken promise of education for all: Findings from the global initiative on out-of-school children*. Retrieved from http://ais.volumesquared.com/wp-content/uploads/2015/01/OOSC-2014-Conflict-and-education-final.pdf.

Kadir, A., Shenoda, S., & Goldhagen, J. (2019). Effects of armed conflict on child health and development: A systematic review. *PLoS ONE, 14*(1), e0210071.

Kambhampati, U. S., & Rajan, R. (2006). Economic growth: A panacea for child labor? *World Development, 34*(3), 426–445.

Kamruzzaman, M., & Hakim, M. A. (2015). Socio-economic status of child beggars in Dhaka city. *Journal of Social Sciences and Humanities, 1*(5), 516–520.

Kar, B. (2018). Child labour: An analysis of work differential across gender in India. *Indian Journal of Geography and Environment Management, 15*(16), 102–116.

Kara, S. (2014). *Tainted carpets: Slavery and child labor in India's hand-made carpet sector*. Boston: Harvard University. Retrieved from https://cdn2.sph.harvard.edu/wp-content/uploads/sites/5/2014/01/Tainted-Carpets-Released-01-28-14.pdf.

Keeley, B., & Little, C. (2017). *The state of the worlds children 2017: Children in a digital world*. UNICEF. 3 United Nations Plaza, New York, 10017.

Khatab, K., Raheem, M. A., Sartorius, B., & Ismail, M. (2019). Prevalence and risk factors for child labour and violence against child issues in Egypt using Bayesian geospatial modelling with multiple Imputation. *BioRxiv*, 546697.

Kielland, A., & Tovo, M. C. (2006). *Children at work: Child labor practices in Africa*. Boulder, CO: Lynne Rienner Publishers.

Kiranmayi, B., & Joseph, G. (2018). *Unit-9 the vulnerable groups: Women and children*. IGNOU.

Klasen, F., Reissmann, S., Voss, C., & Okello, J. (2015). The guiltless guilty: Trauma-related guilt and psychopathology in former Ugandan child soldiers. *Child Psychiatry and Human Development, 46*(2), 180–193.

Koirala, P. (2019, May 19). Ending child labour: Whose concern is it? *The Himalayan Times*. Retrieved from https://thehimalayantimes.com/opinion/ending-child-labour-whose-concern-is-it/.

Kuimi, B. L. B., Oppong-Nkrumah, O., Kaufman, J., Nazif-Munoz, J. I., & Nandi, A. (2018). Child labour and health: a systematic review. *International journal of public health, 63*(5), 663–672.

Kujur, R. (2019). Underdevelopment and patterns of labour migration: a reflection from Bolangir district, Odisha. *Research Journal of Social Sciences, 10*(1).

Kuriakose, F., & Iyer, D. (2018). Technology and the future of bonded child labour in South Asia.

Lahariya, C. (2018). 'AyushmanBharat' Program and universal health coverage in India. *Indian Pediatrics, 55*(6), 495–506.
Laing, K., McWhirter, J., Templeton, L., & Hannah-Russell, C. (2019). M-PACT + : Supporting families affected by parental substance misuse. *Health Education, 119*(1), 63–82.
Lancy, D. F. (2018). Children as laborers. In *Anthropological perspectives on children as helpers, workers, artisans, and laborers* (pp. 189–212). Palgrave Macmillan, New York.
Larmar, S., O'Leary, P., Chui, C., Benfer, K., Zug, S., & Jordan, L. P. (2017). Hazardous child labor in Nepal: The case of brick kilns. *Child Abuse and Neglect, 72,* 312–325.
Lesback, L. (2019, May 6).The makeup industry's darkest secret is hiding in your makeup bag. *Refinery 29.* Retrieved fromhttps://www.refinery29.com/en-gb/2019/05/231987/mica-in-makeup-mining-child-labor-india-controversy.
Lopez-Calva, L. F. (2001). Child labor: myths, theories and facts. *Journal of International Affairs*, 59–73.
Maadad, N., & Matthews, J. (2018). Schooling Syrian refugees in Lebanon: building hopeful futures. *Educational Review*, 1–16.
Maplecroft, V. (2019). *Progress on child labour flatlining in world's manufacturing hubs—Child labour index.* Retrieved from https://www.maplecroft.com/insights/analysis/child-labour-in-worlds-manufacturing-hubs/.
Maconachie, R., & Hilson, G. (2016). Re-thinking the child labor "problem" in rural Sub-Saharan Africa: The case of Sierra Leone's Half Shovels. *World Development, 78,* 136–147.
Macveigh, T. (2019, 30 May). *Boycott North Korea's 'inhumane' mass gymnastic displays, says ex-diplomat. The Guardian.* Retrieved from https://www.theguardian.com/global-development/2019/may/30/boycott-north-koreas-inhumane-mass-gymnastic-displays-says-ex-diplomat.
Malhotra, S. (2015, June 7). Invisible hands. *Business Today*. Retrieved from https://www.businesstoday.in/magazine/features/child-labour-in-india-how-it-being-hidden-from-authorities/story/219448.html.
Marsh, L. (2018). *Report on social security for Canada: New edition* (Vol. 244). McGill-Queen's Press-MQUP.
Mauras, M., Mendez, E. G., & Himes, J. R. (2018). Preface. In Salazar, M. C., & Glasinovich, W. A. (Eds.). (2018). *Child work and education: Five case studies from Latin America*. Oxford: Routledge.
McGregor, G. (2017). Counter-narratives that challenge neo-liberal discourses of schooling 'dis-engagement': Youth professionals informing the work of teachers. *British Journal of Sociology of Education, 38*(4), 551–565.
Mehraj, S. (2019). Why carry bricks when shoulders are intended to carry books? Child labour—A withered bud. *National Journal of Labour and Industrial Law, 1*(1), 21–23.
Meyer, B. D., & Mittag, N. (2019). Using linked survey and administrative data to better measure income: Implications for poverty, program effectiveness, and holes in the safety net. *American Economic Journal: Applied Economics, 11*(2), 176–204.
Ministry of Labour and Employment, Government of India. (2018). *About child labour*. Retrieved from https://labour.gov.in/childlabour/about-child-labour.
Ministry of Labour & Employment, Government of India. (2015). *State wise details of working children in the age group of 5–14 years as per Census 2001 and Census 2011*. Retrieved from https://labour.gov.in/sites/default/files/Census-2001&2011.pdf.
Ministry of Labour & Employment, Government of India. (1987). *National policy on child labour, 1987*. Retrieved from https://labour.gov.in/sites/default/files/PolicyofGovernmenontheissueofChildLabour.pdf.
Ministry of Labour & Employment, Government of India. (1986). *Child and adolescent labour (Prohibition & regulation) Act, 1986*. Retrieved from https://labour.gov.in/sites/default/files/The_Child_and_Adolescent.pdf.
Ministry of Labour and Employment, Government of India. (n.d.). *The factories act, 1948*. Retrieved from https://labour.gov.in/sites/default/files/TheFactoriesAct1948.pdf.

Ministry of Labour and Employment, Government of India. (2016). *National child labour project scheme*. Retrieved from https://labour.gov.in/childlabour/nclp.
Ministry of Law and Justice. (2016). *The Juvenile Justice (Care and Protection of Children) Act, 2015*. Retrieved from http://cara.nic.in/PDF/JJ%20act%202015.pdf.
Ministry of Law and Justice. (2016). *The Child Labour (Prohibition and Regulation) Amendment Act, 2016*. Retrieved from https://pencil.gov.in/THE%20CHILD%20LABOUR%20(PROHIBITION%20AND%20REGULATION)%20AMENDMENT%20ACT,%202016(1).pdf.
Ministry of Law and Justice. (2017). *The Mahatma Gandhi National Rural Employment Guarantee Act, 2005, with schedules as amended in 2017*. Retrieved from https://nrega.nic.in/amendments_2005_2018.pdf.
Ministry of Statistics and Program Implementation. (2019). *Labour and employment statistics*. Retrieved from http://mospi.nic.in/94-labour-and-employment-statistics.
Mishra, M., & Joshi, A. (2016). A study on labour welfare measures and it's effect on employee's job satisfaction in an industry of district Faridabad. *Indian Journal of Preventive & Social Medicine, 47*(1–2), 5–5.
Montgomery, H. (2009). Are child prostitutes child workers? A case study. *International Journal of Sociology and Social Policy, 29*(3/4), 130–140.
Mukherjee, D., & Das, S. (2008). Role of parental education in schooling and child labour decision: Urban India in the last decade. *Social Indicators Research, 89*(2), 305–322.
Mukherjee, C., & Pal, R. (2016). Role of parental expectations in determining child labour and schooling. *Department of Economics, Lund University Working Papers*, 6.
Narayan, N. (1999). International partnerships must reduce the use of child labor. In M. E. Williams (Ed.), *Child labor and sweatshops* (pp. 63–69). San Diego: Greenhaven Press.
Naylor, C. D. (2018). Canada as single-payer exemplar for universal health care in the United States: A borderline option. *JAMA, 319*(1), 17–18.
NCPCR. (n.d.). *Constitutional provisions on child labour*. Retrieved from http://ncpcr.gov.in/showfile.php?lid=74.
Neumayer, E., & De Soysa, I. (2005). Trade openness, foreign direct investment and child labor. *World Development, 33*(1), 43–63.
Nicolella, A., & Kassouf, A. L. (2018). The effect of child labour on children's health in Brazil. *International Journal of Social Economics, 45*(2), 357–371.
NIOSH. (2016). Analyses of the 2014 Childhood Agricultural Injury Survey (CAIS). Morgantown WV: U.S. Department of Health and Human Services, Public Health Service, Centers for Disease Control and Prevention, National Institute for Occupational Safety and Health, Division of Safety Research. Unpublished.
Ochab, E. U. (2019, March 23). The transatlantic slave trade and the modern day slavery. *Forbes*. Retrieved from https://www.forbes.com/sites/ewelinaochab/2019/03/23/the-transatlantic-slave-trade-and-the-modern-day-slavery/#5b6e39e02e55.
O'Driscoll, D. (2017). Overview of child labour in the artisanal and small-scale mining sector in Asia and Africa. *KD4 Helpdesk Report*. Retrieved from https://assets.publishing.service.gov.uk/media/5a5f34feed915d7dfb57d02f/209-213-Child-labour-in-mining.pdf.
O'Sullivan, M. E. (2006, January 01). Review of Kastner, Dieter, Kinderarbeit im Rheinland: Entstehung und Wirkung des ersten preußischen Gesetzes gegen die Arbeit von Kindern in Fabriken von 1839. www.h-net.org. Retrieved 2015-11-14.
Panda, S., Chakraborty, M., & Misra, S. K. (2016). Assessment of social sustainable development in urban India by a composite index. *International Journal of Sustainable Built Environment, 5*(2), 435–450.
Panda, S. S., & Mishra, N. R. (2018). Factors affecting temporary labour migration for seasonal work: A review. *Management Research Review, 41*(10), 1176–1200.
Pandit, A. (2019, May 2018). *Those rescued from child labour, trafficking may not be asked for multiple statements*. Retrieved from https://timesofindia.indiatimes.com/india/those-rescued-from-child-labour-trafficking-may-not-be-asked-for-multiple-statements/articleshow/69543512.cms.

Papastergiadis, N. (2018). *The turbulence of migration: Globalization, deterritorialization and hybridity*. New York: Wiley.
Parker, D. (2016). P070 A public health perspective on child labour. *Occupational and Environmental Medicine, 73*(1), 44.
Patterson, E. G. (2018). Work expectations and the able-bodied adult: Myths and realities in food stamp reform. *Wake Forest JL & Pol'y, 8,* 363.
Pawar, M. (2016). Child labour: An integrated approach. In *Child labour in South Asia* (pp. 63–76). Abingdon: Routledge.
Peled, E. (2019, January 2). We can end child trafficking and forced labor. *Forbes*. Retrieved from https://www.forbes.com/sites/unicefusa/2019/01/02/demanding-an-end-to-child-trafficking-and-forced-labor/#18d4cac27ccd.
Pham, T. T. T., & Nguyen, K. S. (2019). Does microcredit influence parent's decision to send a child to school or to work? Evidence from Vietnamese rural households. *The Journal of Developing Areas, 53*(3).
Pinto, A. (2016). Child labour in India: A critical evaluation of four issues. In *Child labour in South Asia* (pp. 125–144). Abingdon: Routledge.
Prasad, A. N., & Prasad, P. L. (2009). Children in conflict zones. *Medical Journal Armed Forces India, 65*(2), 166–169.
PROBE. (1999). *Public report on basic education in India. The PROBE team*. Oxford: Oxford University Press.
PTI. (2017a, September 26). Over 70,000 missing children rescued under MHA drive: Rajnath Singh. *The Economic Times*. Retrieved from https://economictimes.indiatimes.com/news/politics-and-nation/over-70000-missing-children-rescued-under-mha-drive-rajnath/articleshow/60841260.cms.
PTI. (2017b, August 25). Kids should not be exploited in entertainment industry, says director Amole Gupte. *Scoopwhoop.com*. Retrieved from https://www.scoopwhoop.com/director-amole-gupte-says-children-shouldnt-be-misused-in-films/.
Putnick, D. L., & Bornstein, M. H. (2016). Girls' and boys' labor and household chores in low-and middle-income countries. *Monographs of the Society for Research in Child Development, 81*(1), 104.
Quattri, M., & Watkins, K. (2016). Child labour and education—A survey of slum settlements in Dhaka (Bangladesh). *World Development Perspectives, 13,* 50–66.
Quinlan, M. (2016). We've been down this road before: vulnerable work and occupational health in historical perspective. In *Vulnerable workers* (pp. 41–76). Abingdon: Routledge.
Rahikainen, M. (2017). *Centuries of child labour: European experiences from the seventeenth to the twentieth century*. Abingdon: Routledge.
Ramachandran, P. (2019). School mid-day meal programme in India: past, present, and future. *The Indian Journal of Pediatrics*, 1–6.
Ramos, A. K. (2018). Child labor in global tobacco production: A human rights approach to an enduring dilemma. *Health and human rights, 20*(2), 235.
Rangeela, R. P., & Anil, M. G. (2018). Welfare measures under the factories act: A critical appraisal. *International Journal of Pure and Applied Mathematics, 120*(5), 255–280.
Ranjan, P. (2001). Credit constraints and the phenomenon of child labor. *Journal of Development Economics, 64*(1), 81–102.
Reddy, A. N., & Sinha, S. (2010). School dropouts or pushouts? Overcoming barriers for the right to education.
Reddy, D. N. (2019). Labour rights in globalizing world and India. In *Globalization, labour market institutions, processes and policies in India* (pp. 371–400). Palgrave Macmillan, Singapore.
Rikhof, J. (2019). Child soldiers and asylum–duality or dilemma? In M. A. Drumbl & J. C. Barrett (Eds.), *Research handbook on child soldiers*. Cheltenham: Edward Elgar Publishing.
Rhodes, V. J. (1990). *Child labor in India: Some historical aspects*. Retrieved from https://archives.columbusstate.edu/gah/1990/101-107.pdf.

Rodgers, G. B., & Standing, G. (1981). *Child work poverty and underdevelopment*. Geneva: International Labour Office.

Roggero, P., Mangiaterra, V., Bustreo, F., & Rosati, F. (2007). The health impact of child labor in developing countries: Evidence from cross-country data. *American Journal of Public Health, 97*(2), 271–275.

Ronzoni, M. (2016). Global labour injustice: A critical overview. *Global Justice and International Labour Rights*, 26–52.

Roy, A. K., Singh, P., & Roy, U. N. (2015). Impact of rural-urban labour migration on education of children: A case study of left behind and accompanied migrant children in India. *Space and Culture, India, 2*(4), 17–34.

Rushe, E. (2019, January 19). Tony's Chocolonely brings slave free chocolate mission to UK supermarkets Sainsbury's, Whole Foods. *Forbes*. Retrieved from https://www.forbes.com/sites/elizabethrushe/2019/01/19/tonys-chocolonely-brings-slave-free-chocolate-mission-to-uk-supermarkets-sainsburys-whole-foods/#63dfd4b34096.

Saludes, M. Z. (2015). *"What…if something went wrong?" Hazardous child labour in small-scale gold mining in the Philippines*. Human Rights Watch. Retrieved from https://www.hrw.org/report/2015/09/29/what-if-something-went-wrong/hazardous-child-labor-small-scale-gold-mining.

Save the Children. (2018). *The many faces of exclusion: End of childhood report 2018*. Fairfield: Save the Children. Retrieved from https://www.savethechildren.org/us/about-us/resource-library/end-of-childhood.

Save the Children. (2016). *Every last girl: Free to live, free to learn, free from harm*. Retrieved from https://www.savethechildren.org.uk/content/dam/global/reports/advocacy/every-last-girl.pdf.

Schwartz, S. (2018). *Homeward bound: Return migration and local conflict after civil war*. Columbia Academic Commons. Retrieved from https://academiccommons.columbia.edu/doi/10.7916/D8ZK706X.

Subcommittee on International Human Rights. (2017, November 30). *Minutes of proceedings*. https://www.ourcommons.ca/DocumentViewer/en/42-1/SDIR/meeting-88/evidence.

Shah, M., & Steinberg, B. M. (2015). *Workfare and human capital investment: Evidence from India* (No. w21543). National Bureau of Economic Research.

Sharma. (2017). India's burgeoning youth are the world's future. *Livemint*. Retrieved from https://www.livemint.com/Opinion/2WSy5ZGR9ZO3KLDMGiJq2J/Indias-burgeoning-youth-are-the-worlds-future.html.

Sharma, A., & Chadha, N. (2018). Unit-29 Child Care Services in India. IGNOU.

Sharma, A. (2017, May 30). *All you need to know about the Crèche facility provision*. Retrieved from https://www.peoplematters.in/article/hr-ready/all-you-need-to-know-about-the-creche-facility-provision-15571.

Shields, D. A. (2015). Federal crop insurance: Background. *Congressional research service*, 7-5700.

Singh, S. K., & Parihar, A. (2016). *Child labour in India: A study of Saharsa District of Bihar*. KrishiSanskriti Publications.

Singh, T., & Singh, J. (2016). Direct cash benefit scheme: A review of issues in India. *International Journal of Advanced Multidisciplinary Research, 3*(6), 5–12.

Singal, N. (2006). Inclusive education in India: International concept, national interpretation. *International Journal of Disability, Development and Education, 53*(3), 351–369.

Sinha, S. (2015). Child labour and compulsory education.

Sloth-Nielsen, J. (2016). Worst forms of child labour: A view from out of Africa. In *Children's rights in Africa* (pp. 333–352). Abingdon: Routledge.

Spaull, N. (2015). Schooling in South Africa: How low-quality education becomes a poverty trap. *South African Child Gauge, 12*, 34–41.

Spencer, N. (2018). *Poverty and child health*. London: CRC Press.

Srivastava, A. (2011). *Television shows—Child labour in a new form?* Vidura. Retrieved from http://www.cmsindia.org/mediacoverage/vidura_july.pdf.

Srivastava, V. (2018). *A study on hand knotted carpet industry of Jaipur City*. Retrieved from https://shodhgangotri.inflibnet.ac.in/bitstream/123456789/5595/2/02_synopsis.pdf.

Srivastava, N. (2015). Impact of socio-economic background on school dropout rates in rural India. *National University of Educational Planning and Administration, 29*(1), 29–36.

Srivastava, R. (2017, June 15). *India: Child labour (Prohibition and Regulation) Amendment Act, 2016 of India*. Retrieved from http://www.mondaq.com/india/x/602434/employee+rights+labour+relations/Child+Labour+Prohibition+And+Regulation+Amendment+Act+2016+Of+India.

Stromquist, N. P. (2015). *Out-of-school children: Why gender matters?* Retrieved from https://www.academia.edu/9535568/Out-of-School_Children_Why_Gender_Matters.

The Tribune. (2019, May 30). *Millions at risk of child labour in manufacturing hubs, say researchers*. Retrieved from https://www.tribuneindia.com/news/world/millions-at-risk-of-child-labour-in-manufacturing-hubs-say-researchers/780579.html.

Thirumurthy, P. (2017, July 14). Entertainment or exploitation? The horror which plays out in children reality TV shows. *The News Minute*. https://www.thenewsminute.com/article/entertainment-or-exploitation-horror-which-plays-out-children-reality-tv-shows-65166.

Thomson Reuters Foundation. (2017, January 18). After Brick Kiln, 200 child workers rescued from bangle factories In Hyderabad. *NDTV*. Retrieved from https://everylifecounts.ndtv.com/after-brick-kiln-200-child-labourers-rescued-from-bangle-factory-in-hyderabad-9223.

Tilak, J. B. (2018). Education poverty in India. In *Education and development in India* (pp. 87–162). Singapore: Palgrave Macmillan.

TNN. (2016, March 12). 'By 2020, India will have the largest young workforce'. *The Times of India*. Retrieved from https://timesofindia.indiatimes.com/city/madurai/By-2020-India-will-have-the-largest-young-workforce/articleshow/51368384.cms.

TNN. (2016, August 23). *Class 8 students to get free bicycles*. Retrieved from https://timesofindia.indiatimes.com/city/bengaluru/Class-8-students-to-get-free-bicycles/articleshow/53818709.cms.

Tumino, A., & Taylor, M. P. (2015). *The impact of local labour market conditions on school leaving decisions* (No. 2015-14). ISER Working Paper Series.

UN News. (2015, January 20). *UN lauds Somalia as country ratifies landmark children's rights treaty*. Retrieved from https://news.un.org/en/story/2015/01/488692-un-lauds-somalia-country-ratifies-landmark-childrens-rights-treaty.

United Nations Development Programme. (2019). *Sustainable development goals: Background on the goals*. Retrieved from https://www.undp.org/content/undp/en/home/sustainable-development-goals/background.html.

UNICEF. (2017a). *In the world's poorest countries, around 1 in 4 children are engaged in child labour*. Retrieved from https://data.unicef.org/topic/child-protection/child-labour/#.

UNICEF (2017b). *Percentage of children aged 5–14 years engaged in child labour (by sex, place of residence and household wealth quintile)*. Retrieved from https://data.unicef.org/topic/child-protection/child-labour/.

UNICEF. (2013). *Child labour robbing millions of health, education and growth, UNICEF says* (Press Release). Retrieved from https://www.unicef.org/media/media_69610.html.

UNIGME. (2017). *Levels and trends in child mortality report 2017*. Retrieved from https://www.unicef.org/publications/files/Child_Mortality_Report_2017.pdf.

United Nations Organization. (1989). *Convention on the rights of the child*. Retrieved from https://www.ohchr.org/en/professionalinterest/pages/crc.aspx.

University of Jordan. (2016). *National child labour survey 2016 of Jordan*. Retrieved from https://www.ilo.org/wcmsp5/groups/public/—arabstates/—ro-beirut/documents/publication/wcms_510520.pdf.

United States Department of Labor. (2014). *2013 findings on the worst forms of child labor*. Washington DC: US Department of Labour. Retrieved from: https://www.dol.gov/ilab/reports/child-labor/findings/2013TDA/2013TDA.pdf.

Van Kooten, G. C., Orden, D., & Schmitz, A. (2018). Use of subsidies and taxes and the reform of agricultural policy. In *The Routledge handbook of agricultural economics* (pp. 355–380). Abingdon: Routledge.

Van den Anker, C. (Ed.). (2003). *The political economy of new slavery*. Hampshire: Palgrave Macmillan.

Wahlén, E. B. (2017, September 1). ILO reports find progress on ending child labour insufficient to meet SDG Target. *SDG Knowledge Hub*. Retrieved from http://sdg.iisd.org/news/ilo-reports-find-progress-on-ending-child-labour-insufficient-to-meet-sdg-target/.

Walt, V. & Meyer, S. (2018, August 23). Blood, sweat, and batteries: Inside Congo's cobalt mines. *Fortune*. Retrieved fromhttp://fortune.com/longform/blood-sweat-and-batteries/.

Wanchuk, R. N. (2019, May 23). Their future was a brick kiln, but top cop and NGO ensure 800 kids bag a new destiny. *The Better India*. Retrieved from https://www.thebetterindia.com/183256/ips-hero-education-telangana-mahesh-bhagwat-odisha-migrant-children/.

Wangchuk, R. N. (2019, May 23). *Their Future Was A Brick Kiln, But Top Cop & NGO Ensure 800 Kids Bag a New Destiny*. Retrieved from https://www.thebetterindia.com/183256/ips-hero-education-telangana-mahesh-bhagwatodisha-migrant-children/.

Webb, J. (2019, October 25). *Child workers found in clothing supply chain: ASOS, Marks & Spencer Implicated*. Retrieved from https://www.forbes.com/sites/jwebb/2016/10/25/child-workers-found-in-clothing-supply-chain-asos-marks-spencer-implicated/#1c63db754b12.

WFTO. (2017). *10 principles of fair trade. World Fair Trade Organization | Resolution Document 2*. Retrieved from https://wfto.com/sites/default/files/WFTO%20-10%20Principles%20%20of%20Fair%20Trade%20%282017%29.pdf.

Worstall, T. (2014, July 21). Bolivia legalises child labour and child labour might decline in Bolivia. *Forbes*. https://www.forbes.com/sites/timworstall/2014/07/21/bolivia-legalises-child-labour-and-child-labour-might-decline-in-bolivia/#408a43ba373e.

Worstall, T. (2016, July 20). India's mistake in liberalising child labour—They should legalise it entirely. *Forbes*. Retrieved from https://www.forbes.com/sites/timworstall/2016/07/20/indias-mistake-in-liberalising-child-labour-they-should-legalise-it-entirely/#3fc8bb686ff8.

Wydick, B. (1999). The effect of microenterprise lending on child schooling in Guatemala. *Economic Development and Cultural Change, 47*(4), 853–869.

Chapter 4
Child Labour: A Global Challenge

Abstract Slums are highly populated urban areas, typically characterized by illegal settlements, overcrowding and associated problems, such as law and order issues, poor physical and mental health and poor standards of living. Lopsided developmental efforts across nations and the concentration of resources in the urban pockets have made urban migration from rural areas a major reality—driven by a need to access work opportunities, education and even healthcare. The Indian slum population was estimated to reach as high as 9% of the total population in 2017—a problem further aggravated by the issue of illegal cross-border immigration to India from neighbouring nations. Children, the most vulnerable sections of the society, also tend to be among the worst victims of the slum environment. Prolonged exposure of children to the slum atmosphere has been associated with poor health conditions, inadequate care giving, stunting of development and risks from organized crime, drugs, sexual violence, child labour, denial of resources and other forms of exploitation. While slums have drawn attention of policymakers frequently both as problems to be addressed and unavoidable malaises to be endured, the issue of children in slums often get ignored—leading to less than adequate policy intervention to address their specific vulnerabilities and needs. The present chapter investigates the concerns of the slum children in India and their exposure to threats of child labour, health-damaging conditions, violence inside and outside their homes and inadequate access to even minimal resources. We discuss the major trends in growth and decline of slums in India, the plight of the Indian slum children and identify gaps that may be addressed through focused policy interventions.

Keywords Slum children · Urban migration · Slums

4.1 Introduction

> …hidden inside cities, wrapped in a cloak of statistics, are millions of children struggling to survive. They are neither in rural areas nor in truly urban quarters. They live in squalor, on land where a city has outpaced itself, expanding in population but not in vital infrastructure or services. These are children in slums and deprived neighborhoods, children shouldering the many burdens of living in that grey area between countryside and city, invisible to the authorities, lost in a hazy world of statistical averages that conceal inequality.

S. Deb et al., *Disadvantaged Children in India*,
https://doi.org/10.1007/978-981-15-1318-3_4

Her Majesty Queen Rania Al Abdullah of Jordan, UNICEF Eminent Advocate (UNICEF, 2012)

In April 2019, the human population of the world crossed 7.7 billion (World Population Prospects, 2019). This impact of this is best understood when kept in perspective with other information. More than 85% (85.7%) of this population boom, for instance, has happened within a space of barely 200 years—roughly coinciding with the arrival of modern medicine and science and technology. Further, much of the world's surface is not available for human habitation, owing to extreme inhospitable climates, water bodies, deserts and mountain peaks. This brings down the habitable area of the earth drastically, and as per the World Development Report 2009 (World Bank, 2009), 95% of the people of the world occupy only 10% of the world's land. Overpopulation brings in its wake resource crunches, further aggravated by the phenomenon of urbanization. In 2018, urban settlements were home to 55.3% of human beings. (United Nations, Department of Economic and Social Affairs, Population Division, 2018); whereas the European Commission estimates that the urban population makes up 85% of human beings on earth (Ritchie, 2018). As of 2015, only around 2.8% of land on the earth's surface has been covered by urban land area (SOER, 2015)—roughly translating to 4.47 million square km. These estimates give a rough idea of the magnitude of the problem of overpopulation and urbanization, and the associated phenomena of overcrowding, resource depletion and competition and physical and cognitive overload. As per a 2012 report, 33% of urban people across the world live in slums (United Nations Children's Fund [UNICEF], 2012). The number is expected to increase to 66% by 2050 (UN-Habitat, 2014a), indicating that congested housing, resource scarcity and deterioration of living conditions might turn out to be the most debilitating problems of the future, if not addressed immediately.

Slums are one of the most prominent manifestations of urbanization and overcrowding, characterized by a high concentration of human habitation in small areas, close to the means of livelihood and resources. According to a UN estimate, over 1.4 billion people would be living in slums by 2020 (UN-Habitat, 2006), and the number is expected to reach 2 billion by 2030. Owing to the lack of resources and facilities, slums are typically characterized by less than ideal living conditions, exploitation and high crime rates. Children, being high on vulnerability, are particularly threatened in slum conditions, owing to stiff competition for resources that are essential for their growth and development.

One in every five children in the world lives in India. Roughly 39% of the Indian population constitutes of children (Ministry of Home Affairs [MHA], 2011), and nearly 40% of these children live in vulnerable conditions (Planning Commission, 2012). Nearly 8.1 million children aged six and below live in slums or slum-like conditions. According to a 2015 report, one in every six urban children live in slums in India (PWC & Save the Children, 2015). The development, adjustment, and progress of these children are heavily jeopardized by their living conditions and immediate environment. This, in turn, leaves a long-term impact on the development and prosperity of the nation.

4.2 Definition of Slums

Slums refer to human settlements that may or may not be unauthorized but are lacking in basic resources and setups of health and privileges that are needed for sustainable and dignified living. The United Nations Human Settlements Programme states that a household defined as a slum is lacking in one or more of what are called the *Five Deprivations*: (1) easy access to water, (2) personal/family toilet, (3) secure tenancy and protection from eviction, (4) durable housing providing protection against extremes of climates and (5) living area shared with not more than three people (UN-Habitat, 2014a; UNICEF, 2012). The Slum Areas (Improvement and Clearance) Act, 1956, of India (Government of India, 1956) defines slum areas as places where

> the buildings in that area – (a) are in any respect unfit for human habitation, or (b) are by reason of dilapidation, overcrowding, faulty arrangement and design of such buildings, narrowness or faulty arrangement of streets, lack of ventilation, light or sanitation facilities, or any combination of these factors, are detrimental to safety, health or morals.

Slums are defined by Census of India as residential areas that are "unfit for human habitation owing to dilapidation, overcrowding, faulty arrangements and design of such buildings, narrowness or faulty arrangement of streets, lack of ventilation, light or sanitation facilities or any combination of these factors detrimental to safety and health" (PWC & Save the Children, 2015). In other words, slums are understood to be lacking in the basic civic amenities, thereby jeopardizing the life of the dwellers as well as the general population who commute through those areas and stay in the neighbouring communities.

Slums or slum-like settlements might have one of the two origins. In the first kind, slums build up historically over time through unplanned human settlement before municipal or rural planning legislations and guidelines come in place. Such unplanned old settlements, particularly those in heritage cities, might acquire the characteristic of slums over time. The second kind of slums builds up owing to illegal settlement of people in an empty area, who construct permanent and/or temporary housing, in violation of existing construction rules and norms of the government. As per the Draft National Slum Policy 2001, slums may include settlements on "illegally occupied land, congested inner-city built-up areas, fringe area unauthorized developments, villages within or peripheral to urban areas, irrespective of tenure or ownership or land use" (Ministry of Housing and Urban Poverty Alleviation [MHUPA], 2010; PWC & Save the Children, 2015).

An unsanitary and unplanned settlement gains its designation as a slum through a three-stage process (Chandramouli, 2013):

1. **Identification**: An unplanned and inhospitable residential area gets identified as a slum when there are at least 300 individuals inhabiting the place in around 70 households. As of 2011, 37% of slums in India were identified slums.
2. **Recognition**: Once identified, over time, the area gets recognized officially as a slum 28.5% of slums in India are recognized slums.

3. **Notification**: The area inhabitants receive a notification designating their settlement as a slum under the Slum Act. Notified slums form 34.3% of the total number of slums in India as per the 2011 Census.

While slums are similar across the world in terms of their deprivation from the basic conditions for human living, they vary widely in terms of culture, livelihood, design and development over time. Stokes (1962) distinguished between two kinds of slums based on their upward mobility over time: "slums of despair" are those where there is a progressive decline over time and "slums of hope," where there is development towards non-slum conditions over the years, owing to aspirational nature of the dwellers. Let us have a look at the lives of slum children.

Case Study 1: From Mumbai to Luck now, Children in Indian Slums

"In the Bherkhampur Mohalla of Lucknow, on the banks of the Gomati River, is a colony of maids and rag pickers. Children belonging to the families that reside here pick rags in and around the railway station, and other areas of the city. They start work early morning and go on till late in the evening. The women clean homes, cook for families, and do household work. Sometimes, the children are given the additional responsibility of looking after their younger siblings, and therefore cannot attend a regular school."

Hanumant Singh, In *Slum Children get a Glimpse of School Life* (Singh, 2019)

"In the slum of Dharavi [Mumbai], many children work as garbage collectors, street vendors or begging to help their families survive. Many slum girls and slum boys do not have a roof over their heads and live on the street, including children with disabilities due to childhood illnesses such as polio or other infirmity. They barely have access to medical treatment and state support. Besides, like most of their parents, they are illiterate."

Kristian Bertel, In *Slum Children of Dharavi* (Bertel, n.d.)

4.3 The Nature and Character of Slums in India

India presently ranks second only to China in the overall population and has one of the highest population growth rates worldwide (PTI, 2019c). While China ranked the highest in the world in terms of the number of people living in slums in 2014 (180 million), India ranked second, with 104 million people living in slums (UN-Habitat, 2014a). Further, uneven growth and development of different pockets of the country makes urban immigration a grim reality of India According to data, urban areas in India house 13% of the population but occupies only 0.2% of the land. This results in living conditions that are abysmally crowded, leading to pressure on existing facilities, rapid depletion of resources, competition for facilities and means of livelihood and substandard living. There is no less than 76 million urban poor in India, who are mostly located in the slum settlements (MHA, 2011). The Census of 2011 revealed that one in every six urban Indian households (17.4%) is in a slum. The top state in terms of urban slum population is Andhra Pradesh (35.7%), whereas Kerala, with only 1.5% of urban households in slums, has the most promising picture (PWC & Save the Children, 2015). However, the NSSO reported a downward trend in the number of urban slums in India between 2009 (49,000) and 2012 (33,150)—a sharp fall of almost 33% (Business Standard, 2013).

Conditions of slum also differ on depending on whether the slum is in the urban area or in the rural area. People dwelling in rural slums tend to have lower income than people in urban slums. However, although people in urban slums tend to have greater access to income, their purchasing power remains low owing to the high cost of living in urban area, and scarcity of resources and services owing to high population density in the cities (Usmani & Ahmad, 2018). While slums are usually associated with poverty and penury, the Census data shows that slum dwellers are often as well-endowed as, even slightly better than, non-slum urban dwellers in terms of ownership of assets and access to certain services—such as homeownership (70.2% vs. 69%), mobile phones (63.5% vs. 64.3%), access to treated drinking water (65.3% vs. 62%), or electricity (90.5% vs. 92.7%). Even in terms of access to resources such as ownership or cars or computers, or services such as banking or LPG cooking facilities, non-slum households tend to do only slightly better than slum households, indicating that many of the slum household owners are characterized by decent per capita income, stable sources of revenue and access to modern urban amenities, which attract people to urban settlements in the first place (Sethi, 2013).

The statistics show a grim picture when it comes to health and sanitation. As per a UN-Habitat report, permanent structures form only 28% of slum households (UN-Habitat, 2014a). As opposed to around 72% of non-slum urban households, domestic access to drinking water is available in only 56% of slum households (Sethi, 2013) This leads to daily hassles to access one of the most basic necessities of life, long hours spent in queues before municipality public taps, or money spent in buying water, which could have been invested elsewhere. The victims of this system are, more often than not, the children, who spend time in water queues, dropping out of schools (Subbaraman et al., 2015). Close to 34% of slum homes have no toilet within their premises, and 36.9% have no connectivity to open drainage. This translates into serious issues of hygiene and health hazards for the residents of the neighbourhood (Sethi, 2013).

Another important statistic is that 25% of the urban population in India lives below the poverty line (Usmani & Ahmad, 2018). This section, not surprisingly, is located almost entirely in the slums, owing to lack of affordable housing elsewhere. This makes slum life one of stark contrasts, a mesh of many kinds of livelihoods, and a breeding ground for violence and crimes.

An important observation when it comes to slums is the distinction between income poverty and what is called shelter poverty (HPEC, 2011). Much of the poor, congested living conditions in slums arise out of inflated land prices, and cost of living quarters in urban areas, forcing people to move into less than adequate housing conditions. Another challenge is the pressure of commuting in particularly crowded urban areas, which make people crowd in and around office areas, even at the cost of living in inhospitable conditions. The following case study is a clear illustration of sorry state of slum children:

Case Study 2: Slum Children Working as Rag Pickers in Gujarat

"At our organization we are working for slum children who used to live on the footpath of Indian urban life. Mostly they are born to third generation on the footpath. Mostly they are engaged in collecting garbage. They are earning by collecting garbage only. Our survey report of such 2300 children show some astonishing fact about that their mentality. Whenever we asked, "What is your hand is for?" in response 80 per cent answer is "Hand for collecting garbage and eating."

Slum shine, In *Slum Students Interview* (Slumshine, 2019)

4.4 Slum Children, Street Children and Homeless Children

Children from the slums often end up on the streets. While many of them do so to escape from violence, abuse or neglect at home, about 65% of street children live with their parents in temporary shelters on the street or in the railway premises. There are about 0.27 million homeless children in India aged between 0 and 6, of which 0.11 million reside in urban areas. Most street children are engaged in minor professions such as begging, selling flowers, toys, rag picking or doing odd jobs. About one-fourth (24%) of such children were illiterate, and two out of every five have faced sexual abuse or torture (Tata Institute of Social Sciences & Action Aid, 2013). Street children are heavily exposed to the risk of drug addiction, and most were found to be malnourished (Rajadhyakshya, 2013).

According to the NSSO report of 2007–2008, about 30% of India's population consists of internal migrants, of which over 15 million are children (United Nations Educational, Scientific and Cultural Organization [UNESCO], 2013). Many children in Indian slums are migrants from rural areas, who accompany their parents in the latter's search for work. Children of migrant workers are doubly jeopardized, as they are often deprived of the safety net provided by social security services such as Public Distribution System, BPL cards, or caste cards. Such children also tend to be school dropouts owing to their erratic lifestyles, lack of adult supervision and pressure of domestic chores when the adults of the family go out for work (UN-Habitat, 2014b). Migrant children in urban areas tend to be vulnerable to child labour and exploitation in hazardous and illegal vocations such as child prostitution and sex trafficking. A report by Aide et Action showed that almost 80% of migrant slum children had no access to education and around 40% of them were child labourers (Aide et Action, 2014). The daily life of slum children is painful and inhuman. One can have a better understanding of reality of slum children from the following case study:

Case Study 3: Life of Children from the Slums of Dehradun, India

"Hope is an alien concept if you're born in Dehradun's Bindal slum, lining the side banks of the unpredictable Bindal river. Your parents are mostly daily wage labourers working at construction sites. In most cases, the father is addicted to alcohol. Your parents – if both are working – leave for work early in the morning. The eldest female sibling is left to fend for the younger ones. Food is a luxury. A lot of the earnings, meagre to begin with, are spent on alcohol and it's not uncommon for women to drink either. Addiction to whiteners is found

among children as young as 5 or 6.Your surroundings don't offer much hope either. Filth is your mainstay. Children of all shapes, sizes and ages – unkempt and unattended – scamper around barefoot along with stray dogs and pigs, begging or making their way to the closest temple to find a meal. Garbage heaps abounds; drain water overflows; the stench makes you sick and the shanty dwellings look shaky as paper."

The Better India, *How a Trust Pulled 1800 Slum Kids off Dehradun's Streets and Gave Them Education (The Better India,* 2017*)*

4.5 Problems Assailing Childhood in Slums

A significant portion of the population in the 49,000-odd slums in India is made up of children (UNICEF, 2012). According to Usmani and Ahmad (2018), over one billion children live in urban India, and out of them, over 300 million children, mostly located in slums, are denied of basic healthcare, sanitation, nutrition, or education and development opportunities.

While slum conditions vary depending on its closeness to an urban area, the problems that children encounter in slums also differ in interesting ways depending on whether the slum is urban or rural. Rural slums are characterized by poverty, lack of livelihood and lack of access to resources such as healthcare, education and recreation. However, rural areas tend to be more endowed when it comes to access to playgrounds and open areas, and social network and support structures. Urban slums, on the other hand, mostly see settlement from people who arrive in search of livelihood. Thus, urban slums, on an average, fare slightly better than rural slums when it comes to income or access to quality facilities. However, this is offset by a much higher crunch for space, unhygienic conditions, higher costs of living, no space to play, absence of social support and extended family network, and greater vulnerability to crimes when it comes to the urban and semi-urban settlements. Slum children live in all kinds of polluted environment. For example,

Case Study 4: Rag pickers in Dharavi Slum in Mumbai

"All along the streets one can see hundreds of barefoot children can listen noises of human recycling machines, scurry back and forward. There are hauling bundles of waste plastic, cardboard or glass retrieved from Mumbai's vast municipal dumps. From every alley come the sounds of hammering, drilling and soldering. In every shack, dark figures sit waist-deep in piles of car batteries, computer parts, fluorescent lights, ballpoint pens, plastic bags, paper and cardboard boxes and wire hangers, sorting each item for recycling."

In A Study of Slums in Mumbai with special reference to Dharavi (Kaur, Kaur, & Soni, 2014)

4.6 Health Hazards from Unhygienic Living Conditions

Children tend to have weaker immune systems than adults. They are, therefore, far more vulnerable to exposure to unsanitary conditions. The mortality rate of children under five in urban slums is as high as 72.7 per 1000 births as compared to 41.8 per 1000 births in urban non-slum areas (Usmani & Ahmad, 2018). Slum houses tend to be illegal structures—build without satisfying the necessities for sunlight, open-air, sanitation, drinking water and clean surroundings.

In India, only 6% of the households in the bottom 20% in terms of income have access to piped drinking water (World Bank, 2019). Again, slums, being unplanned and mostly unauthorized, do not come under the coverage of waste disposal systems of the city or the village. Garbage tends to be thrown on the street or dumped in open places close to the neighbourhood. In the absence of sewer systems, the number of modern toilets available is inadequate and open defecation is common, leading to a scary spread of infections in close quarters (Achiego, 2016). Interviews from teenaged girls from slums in Mumbai and Pune reveal the following:

> There are no bins on the road where the waste can be dumped and hence, it gets scattered all over the area that leads to a foul smell. The lack of clean water in the area is also a problem…1800 of us have to share one toilet, which is dirty and unfit for use. Moreover, we don't use it as boys tease us when we go there…There are few useable public toilets in our area. These toilets have neither water nor electricity and women feel scared to use them in the evenings. (UNICEF, 2012)

According to the Report on the Informal Day Care Centres of Karagita, Kenya, poor lighting, congested conditions, poor hygiene and lack of health checkups cause frequent diseases in children living in slums (Gitonga, 2018). Similar findings have been reported from Liberia in 2009, where only one-third of residents in the capital have access to toilets, and 20–30 cases of cholera are reported every week (IRIN, 2013). Again, NFHS-3 data show that children are much less likely to have nutrition deficiencies if the household uses piped water, bottled water, or water from tankers, as opposed to wells and surface water (International Institute for Population Sciences, 2009).

A major risk for slum children is stunting, which is associated with 53% of the deaths in the developing countries (World Bank, 2019). The study shows that in Bangladesh, children from urban slums are 50% more likely to be stunted than other urban children. Childhood stunting affects the school performance and earning potential of an individual, affecting the adult years as well as the future generations (Damania et al., 2017).

The 2012 UNICEF report states that the unsanitary conditions in slum housing lead to diarrhoea and pneumonia, contagious diseases that feature among the leading causes of death for children aged below 5 years, as well as measles, tuberculosis and polio (Chandrasekhar, 2018; George et al., 2019; UNICEF, 2012). According to the Key Population Briefs on Urban Settlements by the Stop TB Partnership ('Key Population Briefs', 2016), slums are breeding grounds for tuberculosis owing to use of the same room for living, cooking and sleeping, which expose children to the smoke from burning fuels and contagion from other family members with respiratory diseases. Non-slum children are nine times less predisposed to contract TB than slum children living in highly congested urban slums in the Philippines (Fry, Cousins, & Olivola, 2002). Another killer is respiratory disease in pneumonia. Children from the poorest families in the rural and urban slums tend to be at the highest risk when it comes to pneumonia, as they tend to be malnourished, non-immunized and less likely to receive early diagnosis and treatment (Elliott, 2019).

Apart from access to healthcare, slum children are often denied healthcare owing to superstitions, traditions and social norms prevalent among poor, uneducated people. Sanghera (2018) reports that women in Dharavi slums avoided ICDS (Integrated Child Development Services), as they believed that weighing their kids would bring ill luck. Immunization is a major challenge in the slums as people may avoid immunization owing to cost or lack of awareness. Poverty plays a role here—only 47.3% of the poor children are fully immunized, as opposed to 75.5% of the rich children (National Institute of Urban Affairs [NIUA], 2016). Zaman, Goswami, and Hassan (2018) reported that the incidence of non-immunized children in the slums is as high as 80%. Thus, improper health-seeking behaviour by caregivers is also a major cause of illnesses among slum children.

4.7 Access to Education

One of the most serious impacts of slum-dwelling comes on the educational status and progress of the children. The 2011 Census showed that 23% of the children in urban India are out of the school, and this section is almost entirely from the slums (EdCIL & SRI, 2014). The 2015 PWC report on children in urban India revealed that 68% of street children are illiterate (PWC & Save the Children, 2015).

One of the major challenges when it comes to the education of slum children is the phenomenon of cultural deprivation. Slums, being crowded, noisy and frequently violent, are often devoid of a healthy environment to stimulate the child's early intellectual growth and social skills. Parents of such children are also often ill-equipped or too hard-pressed for time to provide the children with the needed preparatory training before they join school. Such children find it increasingly difficult to adjust to school environment and keep up with the educational demands that a child from a more privileged household finds easy to handle. Again, while children living in slums tend to be high on practical experience and realities of the world, they are often underprepared with the general concepts of basic science and mathematics. It has also been noted that mixed schools tend to be a constant reminder to children of their inadequacies, causing them to feel alienated. The UNICEF report on children in urban India quotes a boy from a slum in Delhi:

> In the kachcha colony, where I live, the condition is worse. There is no water connection, no parks to play, and the houses here are shanties. I feel discriminated against as people from JJ Colony also ill-treatus. (UNICEF, 2012)

Resource inadequacies make children from slums go for low-cost or free educational options in government-run schools in India, which at times cannot match up with the quality of resources and faculty that may be found in the more affluent schools. Since they come from a challenging and disadvantaged background, children from slums often require specialized assistance and guidance when it comes to learning. Low-cost schools accessible to slum children are often lacking in teachers who have the needed training and qualifications to deal with the specific problems of these children. A 2015 research on schools in Kenya's largest slum revealed that 99% of the teachers in the sampled schools have no training in inclusive education or in teaching people with mental or intellectual disability (Action Foundation, 2015). The result is low engagement among the students, poor attendance and a tendency to drop out of schools. In a survey on Delhi slums, Tsujita (2010) reported that attendance rate for schools in slums is a mere 54.5% as opposed to 90% for the city as a whole.

Data shows that the girls tend to be worse affected than boys when it comes to school education, owing to pressure of domestic work, lack of safety on roads and early marriage. Research on slums in Kenya show that lack of easy access to drinking water force girls to spend their days in helping their mothers fetch water for family consumption, carrying 15–20 L of waters on their backs (Achiego, 2016). Child marriage is not uncommon in slums, where parents marry off young girls as protection against sexual predators (Letsoalo, 2019; Lopez, 2016). Although the number of child marriages in India has fallen by 51% between 2000 and 2018 (Save the Children, 2019), in many states, such as West Bengal, almost 42% of girls face child marriage (Ray, 2019). Only 50% of the girls aged between 15 and 17 in urban India are found to attend schools, and only 14 out of every thousand urban girls reach class 12 (PWC & Save the Children, 2015). Boys tend to drop out of school in search of income to supplement the family earnings.

Migrant children, who form a significant portion of the slum population, tend to another highly deprived group when it comes to education. The Global Educational Report 2019 (UNESCO, 2019) shows that India, like most other countries of the world, fares poorly when it comes to education of migrant children; in one survey, migrant children were unable to perform daily tasks using basic mathematics, even when they have received a formal education in the subject. In another study in Kolkata, the quality of education provided by the free government facilities to migrant children was found to be lacking in quality and effectiveness (Institute of Social Sciences & UNICEF, 2014).

School dropouts in case of slum children have long-term consequences. It affects the employability of the person in the long run, making them continue their lives in poverty and passing on the burden to the next generations. Such children also tend to deviate towards less ostensible means of income, which escalates them in the path of crime, lawlessness and penury (EY, 2019). Researchers have equated the situation of school-dropout slum children and adolescents as 'social dynamite' that may destroy the equilibrium of the civil society.

4.8 Malnutrition

Malnutrition is a chronic problem of children from the poor socio-economic background. Malnutrition is a state of deficiency caused when one's diet lacks essential food components (such as vitamins, minerals, proteins, carbohydrates, etc.) in sufficient quantities. One of the most common malnutrition problems in India is iron deficiency, followed by iodine deficiency, protein deficiency, or various vitamin deficiencies, leading to skin disorders, poor eyesight, poor dental health and low immunity and stunted growth in children. Malnutrition may happen either due to insufficient intake or poor biological utilization (Yadav & Dubey, 2014). Malnutrition may be a consequence of scarce resources, such as in war-ravaged countries, or poverty, but it may also be a consequence of absence of dedicated caregiving or a lack of understanding of what constitutes adequate nutrition for a child.

Malnutrition leads to 2.3 million child deaths every year, and the cost of child malnutrition on the future population worldwide has been estimated at $125 billion (UNICEF, 2012). The National Family Health Survey-3 estimated that a staggering 54% of mortality below age 5 is related to malnutrition of which 44% happen from mild to moderate malnutrition that is easily preventable (IIPS, 2009). The NFHS-4 (Ministry of Health and Family Welfare [MHFW], 2017) showed that more than one-third of the children in India are underweight, the most prominent symptom of malnutrition. The 2016 Baseline Study of the National Institute of Urban Affairs reports that a staggering 79% of the children in India are anemic (NIUA, 2016).

Malnutrition tends to be particularly debilitating when it comes to children from the slums (Yadav & Dubey, 2014). Children in urban slums tend to show symptoms of chronic malnutrition, leading to wasting, underdevelopment of physical and intellectual abilities, and increased susceptibility to diseases. This malnutrition arises partly from poverty, as many slum dwellers may not have access to ostensible means of income. At the same time, the situation also arises from the lack of an adult support network in urban slums when it comes to caregiving. In cases where both parents are working, children in the slum homes are often left alone at home with their siblings and are forced to manage their own meals. Rode (2009) reports that mothers in urban slums are forced to wean their children from exclusive breastfeeding earlier than their rural counterparts, as they must go for work. In rural communities, the support network of extended families and close-knit social circles ensure that children have caregivers even when parents are not at home (Sanghera, 2018). Yadav and Dubey (2014) too state that malnutrition for children from urban slums arise from inappropriate feeding habits for small children, such as early weaning from exclusive breastfeeding, diluting milk, delaying entry of solid and semi-solid food into a child's diet, absence of a regular caregiver at home, lack of nutritional knowledge and insufficient access to public health services such as nutritional counseling. The following case study of slum children is a bright example of their daily struggle for existence:

Case Study 5: What do Street Children Eat?

"In a lane near Colaba market, Anita sleeps on the pavement with her son, two daughters, and her brother's two children. Her husband is a daily wage laborer who earns Rs 200 every day. When I asked her how she manages to feed so many children with such meager earnings, instead of explaining the financial aspect, she gave me a sense of logistics. She said, 'Kabhi ghar pe khana bana letihoon, kabhi bahar kha lete haibachche." (Sometimes I cook at home, and at other times, these kids eat out). Unfortunately, what she calls ghar is a pavement, a footpath that belongs to the public, which they have to vacate in the morning every single day.

*"Unlike rural children, street children in India do not face hunger. They are typically not food deprived. But they do suffer from high levels of malnutrition. One reason is obviously the content of the food that they buy off the street, which is very poor...Their bodies adjust to having lesser nutrition than that which is required. So, their bodies adjust by stunting. When you look at street children, they look obviously malnourished, but also smaller than their age," Harsh Mander, Director of Centre for Equity Studies said. According to an Action Aid and TISS study (*2013*) on Mumbai street children, around 25 percent of the children in the sample survey reported skipping at least one meal a day. Having no money for food was the most cited reason for skipping meals."*

Simantini Dey, In *World Nutrition Day: What Do the Street Children of India Eat?* (Dey, 2018)

4.9 Insecurity and Threat of Eviction

If there is anything greater than the physical strain of living in slums, it is the psychological stress that comes from the stimulation overload caused by overcrowding, tension overshared resources such as water or toilets and sense of deprivation of the necessities (Aishwarya, Samanta, & Dudeja, 2019; Raj, Galhotra, & Roja, 2019). Lack of privacy is one of the major problems, with cramped quarters, that make studying or pursuing hobbies difficult. Further, one of the realities in the lives of the children from slums is the fear of eviction and homelessness. Evictions caused by municipal action or by legal owners of properties, cause significant distress to the meager possessions of slum dwellers. The uncertainty that follows also deprives the children of education and healthcare, until the family settles elsewhere. Evictions also break social value chains within the slums and destroy small entrepreneurship, which take a considerable amount of time to rebuild (Gupte, Lintelo, Patel, Rao, McGregor, & Lakshman, 2019).

Insecurity about the permanence of households acts as a vicious cycle that makes slum problems persists in the long run. Since people are not sure if the status quo would prevail, they are reluctant to invest in the development of the neighbourhood or surrounding areas. This leads to continuance of inhuman living conditions for decades, the onus of which falls on the children who grew up in these neighbourhoods (UN-Habitat, 2014a). Continuous fear of eviction keeps slum children and their family members always disturbed. To some of them, this is a normal phenomenon.

Case Study 6: Forced Eviction in Delhi Slums

"The first time a bulldozer came to our place, I was scared and kept sitting near our belongings that had been thrown out," says Roshni, a ten-year-old whose family migrated from Bihar to Delhi looking for employment. Roshni and her family have been living in a slum in Yamuna Khadar's Belagaon in the capital's eastern region...Children in these fragile communities are amongst the worst hit by slum demolitions. They miss out on education, dropping out of school due to homelessness, uncertainty, and the stigma they face in schools as "slum children" ...Diptesh Singh of LAF explains, "We have been associated with this place since 2012. The area faces around four demolitions per year. One demolition takes place in a staggered manner over several days. So, for the entire period the families, including the children, stay around their homes in case the bulldozers return...Children end up missing many days of school at a stretch or dropping out altogether."

...This year Roshni saw DDA officials in her area again. But this time she was quick to act: "I carefully dismantled our makeshift home, carried the lighter things outside the house with my younger brother, called up my older brother, and waited for him to come and take the heavy stuff out."

Ankita Anand, In Not Seen, Not Heard (Anand, 2019)

4.10 Risks from Crises and Disasters

Children are among the most helpless when it comes to a situation of instability and disorder. Children lack survival skills and ability to fend for themselves and are vulnerable to the ensuing chaos (Save the Children, 2017). Apart from the threat of eviction, slum dwellings, owing to their semi-permanent, makeshift, and non-planned nature, are particularly vulnerable to natural disasters and accidents such as floods, water logging due to heavy rains, earthquakes and fire (Malhotra, 2018). In the slums of north India, cold waves in the winter months is a major killer, leaving families exposed to the mortal danger of hypothermia, particularly young children (Mascarenhas, 2015). Such situations may cause significantly more damage to life and property in slums than in non-slum areas. Further, owing to their limited financial capacity, rebuilding one's shelter is also a slow process. The onus of all these falls on children—who are forced to live under the open sky, in inhospitable and unhygienic conditions, missing out on adequate nutrition and remaining vulnerable to sexual predators (Brown & Dodman, 2014).

4.11 Access to Play Spaces and Recreation Spots

Play is important for the motor, cognitive, and social development of children (NIUA, 2016). By dint of overcrowding, slums, particularly those in the urban areas, lack in open areas and playgrounds for children. This deprives children of exposure to sunlight and open-air and exercise that is crucial for physical health. Such children tend to play on the roads and the lanes, where they are subject to the injury on the concrete roads and risk of traffic accidents (World Vision International, 2014). Achiego (2016) reports children in Kenyan slums playing in trenches filled with waters from bust sewers, exposing the children to severe health hazards. Devoid of healthy recreations, children also deviate to unhealthy activities such as gambling, pornography, or drug addiction (Russell, 2019; Yadav, 2019). In Bolivia, children in urban slums reported issues such as teenage pregnancy, youth criminal gangs and violence against children (World Vision International, 2014).

4.12 Crimes Against Children

Children around the world are frequent victims to several heinous crimes—starting from kidnapping, to sex trafficking, rape and murder. The vulnerability of children rises from their inability to defend themselves physically from an older person, and their incredulousness, which makes them easy targets for criminals. For children living in slums, the situation is worsened by the lack of security in slum settings. Slum areas are usually unauthorized settlements, which make these areas open for thoroughfare by people from different walks of life. Again, slum areas, owing to their congested nature and over crowdedness are less frequented by police, making them hubs of many kinds of criminal activities. According to a study by Banerjee, Pande, Vaidya, Walton, and Weaver (2011), 75% of the slum dwellers surveyed reported law and order problems in their neighbourhood—the most common ones being theft, gambling and substance abuse, violent crimes, domestic violence and vandalism, but only 10% reported seeking help from the police, or the political leaders. Khan, Unnithan, and Dassi (2007) report that slum dwellers tend to high in their Tolerance Quotient towards crimes, making them unmindful of criminal activities in close vicinity and even normalize it as a way of life and livelihood. All these make slums unsafe neighbourhoods for young children, who are exposed to different kinds of illegal elements. In a study done among slum children in Manilla, Philippines, all the 13 children interviewed reported witnessing at least one murder (Dodman, 2014). Another study done in Dhaka describes how slum children and street children are drawn into organized crimes, as a way of earning livelihood, and regularly engage in theft, extortion, illegal occupation of lands and even contract killing (Atkinson-Sheppard, 2018). Crimes are also one of the major challenges when it comes to slum upgrading and cleanup, as there are vested and powerful interests against disturbing the status quo (Weerdt, 2011).

Second, slum households are often run by dual-income couples, where both parents go out to work, often leaving children alone at home without an adult caregiver. This makes children especially vulnerable to sexual predators in the neighbourhood. Also, in the absence of protected playgrounds or space at home, children play on the road and the lanes, making them vulnerable to accidents and kidnapping. In India, between 2015 and 2016, there was a spike in the number of registered child sexual abuse cases by 40% (National Crime Records Bureau, 2016). According to a survey by the Praja Foundation, the number of reported cases in child sexual abuse in

Mumbai went up by 19% between 2016 and 2018 (Natu, 2019), while the number of rapes in Delhi between 2012 and 2018 went up by a staggering 202% ('Cops say all ok', 2019).

Another important reason that increases the vulnerability of slum children to assaults is the lack of education among children and their parents about potential risks and ways to seek help. Slum households often lack in awareness about potential hazards that may happen to the child and therefore are often careless when it comes to monitoring the child's movements and company, teaching them the danger signals, or where to seek help if in trouble. Children rarely have training in self-defense, making them unable to put up any effective resistance when attacked. The problem is aggravated by the lack of empathy from police or from teachers in schools, where the child is most likely to seek shelter. Children from the slums who take up employment, whether as domestic help or in shops, establishments, or factories, are exposed to threats of abuse from their employers. Gross violation of fundamental rights of slum children especially safety needs attention of all concerned especially the policymakers. If they visit police station for lodging a complaint against harassment, police officer should listen to them carefully, ensure justice and safety. Sexual harassment is very common for slum children. For example,

Case Study 7: Crimes against Adolescent Girls in Delhi

"Meena (not her real name) didn't tell her parents when the older boys started harassing her on the hour-long walk to school from her home in Madanpur Khadar, south Delhi – grabbing her hand and shouting "kiss me" – because she knew she would get the blame, as if she had somehow encouraged them. She was right: when her family found out, they banned her from going back to school, worried about the effect on their "honor" if she was sexually assaulted. The plan now is to get her married. She is 16.

Madanpur Khadar, a "resettlement colony" begun in 2000 to house families moved on from newly cleared slums...Meena, who comes from a Dalit family ... had imagined herself working for the police or becoming a teacher. "My parents are looking for a boy for me," she says. "They say I can get married and then I can study. But I know that once I get married, it will become very difficult. My dream will never come true."

Rachel Williams, In Why Girls in India Are Still Missing Out on the Education They Need (Williams, 2013)

4.13 Child Labour

The poor socio-economic conditions of slum households, early school dropouts and the absence of adequate guidance and caregiving at home often steer slum children to another major problem—child labour. More than one-tenth (11.8%) of the children in India are engaged in child labour, and children from slums form a significant portion of this vulnerable group (Save the Children, 2019). Child labour is widely prevalent in the slums, where children are engaged in part-time or full-time vocations as domestic help, apprentices, workers in shops or small manufacturing units, or vendors on the streets and the traffic signals. A survey of slums in Dhaka, Bangladesh showed that almost half of the children in the slums were working, and 15% of the children aged between 6 and 14 were engaged in full-time work, chiefly in the units of the $ 30 billion garment industry of Bangladesh (Quattri & Watkins, 2016).

Given the illegal character of child labour in most countries of the world, these children remain off the radar when it comes to labour rights and safe work conditions. Child worker in Dhaka and Kathmandu reported that their workplaces were unsafe and susceptible to building collapse ('Poorest Urban Children', 2014). Further, since they mostly work in the informal economy, they are denied the basic minimum wage, additional benefits such as medical insurance, holidays and leaves and even protective gear at work. The work, for a bare subsistence level pay, however, keep them away from education and other meaningful vocational training, which might have helped them escape from the traps of poverty. One-third of the children employed illegally in the textile factories of Bangladesh reported extreme fatigue ('Plight of Bangladeshi', 2016).

Case Study 8: Child workers in metal workshops in Moradabad

"From ages 8 to 10, Anas spent 10 h a day, six days a week, working in a smoke-filled metal ware workshop in the slums of Moradabad. In Moradabad, workshops is crowded together with houses in congested slums. Soot, smoke and exhaust fumes fill the air, and open drains line the narrow alleys, leaving barely enough room to walk. There are no places for children to play. This poverty drives children like Anas to work. In India, 42% of people live on less than $1.25 a day, and 12% of children between ages 5 and 14 are involved in labour.

Anas was drawn into the dangerous metal trade out of concern for his family's welfare. His father's work as a rickshaw puller barely met the family's needs, and his grandfather needed medicine they could not afford. The work was perilous. Anas worked inches from a pit of molten metal, and a bad burn to his foot has left him with a permanent scar. And, critically, his time in the workshop kept him out of the classroom."

Patricia Lone, *In Getting at-risk children out of work and into school in the slums of Moradabad, India* (Lone, 2012)

4.14 Interventions for Slum Children Worldwide

Healthy living conditions have been recognized as a crucial necessity for human life and dignity around the world. As early as 1948, the Universal Declaration of Human Rights incorporated the Right to Adequate Standards of Living that included the Right to Adequate Housing (UN-Habitat, 2014b). The Millennium Development Goals (MDG) of the United Nations Organization in 2000 included the goal of Environmental Sustainability. Under Environmental Sustainability, two sub-goals pertain to slums, by 2015, reducing the world's population who does not have access to sanitation and drinking water by 50%, and by 2020, improve the life conditions of at least 100 million people living in the slums.

The Rabat Declaration of 2012 (Rabat Declaration, 2012) further envisaged making slums a thing of the past by 2020, through urban planning, implementing changes and preventing unlawful evictions. Through UN-Habitat, both the sub-goals of the

MDG 7 have been achieved ahead of the timeline ('UN-Habitat and the,' 2012). However, the ever-swelling number of people in the slums necessitates continued interventions in this area. Therefore, the UN-Habitat in 2013 proposed the Sustainable Cities Sustainable Development Goals that sought to improve urban lives through urban planning and ensuring safe drinking water, tenancy security, adequate housing, employment generation, public spaces and public transport (UN-Habitat, 2013). The following case study of another country demonstrates the similar unsafe environment of slum children:

Case Study 9: Life in Slums of Nairobi, Kenya

"Paul Odero, a 27-year-old father of two and a resident of Mathare, told IRIN, "Here we share everything because nobody can afford anything of his own. We share latrines, and these people selling food near the latrine have no space to put their kiosks. It must be near there because that is where you can find space…We have no place to dispose our garbage, and we just throw it anywhere. At times, you find children playing with used sanitary pads because the woman and girls who use it have nowhere to take it to. The children get diarrhoea and many die."

In 2012, in a span of just six months, at least three children died from electrocution while playing with illegally connected power lines. In the same year, an illegal electricity connection caused a fire that destroyed some 300 houses, leaving thousands without shelter."

IRIN (2013)

4.15 Policies and Actions for the Slum Children in India

Being a developing nation with huge seasonal impact on agriculture-based livelihood, limited employment opportunities in non-agricultural sectors, exodus of minorities from neighbouring nations, and even from Indian states having disturbances from time to time (such as the Hindus from East Pakistan, later Bangladesh, the Tibetans from Tibet, and Kashmiri Pandits from Kashmir), and limited resources being accessed by a booming population, India has been facing the problems of urban migration, both seasonal and permanent, unauthorized human settlements, and the ensuing negative effects on human lives, for long. Again, being an ancient land with cities that have been surviving for centuries, urban planning to accommodate the growing population is difficult, particularly in terms of making provisions for modern housing, sewerage, water and electricity and recreational areas.

It was recognized early on that the impact of insanitary housing conditions has a particularly debilitating impact on the well-being of the children. To address the issues of malnourishment, poor health and stunted development among children, in 1975, the Integrated Child Development Services (ICDS) was started in India focusing on (1) physiological, intellectual and social development of children, (2) drop in malnutrition, child mortality and school dropouts, (3) improving nutritional status of children through better access to resources and education of mothers and caregivers and (4) coordination among the various government policies and interventions for the well-being of children (Ministry of Woman and Child Development

[MWCD], 2009). The ICDS functions through a vast nationwide network of 0.13 billion Anganwadi Centres (AWC), ensuring outreach of the government schemes and benefits to the last for the households (MWCD, 2018). The AWCs are operated by trained personnel called Anganwadi workers, who are mostly women. The ICDS is the largest integrated child development programme in the world and has been playing a significant role in improving the condition of the Indian children when it comes to early development and maternal and child health (Andrew et al., 2015).

In 2005, The Jawaharlal Nehru National Urban Renewal Mission was launched, with a focus on modernizing cities. The second phase of this programme, launched in 2011, had its specific focus on making cities slum-free (Williams, Omanakuttan, Devika, & Jagajeevan, 2019). This focused on what was called holistic slum upgrade—in terms of 'security of tenure, affordable housing, water, sanitation, health, education and social security' (MHUPA, 2007).

To ensure Environmental Sustainability, as stated in the Millennium Development Goal 7, the Government of India aimed to ensure by 2020 "a significant improvement in the lives of at least 100 million slum dwellers" (MSPI, 2018). In 2015, the Atal Mission for Rejuvenation and Urban Transformation (AMRUT) was launched, targeted at water drainage, green spaces and parks and non-motorized urban transport in Mission cities' (Ministry of Housing and Urban Affairs [MHUA], 2019). Under AMRUT, the target is to set up at least one new children's park in a year and maintain existing parks and playgrounds. It also targets making special provisions for vulnerable sections of the urban homeless, such as the ill and dependent children, by making special provisions for them in homeless shelters. In addition, it specially focuses on providing food, education and healthcare to urban homeless children, school admission and social security measures (MHUA, 2019).

Another plan adopted by the Government for holistic urban development is the National Heritage City Development and Augmentation Yojana (HRIDAY). This focuses on the 'urban planning/economic growth and heritage conservation in an inclusive and integrated manner with a focus on livelihoods, skills, cleanliness, security, accessibility and service delivery.' (Ministry of Urban Development [MUA], 2014). The target of this plan is twelve identified heritage cities across India, where urban development and livelihood need to be developed while preserving the heritage character of the city. HRIDAY has brought about investments in improvement of the condition of children living in slums in heritage cities, by providing them safe shelters, access to education and access to playgrounds and opportunities for recreation (MHUA, 2019).

Apart from the specific interventions for housing infrastructure development, the Government of India launched the Swachh Bharat Abhiyan[1,2] which envisages a clean India, free from open defecation and unsanitary disposal of garbage. Under this programme, complete coverage of India in terms of individual household latrines was achieved in June 2019. The programme targets an open defecation free India through Universal Sanitation Coverage, by October 2, 2019 ('Budget 2019–20', 2019).

---

[1]http://swachhbharaturban.gov.in/.

[2]https://swachhbharatmission.gov.in/sbmcms/index.htm.

When it comes to child health, a lot of importance is attached to the first 1000 days of the child's life or 0–3 years of age. According to the 2019 Global Childhood Report (Save the Children, 2019), owing to economic and agricultural growth, breastfeeding and other nutritious feeding, stunting among children in India has declined by 30%, thereby brining 23 million children out of the dangers of stunting. The Government of India has launched numerous interventions to take care of the health of the mother and the child, so as to provide the fetus a healthy prenatal environment and post-natal protection and care in the form of immunization, adequate nutrition, physical and intellectual stimulation and an environment that is sanitary, safe and enriching. Some of the most important interventions in these areas are the Family Planning Programme, Universal Immunization Programme[3] for pregnant women, infants and children, maternal health programmes such as the Janani Suraksha Yojana,[4] Mid-Day Meal Scheme,[5] and the Supplementary Nutrition Programme,[6] to name a few. These programmes also have their outreach among the population in the slums, although the vast size of the slums and their relative inaccessibility, as well as the reluctance of the target population to reach out for service and support often jeopardize the access (PTI, 2019a). According to the Save the Children report, child mortality rates in India have been down by 57%, and the effect is seen even among the poorest households (Save the Children, 2019).

In 2017, the Government of India launched the National Nutrition Mission (NMM),[7] also known as the POSHAN (PM's Overarching Scheme for Health and Nutrition) Abhiyan.[8] The POSHAN Abhiyan is a mission involving 14 ministries, which aims to reduce the rate of stunting among children due to malnutrition from 38.4 to 25% by 2022 (Mission 25 by 2022) (Press Information Bureau, 2017). It focuses on improving maternal, child and adolescent health status through a variety of measures such as nutrition, immunization, growth monitoring and food fortification. In addition, the NMM has brought about the digitization of the Anganwadi Ecosystem, use of mobile apps and other ICT for real-time health monitoring and involving the people through *Jan Andolans* (People's Movement) for health and nutrition (POSHAN Abhiyaan, 2018). In July 2018, as a part of the NMM, the Government of India laid out guidelines for setting up Anganwadi centres in slums, so that the benefits of the POSHAN Abhiyaan reach the children from the slums without difficulty (Press Information Bureau, 2018).

---

[3]https://www.nhp.gov.in/universal-immunisation-programme_pg.

[4]http://www.nrhmhp.gov.in/content/maternal-health.

[5]https://mhrd.gov.in/mid-day-meal.

[6]https://icds-wcd.nic.in/supplnutrition.aspx.

[7]https://icds-wcd.nic.in/nnm/home.htm.

[8]http://poshanabhiyaan.gov.in/#/.

4.16 Protection of Children Against Abuse and Neglect

In a large number of cases, slum children are abused by their own parents for their comfort and are not encouraged to study. Sometimes some children from slum struggle a lot to continue their education. For example,

Case Study 10: Children of Garbage Collectors in Miyapur Slum, Telangana

"Sunitha has dropped out of school twice, most recently from a residential school in Telangana. Both her parents are garbage collectors working for the Greater Hyderabad Municipal Corporation (GHMC). When they leave for work at 3 am each morning, Sunitha is left in the care of her aunt, who sends her onto the streets to beg. Her parents return by 4 pm, and many times, the money she collects is used by them to buy alcohol...Somewhere in the middle of all this, Sunitha managed to pass class 5 at the Miyapur Government Primary School near her slum. She moved to the Miyapur Government Secondary School in 2017, but the new school was a little further away and she dropped out as her family couldn't afford transport. [In 2018] Sunitha – now 11 years old - joined a residential school\, far from the domestic disturbances at her home. But just months later, she was back home, and once again made to beg on the streets."

Mithun MK in 'Why the Centre's Scheme to Bring Child Laborers Back to School is Failing in Telengana' (Mithun, 2019*)*

Children are vulnerable to abuse and neglect, from the immediate family members, neighbours, peers, teachers, employers and strangers. Slums exacerbate the conditions of abuse by putting children away from the spotlight of law and even parental vigilance under most conditions. While there is an absence of specific laws addressing this issue for children growing up in the slums, the Indian Penal Code provides for the protection of children by means of several legal measures, many of which are highly relevant for slum children. The Child Labor (Prohibition and Regulation) Amendment Act 2016 (Ministry of Law and Justice [MLJ], 2016b) is the single most important law in this area, given that slums tend to be largest generators of children engaged in labour in some form or other—domestic work, factory labour, work in unorganized sectors, begging or street vending and even prostitution and sale of drugs. The original 1986 Act (Ministry of Labor & Employment, 1986) and its 2016 Amendment prohibit labour for young children and restrict work engagements for children aged between 14 and 18, particularly for hazardous work conditions. In 2013, the Resolution on the National Policy for Children was passed, which made provisions to extend support to projects for child labourers and potential child labourers in urban locations beyond the scope of existing Government programmes, with focus on slum children and street children (Sophy, 2016). In 2017, the Government of India also launched the Platform for Effective Enforcement for No Child Labour (PENCIL)[9] that monitors the conditions of children who have been rescued from child labour and rehabilitated in the education system.

The recently amended Juvenile Justice (Care and Protection of Children) Act 2015 (Ministry of Law and Justice [MLJ], 2016a) is one of the most comprehensive legal measures in India when it comes to protection and rehabilitation of children

[9] https://pencil.gov.in/.

who have entered deviant ways and have come in conflict with the law. This law is highly relevant for the context of the slums because data shows significant prevalence of crimes among children in these areas, owing to the overall social exclusion, peer pressure, deviant adult role models and competition for scarce resources (Ministry of Housing & Urban Poverty Alleviation [MHUPA], 2015). Around 35% of the slum children are into substance abuse (PWC and Save the Children, 2015), and their entry into petty and organized crimes is also common. Although primarily focused on rehabilitation of deviant children, the recent amendment provided for the trial of juveniles aged between 16 and 18 and engaged in heinous crimes as adults. The Juvenile Justice Act 2015 provides for vulnerable witness courts and child-friendly courts across the country so that juvenile delinquents are treated with compassion and given chance to rectify to the extent possible ('Government Must Acknowledge,' 2018). Under the 2015 Act, children living in slums and unauthorized areas form one of the Target groups for rehabilitation and protection in Government-run Children Homes in all districts of the country.

In 2009, the Integrated Child Protection Scheme (ICPS)[10] was launched, which is directed at coordinating the various governmental measures for protecting children from various threats—such as sexual offences (child pornography, molestation or rape), child marriage, or immoral trafficking. The ICPS also aims at creating a government and civil society collaboration to protect children at home or in the community, gather data and knowledge and institutionalize structures to protect child rights. The revised ICPS of 2014 has the provision for Open Shelters for slum children, street children, rag pickers, trafficked children and children from migrant population (Ministry of Women & Child Development [MWCD], 2014). These Open Shelters are not designed to be permanent homes, but rather temporary shelters to supplement the Children's Homes, in order to protect the children from threats at home or deviant ways, enhance their life skills through age-appropriate education, bridge education and vocational training, provide them healthcare and testing for HIV and other STDs, and provide them training and counseling to develop life skills (MWCD, 2014). The programme has been subsequently renamed as the Child Protection Services Scheme (CPSS) that integrates the following interventions (Press Information Bureau, 2019):

a. Statutory Support Services such as Child Welfare Services and Juvenile Justice Boards.
b. Institutional Care Services, such as Open Shelters, Homes and Specialized Adoption Agencies.
c. Inspection and monitoring of Child Care Institutions.
d. Non-Institutional care services such as foster homes, in-country adoption and inter-country adoption.
e. Child Helpline (1098).
f. Child Helpdesks at railway stations to help lost, run away, or trafficked children.
g. Locating missing and sighted children (Khoya-Paya Portal).
h. Online POSCO e-box facility, for filing anonymous complaints about sexual abuse.

---

[10]https://wcd.nic.in/integrated-child-protection-scheme-ICPS.

i. Safe Neighbourhood Campaign for awareness and advocacy.
j. Baal Puraskar (Awards for Children) and activity campaigns to encourage creativity, merit and achievement among children.

4.17 Interventions for Slum Children: Possible Directions

The problem of the children of the slums is a complicated one. Children across social classes and geographies need access to nutrition, healthcare (including immunization), education and security, and children from the slums are no different in this regard. In one respect, much of the issues that assail a child from the slum arise from poverty. Therefore, it seems intuitive to suggest that the solution lies in making available the basic life resources free of cost to children and their caregivers, so that they may live meaningfully. When looked from this perspective, the existing safety net for children in terms of health, nutrition and education appear adequate for the needs of the slum children. However, the real scope of the challenge is seen when one considers the context—the slums. Owing to their unauthorized and unplanned nature, slums see a significant aggravation of all the problems that affect a child's life—threats on health and hygiene, crimes, cognitive overload, lack of access to resources and facilities and lack of opportunities towards growth and development. Also, the unplanned nature of the slums makes it difficult for outreach and inclusion, causing many children to fall out of the safety net. Interventions for slum children, therefore, need to consider the specific context of the slums while upholding child rights.

Case Study 11: From Child Laborer at age 10 to Running Her Own NGO at age 20

"Like most children from the slums, Chandni started earning at a very young age. "From the age of five, I used to travel along with my father to perform street magic shows, dance and play with snakes, even late at night. I also picked up rags during that time," she recalls…When her father met with an untimely death, she became responsible for her family and its survival. "At that time, I had to work under someone else, and earned a mere Rs. 30 in a day…At the age of seven, I had shifted to rag picking. Verbal abuses and dog bites became a part of my daily routine and at the end; I ended up in jail over false accusations of stealing. I kept changing my job, from selling flowers to corn, I was doing it all. During one of these monotonous days, I got lucky and met a few NGO volunteers who were educating children from the slums. It was then I discovered my purpose and enrolled myself with Badhte Kadam," she says. She began her education at the age of 10 and is currently in Class 11. She continued working for Badhte Kadam, helped them open new education centres, and connected more children to these centres. Soon, she was appointed District Secretary and later promoted to National Secretary. The itch to make a difference by starting something on her own was strong and this led Chandni to start Voice of Slum…"to provide street children with basic amenities such as health, education, and shelter. We do this with the help of our contributors, volunteers and mentors."

Rekha Balakrishnan, In *'The girl from the slums who first held a pencil at age 10 is now helping slum children rewrite future'* (Balakrishnan, 2018).

4.18 Comprehensive and Updated Databases

One major challenge when it comes to addressing the problems of the slum children is lack of credible and comprehensive data about the extent of the issue. For instance, the Census has no data on the count of the urban homeless children in urban areas, or the count of children living in urban slums who are aged above 6 (NIUA, 2016). Birth registration is another important service to ensure that the child enters the social security net and receives facilities from the state for his/her survival and growth. However, Usmani and Ahmad (2018) observed that many children in urban slums are missed when it comes to registration of births and deaths, making interventions grossly ineffective. A survey conducted in Delhi showed that only 20% of the street children there had their births registered or had any identity documents that would help them to access services (Save the Children, 2011). While 98% of the adult citizens of India had Aadhar in 2016, only 23% of children below 5 years, and 65% of the children aged between 5 and 18 was enrolled in Aadhar, in other words, over 92% of the Indian citizens without Aadhar are children (Sharma, 2016). Lack of data is also a major challenge before many recent government interventions for children, including the ambitious POSHAN Abhiyan. Since National Family Health Surveys are conducted only once in 10 years, executives are reportedly facing challenges to estimating the scale of the programme at the ground levels (Sharma, 2019). While the gap is being partly addressed by encouraging ICT-based data collection by Anganwadi workers, efforts and education are needed to motivate people to use technology and to collect data ethically.

In the absence of adequate data, interventions are made based on broad estimates, which may turn out to be quite off the mark when it comes to actual requirements. For instance, the PENCIL[11] programme of the Government of India has been questioned in some cases, owing to the poor funding of these rehabilitation schools, and the poor tracking of the rehabilitated children, who tend to drop out and go back to child labour (Mithun, 2019). Hence it is important to have a regular and detailed assessment of the condition of the children in the slums, to assess accurately the depth of the issue, and the impact of the interventions already in place. Further, it is recommended to have disaggregated census of children in the slums, in terms of age group, gender, nature of the household and access to resources, so that it is possible to make focused interventions in areas where they are the most needed (NIUA, 2016).

4.19 Slum Upgrading

Governments across the world have taken many approaches to solve the problems of slums—including forced eviction, relocation to public housing and providing sites for alternative housing (Chandrasekhar, 2018). However, the 2014 report by UN-Habitat states that slum upgrading is one of the most economical ways to improve the

---

[11] https://pencil.gov.in/.

conditions of slum life. Slum Upgrading consists of improving the living conditions of the slums without displacing the people (UN-Habitat, 2014a). It does not jeopardize the investments made by the slum dwellers in their homes and does not disturb the social network and ecosystem that builds up in such close quarters over the period (De Sarkar, 2015; PTI, 2019b). Further, it does not face resistance from the slum dwellers, who are less threatened by the fear of homelessness in this case (Nianias, 2016).

Slum upgrading is a comprehensive process that begins with the regularization of ownership of the land occupied and regularization of the tenancy. This is accompanied by multi-pronged efforts to improve the infrastructure of the area, with the availability of essential resources such as piped water, sanitation, sewerage, roads, electricity and mobile/internet network. Slum upgrading also focuses on ensuring that the facilities such as schools, creches, hospitals, markets and recreation centres become accessible to the people living in these areas, and they are informed about the various governmental and non-governmental initiatives to facilitate health living. Finally, a key focus of slum upgrading is providing incentives for maintenance of the newly build infrastructure through community initiatives and providing means of livelihood to the people in the slums through vocational training, micro-credits (Cities Alliance, 1999). The UN-Habitat launched the Participatory Slum Upgrading Programme in 2008, to assist nations in upgrading their slums through customized initiatives (UN-Habitat, 2014b).

4.20 Education

Education is of prime importance to remedy the plight of the children from the slums and ensure that the negative experiences of early life do not percolate into their adult years. To stop dropouts, education needs to be appealing to the students. To this end, some early interventionists have recommended that children from disadvantaged backgrounds are given a simpler curriculum that is less demanding and challenging for them. However, many educationists criticize this approach. They recommend instead that schools catering to children from disadvantageous backgrounds should instead rely more on oral learning and exchange, encourage children to talk and share rather than force passive learning, and teach subjects such as science and arithmetic in "an intuitive, non-bookish way" (Shaffer, 1964).

To accommodate the students from slums and ghettos, the Government of the USA has adopted several educational reforms. This includes pre-kindergarten programme with children to prepare them for school, outreach with parents to show the latter the value of school education, non-graded customized learning programmes and provisions for graduates from such programme to intern as teachers for future children from the slums. Another interesting intervention is the Home Visitor Programme in Jamaica, where trained social workers visit individual household to deliver a specific curriculum to children who do not turn up schools owing to lack of accessibility or other constraints (Walker, Chang, Powell, Simono, & Grantham-McGregor, 2000). Such measures try to make multi-pronged attempts to address the problem of deprivation and may be adopted, with necessary modifications, in the context of the developing countries. Other places have implemented mentoring programmes for children from slums by successful working people, free schooling and vocational coaching and training (Andrew et al., 2015).

Creches are crucial to let young children access bridge education to prepare them for mainstream schooling, and to keep them safe when parents are not at home. Mobile Creches,[12] set up in 1969, is one such NGO that provides shelter and education to children of construction workers. It has provided shelter to over 0.75 million children till date while their parents are at work.

An important intervention in the area of education is the provision for scholarships and reservations for children from the economically disadvantageous background. Many children tend to drop out of the educational system as education becomes more and more expensive as they grow older. Another challenge is commuting to school. In the absence of schools in the neighbourhood, children often drop out as they cannot afford transport fare or fear for their safety on the way. Thus, it is important to establish easy access to schools and vocational training centres, safe and subsidized provisions for transport and scholarships for the economically challenged children, so that they may stay within the safety net of the formal education system (Banerjee et al., 2011).

4.21 Urban Planning

The recent drives for Smart City building and Urban Development have put renewed impetus on improvement of urban life condition. However, urban development drives often tend to ignore the needs of children as equal citizens. Crowded city centres, busy roads and artificial land use in the form of shopping malls and car parking often lead to the encroachment of playgrounds and open fields needed for the recreation for children. Falling safety standards in the city jeopardize the safety of children, making them vulnerable to accidents, kidnapping and sexual abuse. As per the NSSO survey conducted in 2012, only a minority of urban slums (24%) benefit from Government interventions such as the Jawaharlal Nehru National Urban Renewal Mission (JNNURM) or the RajivAwas Yojana (RAY). Only 32% of the people living in the notified urban slums and as low as 18% of the people living in the non-notified slums benefited from the various government interventions (Basu, 2015; National Sample Survey Office [NSSO], 2014).

PWC India recommends that urban planning to rehabilitate the population from slums and to improve living conditions in slum settlements must include specific interventions and fund allocation with focus on what the children need (PWC & Save the Children, 2011). This includes access to clean drinking water, unadulterated food and pediatric healthcare, schools and creches in close proximity of households so that children do not have to commute long distances to go to school, street lighting

[12]https://www.mobilecreches.org/.

and police patrolling to keep crime rates low, easy access to child protection services and provision of playgrounds, recreational facilities and community cultural forums.

The Post 2015 Developmental Agenda recommends the participation of children in urban planning, to understand their unique issues and challenges and to act on issues that affect their lives. This avoids the issue of tokenism and ensures that the needs of the child are not ignored due to the pressure of adult issues. This agenda thus recommends that children are involved as stakeholders in the urban planning process and are given regular feedback to ensure that their recommendations are indeed being considered. This ensures that the settlements designed for the future are inclusive for the needs of its members and are sustainable in the long run, in keeping with the needs of their future citizens (Post 2015 Developmental Agenda, 2019).

4.22 Social Security Measures

Cash transfer schemes have been found to be useful for urban slum households for ensuring preventive health checkups and growth monitoring for children (Lagarde, Haines, & Palmer, 2009). In a study done on an urban slum in Delhi, India, report that the primary factor that prevented expecting mothers from accessing institutional delivery and subsequent health assistance to their newborns is finance (Dhingra, Adhav, Dhingra, Mehan, & Deswal, 2019).

Nutrition needs to be one of the most important focus areas of social security interventions. Recommends need-based interventions such as training healthcare workers on nutrition, generating awareness about infection control and fortification of food items (Marimuthu, Rao, Sharma, & Pandian, 2016). Kapur, Sharma and Agarwal (2003) reported that nutrition education helped improve deficiency status among children in urban slums of Delhi.

When it comes to improving the nutritional status of slum children, Yadav and Dubey (2014) suggest two important approaches. One is the Positive Deviance Approach, in which one studies and replicated the practices of the best-performing families in the slum areas when it comes to child nutrition. The other approach is to make food available, through vocational training, or through social security measures, such as mid-day meals at schools, which make cooked rationed food available to the children. Similar approaches have been suggested by Rastogi, Maheshwari, Raghav, and Lala (2017), who emphasized on the importance of nutritional education, and access to public healthcare.

Healthcare interventions in slums are crucial for ensuring the health of children. Researchers and policymakers concur that interventions need to start early, with a focus on pregnant women, so that maternal health, effective perinatal and postnatal care and immunization may be ensured. Mothers need to be also taught about the benefits of exclusive breastfeeding, nutrition value of different kinds of food, and ways to maintain hygiene in the surroundings. Also, overreliance on the expensive and scarce private healthcare needs to be combated by improving the quality and reliability of public healthcare (Gupta, Mohapatra, & Kumar, 2015).

Researchers have emphasized the importance of education when it comes to the adoption of best practices in terms of healthcare, nutrition and other essential aspects of life. Khan and Mahmood (2012) stressed on the role of nutrition education to caregivers to combat malnutrition in children from slums in Uttar Pradesh, India. Again, the Ministry of Statistics and Programme Implementation [MSPI], 2012) found that the education level of the mother has an impact on the immunization of the child.

4.23 Shelter Homes

Relief during natural disasters and times of calamity is one of the most crucial interventions to restore safety and order in the lives of children from slums. However, despite being one of the worse-affected in case of any calamity, slums tend to be one of the slowest to recover and return to normalcy, owing to their presence in the margin of the mainstream society, lack of backup plans and poor infrastructure to provide relief. This necessitates additional efforts in the parts of governmental and non-governmental bodies to provide urgent relief in the form of food, non-food items, water tanks, medicines and clothing, to slum areas in case of calamities. Further, specific reliefs interventions need to be designed and executed that take care of the needs of the children. One such intervention is the Child-Friendly Spaces (CFS) by Save the Children (Bal Raksha Bharat, 2017), which are shelter camps specifically meant for children from calamity hit areas, to recover from the stress caused by the destruction. CFSs house the children while their parents are away to rebuild their homes, providing the children with opportunities to play, learn and interact with one another, away from the inhabitable and unsafe slum areas. CFSs have been successfully run during the floods in Andhra Pradesh, Tamil Nadu, Telangana and Assam during the floods. Another interesting intervention is the Urban Disaster Risk Reduction (UDRR) Project by Save the Children in Kolkata slums, where Children's Groups and Mothers' Groups are formed and trained in mock drills for disaster management, early warning signs for disasters, and best relief practices such as first aid (Save the Children, 2017). In addition, the UDRR teams also do vulnerability assessment of school buildings in case of natural calamities and train teachers and parents in disaster management. One such project involves Nokia developing a mobile and web-based early warning system and road accident information system in case of natural disasters (Save the Children, 2016).

4.24 Prevention of Formation of New Slums

While old slums are subjected to a process of upgradation, the efforts will be futile if new slums continually sprout up to take their places. Therefore, there need to be concerted efforts to present the establishment of new slums in the neighbourhoods.

Slums arise owing to a multitude of reasons—the most common ones being over-population, lack of jobs in the rural areas causing urban migration, and high costs of land and housing causing people to live in compromised conditions. When unauthorized encroachments and settlements begin initially, they are often ignored by the police and policymakers, owing to an ineffective monitoring and surveillance system. This leads to an escalation of a problem that could have been easily preventable in the inception. Also, in many instances, growing slums are provided protection for political reasons; in return of votes from the slum dwellers for the political party that backs their encroachment. This gradually leads to change of the demographics of an area, illegal occupation and excess demand on the resources of a place that was not designed to handle settlement behind a certain limit (UN-Habitat, 2014b).

To combat the formation of new slums, there needs to be a multi-pronged approach, involving both e developmental initiatives as well as law and order measures. There needs to be strict vigilance to prevent illegal encroachment of private or public lands, illegal construction, or settlement. At the same time, efforts need to be made towards the upgrading of living standards in non-urban areas, and provision for livelihood, so that urban migration is discouraged. Finally, affordable housing schemes on the part of the government help in discouraging formation of slums.

4.25 A Model for Interventions

Case Study 12: Urban Slum Health Care Project, Andhra Pradesh

"The Urban Slum Health Care Project the Andhra Pradesh Ministry of Health and Family Welfare contracts NGOs to manage health centers in the slums of Adilabad. The basic objectives of the project are to increase the availability and utilization of health and family welfare services, to build an effective referral system, to implement national health programs, and to increase health awareness and better health-seeking behavior among slum dwellers, thus reducing morbidity and mortality among women and children. To serve 3 million people, the project has established 192 Urban Health Centers. Five 'Mahila Aarogya Sanghams' (Women's Wee-Being Associations) were formed under each UHC, and along with the self-help groups and ICDS workers mobilize the community and adopt Behaviour Change Communication strategies. The NGOs are contracted to manage and maintain the UHCs, and based on their performance, they are awarded with a UHC, or eliminated from the program. Additional District Magistrates and Health Officers supervise the UHCs at district level and the Medical Officer is the nodal officer at the municipality level. The District Committee approves all appointments made by the NGOs for the UHC staff. The Govt. of Andhra Pradesh constructs buildings for the UHCs; provide honoraria to the Project

Coordinators of the UHCs, medical officers and other staff; train staff members; and supply drugs, equipment, and medical registers."

—KPMG, In 'Public Private Partnerships in India' (KPMG, n.d.)

The sheer scale of the issues that affect children from the slums makes it clear that any attempt to deal with them should be holistic and multi-pronged. Given the ever-growing spread and density of slums, it is difficult to ensure a government mechanism, no matter how efficient or giant in scope, to make the needed services available to the residents adequately. The last-mile outreach, therefore, requires the private sector to step in (e.g. Chang, 2009). The resulting model is one where the Public sector is primarily responsible for policymaking, surveillance and quality assurance, whereas the private sector partners play a role in outreach and bringing services to one's doorstep. One such case is that of Dharavi slums in Mumbai, the third largest slum in the world (Hutt, 2016), where the NGO Society for Nutrition, Education and Health Action (SNEHA) works in collaboration with the Government of India to implement the Integrated Child Development Services Scheme (ICDS). SNEHA has reportedly increased the access of the Dharavi children to primary healthcare, nutrition and other services assured under the ICDS by 109%, and has brought down wasting among children aged 3 or below by 23% (Sanghera, 2018), by training Anganwadi workers, recruiting and training volunteers from within the slum community, and educating expecting and new mothers about child nutrition, immunization and the importance of visiting ICDS centres and accessing their services. Another example comes from Indonesia, where women micro-entrepreneurs are being organized under Project Baduta to sell water filters to poor households (Chase, Haddad, Montesi, Gambrill, & Gilsdorf, 2017).

One stakeholder that often remains less explored while conceptualizing social interventions in the private sector. The bulk of India's GDP comes from the private sector firms that employ 39% of the total Indian workforce (Data Admin, 2014). Private sector supplements the government's interventions when it comes to essential services, in terms of healthcare, education, electricity and connectivity, water, sanitation, banking and nutrition. Being profit-oriented and self-sustaining, private sector business models and products and services tend to be highly efficient, competitive and sustainable. They relieve the pressure on the public sector and government facilities and in making the overall standards of goods and services in the country competitive. In a vast territory like India, public services are often inadequate to satisfy the demand and provide adequate coverage (Kaur, 2019). Such services are heavily supplemented by access to private, paid services—private hospitals and clinics, schools, colleges, and technical institutions, internet and mobile services, travel facilities, consumer goods and financial services. When planning interventions, it is important that this sector is taken into consideration to ensure delivery of quality service at reasonable prices, and to facilitate outreach and inclusion. The 2009 Right to Education Act[13] reserved 25% of the seats in private, unaided schools for children belonging to the Economically Backward segments (Sharma, 2018).

[13]https://mhrd.gov.in/rte.

Again, the recently launched Ayushman Bharat[14] provides healthcare benefits for financially challenged citizens in public as well as empanelled private hospitals.[15] Data shows that schemes such as Ayushman Bharat, presently the largest in the world among government-run public health insurance schemes, have significant enhanced health-seeking behaviour in rural areas in 22 states of India (Tripathi, 2019). Thus, private sector facilities need to be channelized and sometimes regulated to ensure that essential services reach the population. Further, private sector businesses need to be encouraged through laws that facilitate ease of doing business, efficient corporate tax regimes, necessary infrastructure that support industrial development, and schemes and interventions to encourage entrepreneurship.

The second important contribution of the corporate sector in the context of social interventions is Corporate Social Responsibility (CSR) activities. Under the Companies Act 2013 and the subsequent Companies (Amendment) Act 2019, "companies with a net worth of INR 500 crore (US $70 million) or more, or an annual turnover of INR 1000 crore (US $140 million) or more, or net profit of INR 5 crore (US $699,125) or more, have to spend 2% of their average net profits of three years on CSR." (Dezan Shira & Associates, 2019) In 2018 alone, the corporate sector contributed over one billion USD to various CSR initiatives in India, benefitting education, hunger and poverty eradication, skill development, sanitation, environment protection and rural development—areas that benefit the cause of children both directly and indirectly (Chowdhry, 2017; Save the Children, 2016). Further, to specifically focus the attention of CSR investments on slums, slum development was incorporated as a CSR activity in 2014 (Kably, 2014). However, the Ministry of Corporate Affairs, Government of India, reported in 2017 that slum areas receive the lowest share of CSR funds (John, 2018)—a meagre 9.78 crore INR in 2017 (Zargar, 2017). This lack of interest in slums is said to arise from the questionable legal status of many slums (making the future of intervention projects doubtful), the lack of representative voice in slums and the overbearing of criminal and political elements, that may make any project run intro troubled waters (Zargar, 2017). Thus, future efforts in designing interventions for the children of the slums need to consider the private sector, both by bringing them into the fold of essential services as partner service providers and by encouraging and facilitating the investment of CSR grants in relevant focus areas, through governmental support structures.

The stakeholder that finally needs to be involved actively in the intervention is civil society. The perspective needs to change, from viewing the society as passive recipients of benefits to active co-creators of the transformative changes (Nitti & Dahiya, 2004). This entails education and empowerment of the citizens of the slums and surrounding areas and employing them directly or indirectly in the intervention measures, as grass-root level workers, programme designers and community champions. This ensures that the efforts made are bottom-up, actively shaped by the knowledge and experience of the end-users and having buy-in from the people for

[14]https://www.pmjay.gov.in/.

[15]https://pmjay.gov.in/about-pmjay.

whom the interventions are made (Dhabhalabutr, 2016). Further, involving the end-users as the change agents ensure that a self-sustaining ecosystem of interventions is built, generating employment and ensuring targeted solutions at the same time (Bhatkal & Lucci, 2015).

Figure 4.1 presents a holistic model for interventions in slums to improve the lives of children. Interventions need to have two drifts: the inner circle focused interventions that address the immediate needs of a generation of children—nutrition, healthcare, education, recreation and security, and the outer circle focusing on interventions with relatively wider scope and long-term impacts, such as urban planning, rural upliftment, slum upgrading and prevention of new slums, population control

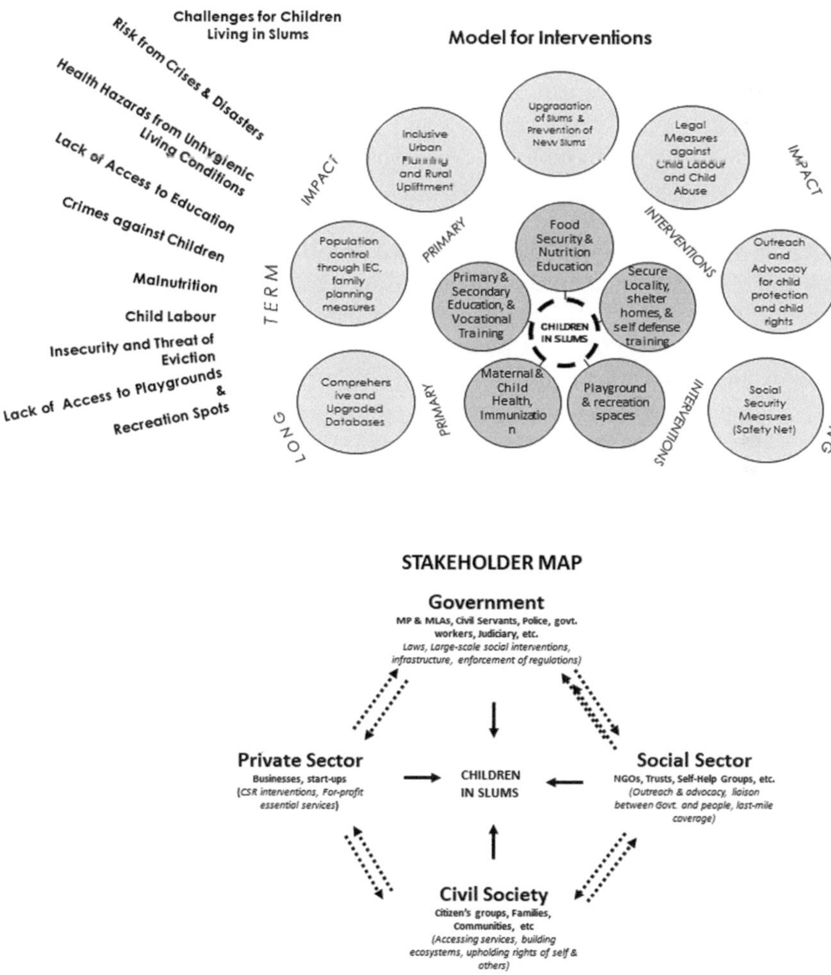

Fig. 4.1 Schematic model of need-based interventions for children in slums and stakeholder map

and family planning, protecting child rights for sustainable growth and development and against exploitation and abuse. The interventions, both focused and long-term, require active participation from all the four major stakeholders in the process—the government and the public and the private sectors, the social sector, and the society in general, through active involvement in the welfare of the children from the slums and through information and resource sharing with each other in the process.

4.26 Role of Public Representatives for Improving the Quality of Life of Slum Children

Public representatives like the local counsellor, MLA and MP have a bigger role to play to improve the living condition and overall quality of life of people living in slum areas through active involvement and participation of the slum people, support from local NGOs and people of larger neighbouring community. The public representative should take the initiative to mobilize the local and neighbouring community and local NGOs. There is a need to sit with slum people to review the situation and prioritize their basic needs by them. Based on inputs from slum people, public representatives should plan slum development activities based on priority and implement them in phased manner. They should use the fund allocated to them for slum improvement. In general, the issues which need attention include common sanitation facilities, sewage system, safe drinking water, electricity and school for children, safety issue, cleanliness and a place for children for games. Unfortunately, slum areas did not receive minimum attention from the public representative and local municipality in most of the areas across the country and denied from basic facilities including safe drinking water as they do not have legal entitlement in the handmade house and they do not have their representative in policy-making bodies. But there is a need to look at the issue from humanitarian angle and provide the basic amenities so that they can lead minimum quality of life including welfare and well-being of children. Most of the children in slum areas do not attend school or become school drop out after attending primary school and gradually get involvement in socially undesirable activities under the peer group influence on account of lack of guidance and support. In turn, larger society loses huge human resources. A positive gesture from the public representatives can bring positive changes in the lives of poor people living in slums.

4.27 Conclusion and Implications

Healthy living conditions are one of the primary privileges to which a child is entitled. Environment goes a long way in building one's physical capacities—through exercise, nutrition and limiting exposure to preventable fatalities. At the same time, environment crafts one's mental capacities—developing one's attitude towards ethics, competition and collaboration and creativity, building one's intellectual abilities, knowledge and skills. Finally, environment provides one with the social capital—network of friends, mentors and partners—to which one depends lifelong for support and resources. It is not surprising therefore that slum environments are one of the major correlates of disadvantaged children—being a breeding ground for other violation of rights such as child labour, child abuse, abandonment, denial of resources and crimes against children.

There is a tendency to view slums as homogenous entities when it comes to their challenges and needs for support. However, although the problems across slums of the world and even those within a country tend to be broadly similar, slums themselves vary widely in terms of local culture, ecosystems and openness to interventions, outreach and problems that are perceived as pressing. Therefore, it is important to understand the local character of the slum before any change intervention is carried out (Unger & Riley, 2007). It may often be necessary to solve what is apparently a less pressing problem, such as access to television networks, in order to win over the trust and the openness of the denizens of the slums and win their support to solve more pressing issues on healthcare, living standards and crime rates.

The sheer scale of the problem of the slums and the complex web of many socio-political and economic issues that give rise to them, make them an intimidating challenge to change-makers. The spread of the problem grows as we speak, so the efforts to address them, no matter how well-engineered, often fall short. It hardly helps that many transnational efforts to address the challenge often end up being little more than making a spectacle of the poverty (Antony, 2012)—leading to controversial and questionable practices such as slum tourism (e.g. Shepard, 2016). Children growing up in these slums fall victim to the resulting mayhem that jeopardizes their dignity, development and even survival. It requires not only a multi-pronged approach of infrastructure development, equitable economic growth and strengthening of social security nets, but also sincere buy-in from all the stakeholders concerned to ensure that children from the slums, like their counterparts in other neighbourhoods, have a healthy, happy and productive childhood.

References

Achiego, R. (2016). *A single scholarship educated 400 children in a Kenyan slum*. Retrieved from https://www.globalsistersreport.org/news/ministry/single-scholarship-educated-400-children-kenyan-slum-41781.

Action Foundation. (2015). *Report of baseline survey on knowledge attitudes and practices (kap) towards inclusion of children with disabilities in education in Kibera*. Retrieved from http://www.globi-observatory.org/wp-content/uploads/2017/04/KAP_TAF_E-version.pdf.

Aide et action. (2014). *Young lives at worksite: A study on the status of the children of the migrant workers in seven cities of India*. Retrieved from https://www.researchgate.net/publication/261921759_Young_Lives_at_Worksite.

Aishwarya, C. S., Samanta, I., & Dudeja, P. (2019). Psychosocial determinants of stress among adolescents in an urban slum in a city of Western Maharashtra: A cross-sectional study. *International Journal of Adolescent Medicine and Health*.

Anand, A. (2019, January 31). Not seen, not heard: In slum evictions, children are some of the worst hit. *Beyond Headlines*. Retrieved from https://beyondheadlines.in/2019/01/not-seen-not-heard-in-slum-evictions-children-are-some-of-the-worst-hit/.

Andrew, A., Attanasio, O., Augsburg, B., Grantham-McGreggor, S., Pahwa, S., Meghir, C., & Rubio-Codina, M. (2015, April 28). *Early childhood development in the slums of Cuttack, Odisha, India: Baseline report*. Retrieved from https://www.ifs.org.uk/uploads/publications/comms/ECD%20India%20-%20Cuttack%20-%20Baseline%20Report_FINAL_noappendix-1.pdf.

Antony, M. G. (2012). "Slum-Pups No More": Rescuing India's slum children. *Journal of Intercultural Communication Research, 41*(1), 17–36.

Atkinson-Sheppard, S. (2018, March 18). When crime is the best of many bad options. *Development and Cooperation*. Retrieved from https://www.dandc.eu/en/article/street-children-are-involved-organised-crime-bangladesh.

Balakrishnan, R. (2018, March 1). The girl from the slums who first held a pencil at age 10 is now helping slum children rewrite future. *Your Story*. Retrieved from https://yourstory.com/2018/03/girl-slums-first-held-pencil-age-10-now-helping-slum-children-rewrite-future.

Bal Raksha Bharat. (2017). *A future for every child: Annual report 2017*. Retrieved from https://www.savethechildren.in/sci-in/files/60/60c56fc8-e492-4cdd-916e-028e33503902.pdf.

Banerjee, A., Pande, R., Vaidya, Y., Walton, M., & Weaver, J. (2011). Delhi's slum-dwellers: Deprivation, preferences and political engagement among the urban poor. In *International growth centre conference proceedings (growth week 2011)*. Retrieved from https://www.theigc.org/wp-content/uploads/2014/10/Banerjee-Et-Al-2012-Working-Paper.pdf.

Basu, S. (2015, September 17). Welfare schemes benefited only a quarter of urban slums: NSSO. Retrieved from https://www.downtoearth.org.in/news/welfare-schemes-benefitedonly-a-quarter-of-urban-slums-nsso--43175.

Bertel, K. (n.d.). *Slum children of Dharavi*. Retrieved from http://www.kristianbertel.dk/archive/slum-children-of-dharavi.html.

Bhatkal, T., & Lucci, P. (2015). *Community-driven development in the slums: Thailand's experience*. ODI Development Progress. Retrieved from https://www.odi.org/sites/odi.org.uk/files/odi-assets/publications-opinion-files/9669.pdf.

Brown, D. & Dodman, D. (2014). *Understanding children's risk and agency in urban areas and their implications for child centred urban disaster risk reduction in Asia: Insights from Dhaka, Kathmandu, Manila and Jakarta*. Asian Cities Climate Resilience Working Paper Series 6: 2014. Retrieved from https://pubs.iied.org/pdfs/10652IIED.pdf.

Business Standard. (2019, July 5). *Budget 2019–20: India will be open-defecation free on October 2 this year, says Sitharaman*. Retrieved from https://www.business-standard.com/article/news-ani/budget-2019-20-india-will-be-open-defecation-free-on-october-2-this-year-says-sitharaman-119070500468_1.html.

Business Standard. (2013, December 25). *Slums fading from cities: NSSO*. Retrieved from https://www.business-standard.com/article/economy-policy/slums-fading-from-cities-nsso-113122400812_1.html.

Chandramouli, C. (2013). *Housing Stock, amenities & assets in slums—census 2011*. Subaltern Urbanisation in India. Retrieved from https://suburbin.hypotheses.org/754.

Chandrasekhar, V. (2018 April 26). 'Designed for death': The Mumbai housing blocks breeding TB. *The Guardian*. Retrieved from https://www.theguardian.com/cities/2018/apr/26/mumbai-housing-blocks-breeding-tuberculosis-death.

Chang, T. (2009). *Improving slum conditions with public private partnerships*. Retrieved from http://www.shram.org/uploadFiles/20140609033101.pdf.

Chase, C., Haddad L., Montesi, B., Gambrill, M. P., & Gilsdorf, R. J. (2017). *Starting life strong in slums: The role of engaging vulnerable groups on sanitation and nutrition*. Retrieved from https://blogs.worldbank.org/water/starting-life-strong-slums-role-engaging-vulnerable-groups-sanitation-and-nutrition.

Chowdhry, S. (2017, October 17). *How companies are spending on CSR projects*. Retrieved from https://www.livemint.com/Companies/oyHdaJdn96pnmzdIFUIFNO/How-companies-are-spending-on-CSR-projects.html.

Cities Alliance. (1999). Cities without slums: Annual Report 2012. Washington DC: Cities Alliance. Retrieved from http://documents.worldbank.org/curated/en/381481468336839270/pdf/761320AR0Citie00Box374363B00PUBLIC0.pdf.

Cops Say All OK, But Rapes Surge Since Nirbhaya Case. (March 8, 2019). *The Times of India*. Retrieved from https://epaper.timesgroup.com/Olive/ODN/TimesOfIndia/shared/ShowArticle.aspx?doc=TOIDEL%2F2019%2F08%2F08&entity=Ar00908&sk=AD3407FA&mode=text.

De Sarkar, D. (2015, December 18). Why Indian slums are allowed to grow, and then demolished. *Livemint*. Retrieved from https://www.livemint.com/Opinion/QkIgZjo9VO5edqjwqwfuFP/Why-Indian-slums-areallowed-to-grow-and-then-demolished.html.

Damania, R., Desbureaux, S., Hyland, M., Islam, A., Moore, S., Rodella, A., Russ, J., et al. (2017). *Uncharted waters: The new economics of water scarcity and variability*. World Bank, Washington, DC. Retrieved from https://openknowledge.worldbank.org/handle/10986/28096 License: CC BY 3.0 IGO.

Data Admin. (2014, May 20). *Employment in the public and private sectors in India during 2000–2011*. Retrieved from https://community.data.gov.in/employment-in-the-public-and-private-sectors-in-india-during-2000-2011/.

Dezan Shira & Associates. (2019, August 22). Corporate social responsibility in India. *India Briefing*. Retrieved from https://www.india-briefing.com/news/corporate-social-responsibility-india-5511.html/.

Dey, S. (2018, May 28). *World nutrition day: What do the street children of India eat?*.

News18. Retrieved from https://www.news18.com/news/india/world-nutrition-day-what-do-the-street-children-of-india-eat-1762007.html.

Dhabhalabutr, K. (2016). The empowerment of the slum inhabitant as a primary agent of low-income housing: Slum upgrading in Thailand between 1980 and 2011. *Procedia-Social and Behavioral Sciences, 216*, 428–439.

Dhingra, M. K., Adhav, P., Dhingra, R., Mehan, A., & Deswal, B. S. (2019). Barriers of institutional delivery in an urban-slum of Delhi. *International Journal of Scientific Research, 8*(5). Retrieved from http://worldwidejournals.co.in/index.php/ijsr/article/viewFile/2377/2378.

Dodman, D. (2014). *Poorest urban children failed in disasters, says report*. International Institute for Environment and Development. Retrieved from https://www.iied.org/poorest-urban-children-failed-disasters-says-report.

EdCIL (India) & SRI. (2014). *National sample survey of estimation of out-of-school children in the age 6–13 in India*. Retrieved from https://mhrd.gov.in/sites/upload_files/mhrd/files/upload_document/National-Survey-Estimation-School-Children-Draft-Report.pdf.

Elliott, L. (2019, January 20). Action not words needed over biggest public health failure of our time: pneumonia. *The Guardian*. Retrieved from https://www.theguardian.com/business/2019/jan/20/action-not-words-needed-over-biggest-public-health-failure-of-our-time-pneumonia-davos-2019.

EY. (2019, March). *Child vulnerability can data help to identify "Children at-risk"*. Retrieved from https://www.ey.com/Publication/vwLUAssets/ey-child-vulnerability/$File/ey-child-vulnerability.pdf.

Fry, S., Cousins, B., & Olivola, K. (2002). *Health of children living in urban slums in Asia and the near east: Review of existing literature and data*. Washington, DC: Environmental Health Project, US Agency for International Development.

George, C. E., Norman, G., Wadugodapitya, A., Rao, S. V., Nalige, S., Radhakrishnan, V., … de Witte, L. (2019). Health issues in a Bangalore slum: Findings from a household survey using a mobile screening toolkit in Devarajeevanahalli. *BMC Public Health, 19*(1), 456.

Gitonga, A. (2018). Report: Filth, congestion exposes children to diseases. *The Standard*. Retrieved from https://www.standardmedia.co.ke/article/2001307601/why-children-in-slum-centres-fall-sick.

Govt must acknowledge that children too have rights: Supreme Court. (2018, February 9). Moneycontrol.com. Retrieved from https://www.moneycontrol.com/news/india/govt-must-acknowledge-that-children-too-have-rights-supreme-court-2504945.html.

Government of India. (1956). *The slum areas (improvement and clearance) act, 1956*. Retrieved from http://delhishelterboard.in/main/wp-content/uploads/2011/12/SLUMACT_14FEB17.pdf.

Gupta, V., Mohapatra, D., & Kumar, V. (2015). Nutritional assessment among children using various anthropometric indices. *International Journal of Biomedical Research, 6*(9), 629–634.

Gupte, J., te Lintelo, D., Patel, S., Rao, V. K., McGregor, A., & Lakshman, R. (2019). *Demolition, forced evictions and wellbeing in the city*. Background paper to the main report. Institute of Development Studies. Retrieved from http://www.internal-displacement.org/global-report/grid2019/downloads/background_papers/Jaideep_FinalPaper.pdf.

Hutt, R. (2016). These are the world's five biggest slums. Retrieved from https://www.weforum.org/agenda/2016/10/these-are-the-worlds-five-biggest-slums/.

HPEC. (2011). *Report on Indian urban infrastructure and services*. Retrieved from http://icrier.org/pdf/FinalReport-hpec.pdf.

Institute of Social Sciences & UNICEF. (2014). *Children of migrant poor in Kolkata: A study on human development perspectives*. Retrieved from http://www.indiaenvironmentportal.org.in/files/file/Study%20on%20Migration%20and%20Children%20in%20Kolkata.pdf.

International Institute for Population Sciences [IIPS]. (2009). *Nutrition in India, National Family Health Survey (NFHS-3), India, 2005–06*. Ministry of Health and Family Welfare, Government of India.

IRIN. (2013, December 4). *The hidden crisis in urban slums*. Retrieved from https://www.refworld.org/docid/52a5a7354.html.

John, E. A. (2018, February 14). Slum area development gets least share of CSR funds. *The Times of India: Business*. Retrieved from https://timesofindia.indiatimes.com/business/india-business/slum-area-development-gets-least-share-of-csr-funds/articleshow/62916215.cms.

Kably, L. (2014, June 26). Slum redevelopment a CSR activity: Ministry of corporate affairs. *The Times of India: Business*. Retrieved from https://timesofindia.indiatimes.com/business/india-business/Slum-redevelopment-a-CSR-activity-Ministry-of-corporate-affairs/articleshow/37207352.cms.

Kapur, D., Sharma, S., & Agarwal, K. N. (2003). Effectiveness of nutrition education, iron supplementation or both on iron status in children. *Indian Pediatrics, 40*(12), 1131–1144.

Kaur, B. (2019, July 4). Economic survey 2018–19: Healthcare still inaccessible in rural India. *Down to Earth*. Retrieved from https://www.downtoearth.org.in/news/health/economic-survey-2018-19-healthcare-still-inaccessible-in-rural-india-65443.

Kaur, G., Kaur, S., & Soni, V. (2014). A study of slums in Mumbai with special reference to Dharavi. *International Research Journal of Management Sociology & Humanity, 5*(5), 159–166. Retrieved from https://www.academia.edu/9837355/A_Study_of_Slums_in_Mumbai_with_special_reference_to_Dharavi.

Key Population Briefs: Urban Populations. (2016). *Stop TB partnership*. Retrieved from http://www.stoptb.org/assets/documents/resources/publications/acsm/KPBrief_UrbanPopulations_ENG_WEB.pdf.

Khan, M. Z., Unnithan, N. P., & Dassi, A. (2007). Delinquency, deviance, and tolerance in a slum in India: A quantitative model. *Criminal Justice Studies, 20*(3), 269–280. Retrieved from https://www.tandfonline.com/doi/abs/10.1080/14786010701617664?scroll=top&needAccess=true&journalCode=gjup20.

Khan, S., & Mahmood, S. E. (2012). Vitamin A deficiency among school children of Bareilly: Crucial role of nutrition education. *National Journal of Medical Research, 2*(2), 188–190.

KPMG. (n.d.). *Public private partnerships in India*. Retrieved from https://www.ibef.org/download/PublicPrivatePartnership.pdf.

Lagarde, M., Haines, A., & Palmer, N. (2009). The impact of conditional cash transfers on health outcomes and use of health services in low and middle income countries. *Cochrane database of systematic reviews*, 4. Retrieved from CD 008137. Retrieved from https://researchonline.lshtm.ac.uk/4671/1/haines.pdf.

Letsoalo, I. (2019, July 10). Meet the women who are fighting child marriage one African country at a time. *Global Citizen*. Retrieved from https://www.globalcitizen.org/en/content/child-marriage-women-activists-africa/.

Lone, P. (2012). *Getting at-risk children out of work and into school in the slums of Moradabad, India*. Retrieved from https://www.unicef.org/infobycountry/india_61865.html.

Lopez, A. X. (2016). Child marriages rampant in slums. *The Hindu*. Retrieved from https://www.thehindu.com/news/cities/chennai/child-marriages-rampant-in-slums/article4337139.ece.

Malhotra, A. (2018, September 5). Devastated and destroyed: Delhi slums struggle to recover from frequent fires. *The Guardian*. Retrieved from https://www.theguardian.com/cities/2018/sep/05/devastated-destroyed-delhi-slums-recover-fires.

Marimuthu, P., Rao, G. N., Sharma, M. K., & Pandian, R. D. (2016). Perceptions on public health facilities by slum dwellers in the Metropolitan Cities of India. *Health, 8*(01), 93.

Mascarenhas, A. (2015, July 17). Urban children living in slums vulnerable to variety of risks: Report. *The Indian Express*. Retrieved from https://indianexpress.com/article/india/india-others/urban-children-living-in-slums-vulnerable-to-variety-of-risks-report/.

Ministry of Housing and Urban Affairs [MHUA], Government of India. (2019). *Handbook of urban statistics 2019*. Retrieved from http://mohua.gov.in/pdf/5c80e2225a124Handbook%20of%20Urban%20Statistics%202019.pdf.

Ministry of Housing & Urban Poverty Alleviation [MHUPA], Government of India. (2007) *National urban housing and habitat policy 2007*. New Delhi: Government of India. Available at: http://mhupa.gov.in/writereaddata/NUHHP_2007.pdf. Accessed October 11, 2016.

Ministry of Housing & Urban Poverty Alleviation [MHUPA], Government of India. (2010). *Report of the committee of slum statistics/census*. National Buildings Organization. Retrieved from https://books.google.co.in/books/about/Report_of_the_Committee_on_Slum_Statisti.html?id=uUj9ygAACAAJ&redir_esc=y.

Ministry of Housing & Urban Poverty Alleviation [MHUPA], Government of India. (2015). *Slums in India: A statistical compendium 2015*. National Buildings Organization. Retrieved from http://www.indiaenvironmentportal.org.in/files/file/SLUMS_IN_INDIA_Slum_Compendium_2015_English.pdf.

Ministry of Health and Family Welfare [MHFW]. (2017). *National family health survey—4: 2015–2016*. International Institute of Population Sciences. Retrieved from http://rchiips.org/NFHS/NFHS-4Reports/India.pdf.

Ministry of Home Affairs (MHA), Government of India. (2011). *Census 2011*. Retrieved from http://censusindia.gov.in/2011-Common/CensusData2011.html.

Ministry of Labor & Employment, Government of India. (1986). *Child and adolescent labor (prohibition & regulation) act, 1986*. Retrieved from https://labour.gov.in/sites/default/files/The_Child_and_Adolescent.pdf.

Ministry of Law and Justice [MLJ]. (2016a). *The Juvenile justice (care and protection of children) act, 2015*. Retrieved from http://cara.nic.in/PDF/JJ%20act%202015.pdf.

Ministry of Law and Justice [MLJ]. (2016b). *The child labor (Prohibition and Regulation) amendment act, 2016*. Retrieved from https://pencil.gov.in/the%20child%20labour%20(prohibition%20and%20regulation)%20amendment%20act,%202016(1).pdf.

Ministry of Statistics and Program Implementation [MSPI], Government of India. (2012). *Children in India 2012—A statistical appraisal*. Retrieved from http://mospi.nic.in/sites/default/files/publication_reports/Children_in_India_2012-rev.pdf.

Ministry of Statistics and Program Implementation [MSPI], Government of India. (2018). *India in Figures 2018*. Retrieved from http://mospi.nic.in/sites/default/files/publication_reports/India_in_figures-2018_rev.pdf.

Ministry of Urban Development [MUA]. (2014). *Heritage city development and augmentation Yojana (HRIDAY)*. Retrieved from https://smartnet.niua.org/content/7663306a-7610-46a0-919f-d0688d9493e8.

Ministry of Woman and Child Development [MWCD]. (2009). *Integrated child development services (ICDS) scheme*. Retrieved from https://icds-wcd.nic.in/icds.aspx.

Ministry of Women & Child Development [MWCD]. (2014). *Revised integrated child protection scheme (ICPS)*. Retrieved from https://bettercarenetwork.org/sites/default/files/Revised%20Integrated%20Child%20Protection%20Scheme%202014.pdf.

Ministry of Woman and Child Development [MWCD]. (2018, July 30). *Integrated Child Development Services (ICDS) Scheme. 13.63 lakh Anganwadi Centres (AWCs) of the 14 lakh AWCs sanctioned across the country are operational as on 01.06.2018*. Press Information Bureau, Government of India. Retrieved from https://pib.gov.in/newsite/PrintRelease.aspx?relid=181218.

Mithun, M. K. (2019, September 1). Why the centre's scheme to bring child labourers back to school is failing in Telengana. *The News Minute*. Retrieved from https://www.thenewsminute.com/article/why-centre-s-scheme-bring-child-labourers-back-school-failing-telangana-107956.

National Crime Records Bureau, Ministry of Home Affairs. (2016). *Crime in India 2016: Statistics*. Retrieved from http://ncrb.gov.in/StatPublications/CII/CII2016/pdfs/NEWPDFs/Crime%20in%20India%20-%202016%20Complete%20PDF%20291117.pdf.

National Institute of Urban Affairs [NIUA]. (2016). *Status of children in urban india baseline study-2016*. Retrieved from https://cfsc.niua.org/sites/default/files/Status_of_children_in_urban_India-Baseline_study_2016.pdf.

National Sample Survey Office [NSSO] (2014). Drinking Water, Sanitation, Hygiene and HousingCondition in India. Retrieved from http://mospi.nic.in/sites/default/files/publication_reports/nss_rep_556_14aug14.pdf.

Natu, N. (2019, March 6). South Mumbai sees highest spike in rape cases. *The Times of India*. Retrieved from https://timesofindia.indiatimes.com/city/mumbai/south-mumbai-sees-highest-spike-in-rape-cases/articleshow/68279473.cms.

Nianias, H. (2016). Refugees in Lesbos: are there too many NGOs on the island. The Guardian, 5.

Nitti, R., & Dahiya, B. (2004). *Community driven development in urban upgrading* (No. 11263). The World Bank.

POSHAN Abhiyaan. (2018, October 22). *PM's overarching scheme for holistic nourishment*. Retrieved from https://www.india.gov.in/spotlight/poshan-abhiyaan-pms-overarching-scheme-holistic-nourishment.

Post-2015 Development Agenda (2019). United Nations Office on Drugs and Crime. Retrieved from https://www.unodc.org/unodc/en/about-unodc/post-2015-developmentagenda.html.

Planning Commission, Government of India. (2012). *Report of the steering committee on women's agency and child rights for the twelfth five year plan (2012–2017)*. Retrieved from http://planningcommission.gov.in/aboutus/committee/strgrp12/str_womagency_childrights.pdf.

Plight of Bangladeshi slum children who work 64 hours a week instead of going to school. (2016, December 7). Retrieved from https://theirworld.org/news/plight-of-bangladeshi-slum-children-who-work-instead-of-being-in-school.

Press Information Bureau, Government of India. (2017, December 1). *Cabinet approves setting up of National Nutrition Mission*. Retrieved from https://icds-wcd.nic.in/nnm/NNM-Web-Contents/UPPER-MENU/AboutNNM/PIB_release_NationalNutritionMission.pdf.

Press Information Bureau, Government of India. (2018, July 25). *2nd meeting of National Council on India's Nutrition Challenges under POSHAN Abhiyaan held on 24th July, 2018: Month of September to be celebrated as National Nutrition Month every year*. Retrieved from https://pib.gov.in/newsite/PrintRelease.aspx?relid=180992.

Press Information Bureau, Government of India. (2019, January 17). *Ministry of women & child development-year end review 2018*. Retrieved from https://pib.gov.in/newsite/PrintRelease.aspx?relid=187560.

PTI. (2019a, February 28). India's child nutrition programme excludes poorest households: Study. *The Economic Times*. Retrieved from https://economictimes.indiatimes.com/news/politics-and-nation/indias-child-nutritionprogramme-excludes-poorest-households-study/articleshow/68196603.cms?from=mdr.

PTI. (2019b, March 19). Forced, unannounced eviction of slum dwellers contrary to law: High court. Retrieved from https://www.ndtv.com/delhi-news/high-court-says-forcedunannounced-eviction-of-slum-dwellers-contrary-to-law-2009800.

PTI. (2019c, June 7). India likely to add 273 million people between 2019 and 2050: UN Report. *The Economic Times*. Retrieved from https://economictimes.indiatimes.com/news/politics-and-nation/india-likely-to-add-273-million-people-between-2019-and-2050-un-report/articleshow/69830509.cms?from=mdr.

PWC & Save the Children. (2015). *Forgotten voices: The world of urban children in India*. Retrieved from https://www.pwc.in/assets/pdfs/publications/urban-child/urban-child-india-report.pdf.

Quattri, M. & Watkins, D. (2016). *Child labor and education: A survey of slum settlements in Dhaka*. Retrieved from https://www.odi.org/publications/10654-child-labour-and-education-survey-slum-settlements-dhaka.

Rabat Declaration. (2012). *Making slums history: A worldwide challenge for 2020*. Retrieved from http://mirror.unhabitat.org/documents/docs/Rabat_Conference/Rabat%20Declaration_EN.pdf.

Raj, U., Galhotra, A., & Roja, V. R. (2019). A study of utilization of sanitary facilities by adolescent girls in an urban slum of Central India. *Journal of family medicine and primary care, 8*(4), 1396.

Rajadhyaksha, M. (2013, December 3). Over 37,000 kids fending for themselves on city's roads: First street children census. *The Times of India*. Retrieved from https://timesofindia.indiatimes.com/city/mumbai/Over-37000-kids-fending-for-themselves-on-citys-roads-First-street-children-census/articleshow/26756505.cms.

Rastogi, S., Maheshwari, C., Raghav, S. K., & Lala, M. K. (2017). Assessing burden of under-nutrition among under five children of urban slum by using composite index of anthropometric failure in Ahmedabad City, Gujarat, India. *National Journal of Community Medicine, 8*(8), 496–500.

Ray, U. K. (2019, April 16). Child marriage rampant in West Bengal's Malda, but parties believe addressing social evil would be political suicide. *Firstpost*. Retrieved from https://www.firstpost.com/india/child-marriage-rampant-in-west-bengals-malda-district-but-parties-believe-addressing-social-evil-would-be-political-suicide-6457521.html.

Ritchie, H. (2018, September 8). *How urban is this world?* Our World in Data. Retrieved from https://ourworldindata.org/how-urban-is-the-world#note-7.

Rode, S. (2009). Does demolition of slums affects on pre-school children's health in Mumbai? *Theoretical & Empirical Researches in Urban Management, 1*(10), 63–74.

Russell, L. (2019). *Child maltreatment and psychological distress among urban homeless youth*. New York: Routledge.

Sanghera, T. (2018, September 8). *In a Mumbai slum, children become healthier, as their parents learn to tackle malnutrition*. Retrieved from https://www.indiaspend.com/in-a-mumbai-slum-children-become-healthier-as-their-parents-learn-to-tackle-malnutrition-25128/.

Save the Children. (2011). *Surviving the streets: A study on street children in Delhi*. Retrieved from https://www.savethechildren.in/news/surviving-the-streets-a-census-of-street-children-in-delhi.

Save the Children. (2016, October 14). *Nokia and save the children launch rescue app for future disasters to save children*. Retrieved from https://www.savethechildren.in/news/nokia-and-save-the-children-launch-rescue-app-for.

Save the Children. (2017). A future for every child: Bal Raksha Bharat Annual Report 2017. Retrieved from https://www.savethechildren.in/sci-in/files/60/60c56fc8-e492-4cdd-916e-028e33503902.pdf.

Save the Children. (2019). *Global childhood report 2019*. Retrieved from https://reliefweb.int/sites/reliefweb.int/files/resources/global-childhood-report-2019-pdf%20%281%29.pdf.

Sethi, N. (2013). Urban slums data reinforces India's consumption story. *Livemint*. Retrieved from https://www.livemint.com/Politics/jMYppv9iGGknRWep7H0yrI/Urban-slum-dwellers-own-assets-permanent-houses-Census-201.html.

Shaffer, H. B. (1964). Education of slum children. Editorial research reports 1964 (Vol. II). Washington, DC: CQ Press. Retrieved from http://library.cqpress.com/cqresearcher/cqresrre1964102800.

Sharma, A. (2016, August 22). Government plans to link Aadhaar with five big schemes focussed on children. *The Economic Times*. Retrieved from https://economictimes.indiatimes.com/news/economy/policy/government-plans-to-linkaadhaar-with-five-big-schemes-focussed-on-children/articleshow/53801621.cms?from=mdr.

Sharma, K. (2018, December 21). *20 lakh seats reserved in private schools for poor children but only 20% get filled*. Retrieved from https://theprint.in/india/governance/20-lakh-seats-reserved-in-private-schools-for-poor-children-but-only-20-get-filled/166749/.

Sharma, N. C. (2019, July 10). Intent of nutrition policy is clear but achieving its goals may be a challenge. *Livemint*. Retrieved from https://www.livemint.com/politics/policy/intent-of-nutrition-policy-is-clear-but-achieving-its-goals-may-be-a-challenge-1562698332423.html.

Shepard, W. (2016, July 16). *Slum tourism: How it began, the impact it has, and why it became so popular*. Forbes. Retrieved from https://www.forbes.com/sites/wadeshepard/2016/07/16/slum-tourism-how-it-began-theimpact-it-has-and-why-its-become-so-popular/#4cd423dc297d.

Singh, H. (2019). *Slum children get a glimpse of school life*. Art of Living. Retrieved from https://www.artofliving.org/in-en/slum-children-get-glimpse-school-life.

Slumshine. (2019). Slum students interview. Retrieved from http://www.slumshine.org/slum_students_interview.php.

SOER. (2015, February 18). *Towards a more urban world (GMT-2)*. European Environment Agency. Retrieved from https://www.eea.europa.eu/soer-2015/global/urban-world#tab-figures-used.

Sophy, K. J. (2016). The child labor amendment bill: Legal dilution of efforts at elimination of child labor? *Journal on Rights of the Child, 1*(1), 65–74. Retrieved from https://www.nluo.ac.in/wp-content/uploads/2019/05/Journal-on-the-Rights-of-the-Child.pdf.

Stokes, C. (1962). A theory of slums. *Land Economics, 38*(3), 187–197.

Subbaraman, R., Nolan, L., Sawant, K., Shitole, S., Shitole, T. Nanarkar, M., et al. (2015, August 27). *Water poverty in Mumbai slum*. India Water Portal. Retrieved from https://www.indiawaterportal.org/articles/water-poverty-mumbai-slum.

Tata Institute of Social Sciences & Action Aid. (2013). *Making street children matter a census study in Mumbai City*. Retrieved from https://www.actionaidindia.org/wp-content/uploads/2018/06/Mumbai-street-children-V3-Making-Street-Children-Matter1.pdf.

The Better India. (2017). *How a trust pulled 1,800 slum kids off Dehradun's streets and gave them education*. Retrieved from https://www.thebetterindia.com/117061/dehradun-slum-children-education-trust-aasraa/.

Tripathi, D. (2019, July 25). Government's thrust on healthcare pays off in rural India. *Livemint*. Retrieved from https://www.livemint.com/politics/policy/government-s-thrust-on-healthcare-pays-off-in-rural-india-1563992840042.html.

Tsujita, Y. (2010). Deprivation of education: A study of slum children in Delhi, India. *Paper commissioned for the EFA Global Monitoring Report*, 4.

United Nations Children's Fund (UNICEF). (2012). *The state of the world's children 2012: Children in an urban world*. Retrieved from https://www.unicef.org/publications/files/SOWC_2012-Main_Report_EN_13Mar2012.pdf.

United Nations Educational, Scientific and Cultural Organization [UNESCO]. (2013). *Internal migration in India initiative*. Retrieved from https://unesdoc.unesco.org/ark:/48223/pf0000221486.

UNESCO. (2019). *Global education monitoring report 2019. Migration, displacement and education: Building bridges, not wall*. UNESDOC Digital Library. Retrieved from https://unesdoc.unesco.org/ark:/48223/pf0000265866.

Unger, A., & Riley, L. W. (2007). Slum health: from understanding to action. *PLoS Medicine, 4*(10), e295. Retrieved from https://journals.plos.org/plosmedicine/article?id=10.1371/journal.pmed.0040295.

UN-Habitat. (2013). *Revised compilation for sustainable cities & human settlements in the sustainable development goals (SDGs) within the Post-2015 development agenda*. http://mirror.unhabitat.org/downloads/docs/11858_1_595548.pdf.

UN-Habitat. (2014a). *World Habitat Day 2014 background Paper*. Retrieved from https://unhabitat.org/wp-content/uploads/2014/07/WHD-2014-Background-Paper.pdf.

UN-Habitat. (2014b). *A practical guide to designing, planning, and executing citywide slum upgrading programmes*. Retrieved from https://unhabitat.org/wp-content/uploads/2015/A%20Practical%20Guide%20low%20res.pdf.

UN-Habitat. (2006). *State of the world's cities 2006/7. The millennium, development goals and urban sustainability: 30 years shaping the habitat agenda*. United Nations Human Settlements Programme, Earth Scan Publications Ltd: London and Sterling.

UN-Habitat and the Millennium Development Goals. (2012). Retrieved from http://mirror.unhabitat.org/categories.asp?catid=312.

United Nations, Department of Economic and Social Affairs, Population Division. (2018). *World urbanization prospects: The 2018 revision, Online Edition*. Retrieved from https://population.un.org/wup/Download/.

Usmani, G., & Ahmad, N. (2018). Health status in India: A study of urban slum and non-slum population. *Journal of Nursing Research and Practice, 2*(1), 9–14. Retrieved from https://www.pulsus.com/scholarly-articles/phealth-status-in-india-a-study-of-urban-slum-and-nonslum-populationp-4137.html.

Weerdt, D. S. (2011). *Slums, violence and health: a critical discussion of the interactions and effects of violence and slum settings on health and their inclusion in contemporary urban health interventions & recommendations*. Royal Tropical Institute Development, Policy and Practice Vrije Universiteit Amsterdam. Retrieved from https://pdfs.semanticscholar.org/c0d6/508ef97312afcd91c8809352658c39eb07c8.pdf.

Williams, G., Omanakuttan, U., Devika, J., & Jagajeevan, N. (2019). Planning a 'slum free' Trivandrum: Housing upgrade and the rescaling of urban governance in India. *Environment and Planning C: Politics and Space, 37*(2), 256–276. Retrieved from https://journals.sagepub.com/doi/pdf/10.1177/2399654418784305.

World Vision International. (2014). *Just cities for children: Voices from urban slums*. Retrieved from https://www.wvi.org/sites/default/files/Just%20Cities%20for%20Children-Voices%20from%20Urban%20Slums.FINAL_.pdf.

Walker, S. P., Grantham-Mcgregor, S. M., Powell, C. A., & Chang, S. M. (2000). Effects of growth restriction in early childhood on growth, IQ, and cognition at age 11 to 12 years and the benefits of nutritional supplementation and psychosocial stimulation. *Journal of Periatrics, 137*, 36–41.

Williams, R. (2013, March 11). Why girls in India are still missing out on the education they need. *The Guardian*. Retrieved from https://www.theguardian.com/education/2013/mar/11/indian-children-education-opportunities.

World Bank. (2019). *Water supply, sanitation, and hygiene (WASH) poverty diagnostic initiative*. Retrieved from https://www.worldbank.org/en/topic/water/publication/wash-poverty-diagnostic.

World Bank. (2009). *World development report 2009: Reshaping economic geography*. World Bank. Retrieved from https://openknowledge.worldbank.org/handle/10986/5991. License: CC BY 3.0 IGO.

World Population Prospects 2019: Highlights. (2019, June 17). United Nations Department of Economics and Social Affairs. Retrieved from https://www.un.org/development/desa/publications/world-population-prospects-2019-highlights.html.

Yadav, P., & Dubey, B. N. (2014). Nutritional Problems among Children in Urban Slum Area. *Man in India, 97*(2), 349–362.

Yadav, S. K. (2019). Group work with rag picker children in India: finding social justice. *Social Work with Groups*, 1–6.

Zaman, T. U., Goswami, H. D., & Hassan, Y. (2018). The impact of growth and development of slums on the health status and health awareness of slum dwellers. *Health Sciences, 7*(3), 55–65.

Zargar, H. (2017, October 17). Slums find few takers for CSR programmes. *Livemint*. Retrieved from https://www.livemint.com/Companies/Y23WWONfnpswZ8xy7r0twL/Slums-absent-from-companies-CSR-programmes.html.

Chapter 5
Children Under Institutional Care: Ensuring Quality Care and Safety

Abstract A large number of children worldwide live in institutions and their number is increasing every day. It is very unfortunate that a large number of children live in institutions while they are supposed to be with their parents and enjoying their love and affection and all other needs for their overall healthy growth and development. A number of factors are responsible for being thrust into institutional care and they include poverty, broken homes and remarriage, irresponsible behaviour of parents, parents' dependence on substance, lack of support from extended family members during crisis, absence of parents on account of death, abandonment by parents and children in conflict with the law and so on. The main focus of the chapter is to define the institutions, their objectives and the nature of services rendered. Further, the chapter highlights the reasons for taking shelter in institutions, the profile of children and their perception of the nature of support services. The perception of the parents/guardians is also captured in the discourse. The chapter also discusses the safety measures and adversities experienced by the children and the reasons thereof. Finally, the chapter discusses the nature of crimes committed by juvenile delinquents, its magnitude, causes behind juvenile delinquency and preventive measures, based on first-hand experience and how to improve the quality of care and support services, in addition to discussing about legislative and social measures for the protection of the rights of children under institutional care in the light of the UN Convention on the Rights of The Child 1989.

Keywords Children · Institution · Care · Support services · Perception · Abuse · Maltreatment

5.1 Introduction

A child is to be reared within a family under the care and protection of the biological parents for their healthy growth and development. In a family, a child gets the orientation on socialization process and the emotional bondage between a child and his/her parents and siblings become very strong and in turn, a child feels emotionally secured. Similarly, family ensures adequate nutrition, medical care and education in addition to safety and security of a child, thus facilitating a smooth transition from

S. Deb et al., *Disadvantaged Children in India*,
https://doi.org/10.1007/978-981-15-1318-3_5

childhood to adulthood and becoming an independent person with knowledge and skills. Within a family, parents' love and affection and facilities for games and sports ensure a child to enjoy childhood. Therefore, in the UN convention on Rights of the Child, it is clearly stated that family is the natural environment and a child should be grown within the family.

Unfortunately, a large number of children worldwide live in institutions and their number is increasing day by day. It is very unfortunate as they are supposed to be with their parents and enjoy the love and affection of their parents and all of their needs for their overall healthy growth and development.

5.2 Definition and Types of Institutions and Their Objectives

An institution or observation home is an alternative living arrangement for children in need of care and for children in conflict with the law. It is run by governmental and non- governmental organizations. There are different categories of institutions and they include Shelter Homes, Children's Homes, Halfway Homes and Special Homes. Shelter homes are either day care centers or night shelters or both. Children are forwarded to these types of homes for a short period of time since they need a safe shelter during the inquiry process of their background. Observation homes are meant for children in conflict with the law, for short duration, till the completion of the pendency of inquiry or up to 18 years of age, which is, until they become adults.

Series of empirical studies were carried out across the world on the ecology of institutional life for young children (Muhamedrahimov, 1999; Provence & Lipton, 1962; Smyke et al., 2007; The St. Petersburg-USA Orphanage Research Team, 2008). It has been observed that the institutions differ to a great extent in terms of infrastructure and nature of care and support services, with special reference to children and caregiver ratio, unskilled caregivers and their poor wages, lack of individual care and poor psychological support services (The St. Petersburg-USA Orphanage Research Team, 2008; Zeanah et al., 2003). The findings of previous studies raised questions about the quality of services and its impact on children's development (Nelson, 2007; Zeanah, Smyke, & Settles, 2006). Similarly, there are some similarities with respect to some activities and styles of functioning. There is a clear distinction between institutions in the developed and developing countries. Quality of care and support services is much better in the developed countries as compared to the developing countries. What are needed in all the institutions, in the developing countries, are close and consistent interactions with children in addition to close monitoring of the functioning of the institutions. In this regard, the committed caregivers can ensure healthy social and psychological development of young children under institutional care.

The primary objectives of such institutional cares for children include the following:

- To meet the basic needs of destitute and neglected children who do not have parents or, children from poor socio-economic families.
- To provide safe shelter, non-formal or formal education and skill-based training.
- To rehabilitate children coming from difficult circumstances including ill-health, disability, abuse and neglect.
- To support the children for integration into the mainstream of the society aftercare.

5.2.1 Why Is Institutional Care More Prevalent?

Institutional care is very important for disadvantaged children, especially for those who have lost both their parents due to natural calamities or had died in an accident or in war or for those who have nobody to look after them, who were abandoned by their biological parents and for those who are orphans.

Children are coming to institution for various reasons and they include family disorganization, single parenthood, poverty, parental dependence on substance, domestic violence and mental health challenges of parents, safety of girl children and non-availability of educational facility and lack of guidance at home. McCall (2012) broadly categorized the disadvantaged children under institutional care into two major categories based on the presence or absence of parents—"true orphans" are children who do not have living parents and "social orphans" are children who have both parents or one parent but who are unable, unwilling or unfit to take care of their offspring.

5.3 Profile of the Children and Their Background

Children in need of care and protection and children in conflict with the law live in different institutions. Children in need of care and protection and children in conflict with the law mostly live in government observation homes forwarded by the Juvenile Court while children in need of care and protection mostly live in different institutions run by NGOs or Charitable Trusts. They live in institutions exclusively meant for boys or girls. In some institutions, run by NGOs, both boys and girls live together and living arrangements are separate for them. They belong to different castes, religions and age groups.

One recent study in Puducherry covering 26 institutions revealed that more than two-third of the children (64%) were female and mostly belonged to 14–16 years of age and were studying in the Ninth, Tenth and Eleventh standards respectively. The majority of the children belonged to the Hindu religion community (64%), followed by Christians (34%) and the remaining percentage belonged to the Muslim community (Bhuvaneswari, 2017).

So far as type of family is concerned, around 63% of the children came from nuclear families while 33% belonged to joint families. About 3% of them were orphans and were brought up by the institutions and they did not have any contact with their biological parents. However, parents of about two-fifths (42%) were found to be living together, 35% children had lost their fathers, and parents of 7% of the children were re-married or in a relationship with another person. Most of the children had two or more siblings while about one-third had one sibling. The majority of the parents were daily-wage earners, followed by working in private sectors, self-employment and some were unemployed. In case of 40% children, fathers were no more or they were untraceable (Bhuvaneswari, 2017). Sadly, about one-third of the children reported witnessing violence in the family. Perhaps alcoholism was one of the factors responsible for family violence as 43% of the fathers were dependent on alcohol. A large number of parents were reported to be suffering from various health problems. Further, primary research disclosed that academic performance of 43% of the children was reported to be good while it was bad for the remaining 57% (Bhuvaneswari, 2017).

5.3.1 *Magnitude of the Children Under Institutional Care*

It is very difficult to estimate the total number of children in need of care and protection in different institutions internationally and in India. However, according to UNICEF, there were 25 million orphaned children in India in 2007 (Source: http://childlineindia.org.in/children-without-parental-care-india.htm).

As per the prediction of Save the Children (2014), around eight million children worldwide spend their lives in institutions despite having one or both parents alive (Save the Children, 2014). Given the local situation and socio-economic conditions, many countries promote institutional care for children, in helpless conditions, for their upbringing. From the above two different estimations about disadvantaged children, it is clear that the estimation varies to a great extent. In reality, the number of street or disadvantaged children could be more.

Crime in India data reported that the number of juvenile delinquents is increasing every year in India. For example, the number of juvenile delinquents has increased from 18,939 to 31,396, in the category of Juveniles in conflict with law, and from 1,822,602 to 2,949,499, under total cognizable IPC Crimes (Crime in India Report, 2005–2015) during 2005–2015. This issue requires immediate attention of concerned government departments for taking appropriate measures for prevention of juvenile delinquency in India. Diagnostic studies should be carried out in different locations to ascertain the causes behind the increasing number of crimes committed by juvenile delinquents.

5.4 Reasons for Staying in Institutions

The reasons for children staying in institutions may broadly be categorized into two groups. First, the children who are in conflict with laws are forwarded to the government-run observation homes for behaviour modification and skill development, so that, after release from the homes, they may get a job for survival and for leading a decent life. The second categories of children are those in need of care and protection for their healthy growth and development.

From the first-hand field experience of the first author, while working with children in conflict with the law in West Bengal, it has been observed that most of the children from poor families crossed the India–Bangladesh border without valid documents, intentionally, for getting a shelter in the Observation Home where they will have proper food for survival. Financial conditions of the families along the border of Bangladesh is so pathetic that parents indulge their children to cross the India–Bangladesh border, knowing it fully well that their child will be arrested by the Border Security Force (BSF) of India and will produce them in the Juvenile Court and finally, the Juvenile Court will hold them responsible for crossing the border, which is a crime as per law. In reality, it is a struggle of existence for some poor children. Most of the children in the Observation Homes in West Bengal are of similar backgrounds. Therefore, poverty is one of the main causes for children coming into institutional care. However, the reasons for staying in institutions might vary in case of children of other states and other countries.

For the second category of children, factors are somewhat similar for being under institutional care. In addition to poverty, other factors which force children to come under institutional care include broken homes and remarriage, family violence, irresponsible behaviour of parents, parents' dependence on substance, and lack of support from extended family members during crisis, absence of parents on account of death, abandonment by parents and children in conflict with the law and so on.

The other probable reasons for some children staying in different institutions include challenging behaviour or existence of vulnerability towards mental health problems of socio-economically disadvantaged sections or the presence of abuse or emotional neglect in the family or, a combination of two or more factors. Children with intellectual disability, visual impairment, hearing impairment and children with HIV are considered as those who need intensive and perceived care as the institution is the best mode of service delivery. Normally, children with special needs are perceived to be a burden by the family. As a result, family members look for an alternative arrangement for sending their children, by paying money.

Evidence highlights that some children move to residential care because of their unmanageable and challenging behaviour, by the family or foster family (Berridge, Blehal, & Henry, 2012). Findings of studies carried out by Escueta et al. (2014) clearly indicated that the risk from mental health problems is higher among children from socio-economically disadvantaged backgrounds.

Running a private institution is a business for some people. As a result, availability of institutions is an encouragement for some parents to send their child to those places.

Some of the institutions fail to extend quality care to the children for their overall growth and development. Parwon (2006) remarked that "investment and regular resource from government and non-government serves as a driving force for them to continue and develop the institution."

The reason for sending juvenile delinquents to Observation Homes is behavioural change and to impart vocational skills so that after completion of the penalty term, they can lead an independent life in the society and look after their own needs.

5.5 Nature of Care and Support Services Available for Children Under Institutional Care

The nature and categories of support services provided to the children across institutions are almost similar, with some variations. Broadly, the services rendered in the institutions may be grouped under following categories:

- Safe Shelter
- Nutrition
- Medical Care
- Education
- Vocational/Skill-based Training
- Group Activities
- Games and Sports
- Meditation and Prayer

Quality of care and support services depends upon the leadership of an institution and their staff. A person with passion and vision as well as with past work experience in the same field will be more active in designing, planning and delivery of quality care and support services for the best interest of the children. If the leader of an institution is active and engaged in the work, it will have tremendous positive impact on other staff of the institution and they will work sincerely and actively. In addition to physical service delivery, accepting children psychologically and listening to them from time to time will give them a feel of psychological acceptance and love and affection, which will make them happy. By creating that affectionate relationship with the children, the support staff of the institution can make children norm-bound, disciplined and studious, in addition to altering the behaviour of some of the children who were wayward and possessed contra-cultural views and attitudes. Appreciating their performance, by the teachers and staff of the institution will be highly motivating for them and in turn, the children will take up studies more seriously and compete with the children of the larger society and probe their talent, who are equally capable of doing good in their respective fields.

Some of the institutions have created opportunities for learning extra-curricular skills for the children, which included yoga, dance, drawing, music, drama and so on, while some have family strengthening programs, wherein children were offered psychosocial support in the community itself and institution-based care, thus simulating a family-like environment. All these programs benefitted the children in gaining additional skills which would help them in later life.

5.5.1 Institutional Care: Positive Outcomes, Issues and Concerns

Undoubtedly, there are numerous positive outcomes of institutional care for the disadvantaged children. Nature of care-wise benefits is discussed in the following section.

Positive Outcomes

Broadly, positive outcomes could be grouped under four/five categories and they include the following:

- **Safe Accommodation**: A larger number of children get a safe accommodation for living, along with a sense of belongingness. All the children get friends, can play with other children, exchange their joy, sorrow and views with other children, in respect to various issues and learn from each other.
- **Improved Health Status**: Regular nutrition and medical facilities, within the institutions or through referral sources, improve the health status of the children which were missing prior to joining the institution.
- **Educational Facilities**: Almost every institution imparts either non-formal or formal education to all the children or both, depending upon availability of facilities and/or child interest. Some institutions ensure skill-based training programs for empowering the children with skills so that after release from the institution, after 18 years of age, they get some work for survival. In fact, education in any form helps an individual to lead an improved quality of life in all respects. For example, a person becomes more logical, well mannered and behaves in a socially desirable fashion. The children who are interested in studies, with minimal educational facilities and support from the school or institution, they can perform better and move ahead in life and occupy positions in different organizations. Therefore, individual motivation and a little encouragement from the staff of the institutions and school teachers make a big difference in the life of disadvantaged children.
- **Enhanced Psychological Competence**: An institution provides a platform to a child who is homeless or is coming from a very poor family, where he/she gets friends, mingles with them and shares their feelings and views and in turn, they get mental support. Normally, when individuals come in contact with similar group of people, they feel psychologically more comfortable and confident. Enhanced psychological competence encourages a child to take part in all social, educational, cultural and physical activities (like games and sports) actively along with

other children and makes them happy. Arrangements of individual and group counselling by professional psychologists in some institutions addresses the psychological needs of a child as well common issue. In fact, counselling helps a child to overcome stress, anxiety, depression and maladjustment. Further, psychological inputs from the staff of an institution and/or psychologist play an important role to strengthen the relationship with available parents and parents are also benefitted after attending some programs in the institutions.

- **Facilities for Games and Sports and Group Activities**: Most of the institutions have adequate space for games, sports and group activities. These types of physical activities refresh the minds of the children, keeps them physically fit and develop a sense of group cohesiveness. Some institutions arrange outings for picnics or arrange educational tours. Picnic gives a lot of joy and excitement while educational tours become educative in gaining knowledge.

Although evidences are limited, few studies highlighted the positive outcomes of institutional care in terms of meeting the basic needs of the children, which the families fail to do.

For example, in a large scale cohort study covering 2871 children who were orphaned and separated in sub-Saharan Africa, authors found that "institutional care were more likely to meet the basic material needs of children and each model of care had its own strength and weakness, hence tailor-made care environment can be opted for meeting the needs and fulfilling the rights of the children" (Embleton et al., 2014). In another study covering five low and middle-income countries including India, authors made an attempt to assess physical health, growth and emotional well-being through strength and difficulties questionnaire (self-report version and caregiver version), learning ability and memory through Kaufman Assessment Battery for Children-II (KABC-II). The findings disclosed that the children did perform better in institutions compared to the deprived family setting after a36-month follow-up of orphaned and separated children (Whetten et al., 2014). Loman, Johnson, Quevedo, Lafavor and Gunnar (2014) studied the risk-taking and sensation-seeking propensities of 12 and 13-year-old post-institutionalized adolescents and found that adolescents with history of early institutional care exhibited less risk-taking and sensation-seeking behaviours. However, higher levels of conduct problems among post-institutionalized adolescents were recorded and did not differ in terms of depressive symptoms.

Issues and Concerns

As there are a number of positive outcomes, there are disadvantages for children living in an institution too. The nature of challenges, issues and concerns vary from institution to institution. When we look at the challenges, issues and concerns of an institution, we need to examine the same considering the social and economic background of the society or the country.

Institutional care is the immediate need for children who are in crisis situations and for some, it becomes a relatively permanent care who are homeless and who need temporary shelters. General observations about institutions are that staffs are not professionally qualified or they are not trained but, one should look at the issue from another angle, that is, job status. If an institution offers reasonably good salary, one might get qualified and trained staff. Until reasonably good salary is offered, people with low education and inadequate skills will apply for different positions of institutions. Therefore, there is a need to re-look at the salary issue for getting skilled and motivated staff for childcare institutions.

For developing countries, institutional support for disadvantaged children is a great help since poverty is a serious issue while, in the developed countries, the issues are different. Since there is no financial crisis or fund scarcity in the developed countries, they give more emphasis on psychological happiness and quality of care by professionals.

One school of thought says that the standard of care in most of the institutions in the developing countries like India is very poor or substandard. In a good number of institutions, gross violation of child rights is reported in terms of neglect, child labour, child sexual abuse and physical abuse. For example, the Central Bureau of Investigation (CBI) has registered two fresh FIRs concerning sexual abuse of children in two shelter homes in Gaya and Bhagalpur in Bihar. In another similar case, investigation is going on at the Muzaffarpur shelter home (Hindustan Times, New Delhi, Jan. 17, 2019). These are not isolated incidents. There are a number of reports regarding sexual abuse of children in different institutions across the country.

Famous psychologist like Bowlby (1952) opinioned that "children's attachment gets disturbed in institutional care despite availability of adequate physiological needs met." Further Ainsworth identified in various studies, the higher rates of insecure attachment and disorganized attachment among institutionalized children (as cited in van IJzendoorn et al., 2011). In another study, Fischer et al. (2016) examined the relationship between interpersonal traumatic experiences and specific psychopathological symptoms among children living in youth welfare institutions. The children were grouped into three viz., no interpersonal trauma, single interpersonal trauma and multiple interpersonal trauma. The study found that trauma-induced psychological disturbances were more among male children while affective disorders were more prevalent among female children.

Evidence highlights that children under institutional care experience a range of challenges and it finally affects their mental health. For example, Jiménez-Morago, León and Román (2015) undertook a study to examine the adversity and adjustment in a group of 230 children aged from 4 to 10 years in different care centers viz., international adoption, institutional care, non-kin foster care, kinship care, using the Parent version of Strength and Difficulties Questionnaire and concluded that children in institutional care had experienced most problems and difficulties. Based on a secondary research McCall, Groark and Rygaard (2014) concluded that the "major reason for increasing number of children in institution as well as mushrooming of institution itself is the lack of widespread message about foster care or group home. Presence of warm, sensitive and responsive care is not noted in most of the institutions and the provision of basic physical essentials of adequate food, safety is not noted in some of the institution." Oriol, Sala-Roca and Filella (2014) undertook a study on emotional competencies of three groups of adolescent viz., adolescents living in residential care, adolescents from normative population and adolescents from disadvantaged family environments, by using Emotional quotient Inventory (EQ-i). The findings revealed that "there is no significant difference in level of emotional intelligence. Nevertheless, girls in the residential care scored high in total EQ-i and on the interpersonal and adaptability components than the other two groups of children." In the same year another study by Gleason et al. (2014) reported that "younger children with a history of long-term institutional care exhibit socially indiscriminate behaviours compared to children who were never institutionalized."A cross-sectional study found that "sleep problems such as bedtime resistance, daytime sleepiness and night awakening were common among the institutionalized children" (Abou-Khadra, 2012). Ayaz et al. (2012) conducted the study to understand the prevalence of mental disorders and associated factors in institutionalized 3- to 5-year-old children by comparing them with children from the community. The findings unearthed that "severity in symptoms of attention deficit hyperactivity disorder, reactive attachment disorder, oppositional deficient disorder and pervasive developmental disorder were highly present in children under institutional care compared to children reared in families and predictive factors included the duration of institutional stay, presence of abuse before institutionalization." Wiik et al. (2011) found that "children with history of institutional care had increased level of ADHD symptoms." Regarding stereotypes in children, Bos, Zeanah, Smyke, Fox and Nelson (2010) undertook a study following randomized controlled trial method in Romania and concluded that there is more prevalence of stereotypes in children with a history of institutional care. Further, the authors observed significant association with lower performance on language and cognitive developmental scales. Merz and McCall (2010) investigated the behaviour problems in children aged between 6 and 18 years adopted from psychosocially deprived Russian institutions. Children of post institutionalization were compared with non-institutionalized children. Findings reported that "the children reared in the psychosocially depriving institutions had lesser behaviour problem than the severely depriving institutions." In a secondary study McCall (2013) observed that "the risk for developmental delay and psychological problems are higher when children get admitted to an institution at an early age. The adverse effect of lack of requisite warm, supportive and responsive caregiving during the first years of children's lives leads to problems in developmental milestones. Psychosocial deprivations in early years of life affect the motor development of children with low intelligence and a history of institutionalization."

Abuse and maltreatment of children in the institutions have been reported by a number of studies across the world. It is unfortunate that the custodian becomes the perpetrators. In such a situation, children are helpless and struggle a lot, which affect their overall growth and development. In this regard, Euser et al. (2013) disclosed the high prevalence rate of sexual abuse or maltreatment in institutional care among children and youth aged between 12 and 17 years and the rate was higher in institutional care than foster care. The study also highlighted the greater need for protection against violence which is more prevalent in institutional care compared to the general population. Similarly, Hermenau et al. (2014) examined the safety issue of children under institutional care among Tanzanian children and found that "maltreatment in institutional care increases the vulnerability for problems in mental health of children particularly for those who were institutionalized early. Tanzania is a country where institutional care is common and protection of children from harm is uncommon. Further, it was observed that maltreatment is an influencing factor for mental health problems in children who are institutionalized early and does not have relation with mental health problem when children are institutionalized in later years."

Some of the studies carried out in India on the same issue highlights similar observations. Based on the findings of an empirical study, authors suggested mental health support services for children under institutional care in addition to maintaining contact with the biological parents or guardians. More specifically, they recommended individual psychotherapy and/or counselling, life skill training, sex education, mental health checkup at the time of admission and a separate mental health care unit in each home. In addition, periodic physical and mental health checkups were recommended by the authors (Sagar et al., 2017). Prior to this study, Mukhopadhyay and Bhalla (2016) conducted a case study on compliance of Juvenile Justice Rules 2007 by the juvenile institutions in Kolkata. The institutions were surveyed on the parameters of health care, nutrition, education, infrastructure and treatment. The findings of the study observed that "many of the child care institutions did not follow the standards as mentioned in the rules thus creating a milieu which impedes and worsens the mainstreaming process of children in society. The major reason for negative impact on children's well-being in institutional care was the non-compliance of the rules prescribed in JJ Act as reported by the authors."

5.6 Status of Mental Health of the Children Under Institutional Care

So far as mental health of the children under institutional care is concerned, a number of studies were carried out in India and internationally. Most of them reported higher behavioural problems among children under institutional care as compared to children living with families. For instance, Padmaja, Sushma and Agarwal (2014) explored psychosocial problems and well-being among institutionalized children by comparing them with children living with their parents and observed that emotional difficulties, hyperactivity, internalizing and externalizing problems, high depression and low well-being were higher among children living in institutions than with children living in families. Another study reported higher rates of social problems, rule-breaking behaviour, aggressive behaviour and externalizing problems among post-institutionalized children (Muhamedrahimov et al., 2014). Further, the researchers noted that "the transition from institution to family care developed complexity in adaptation to the family environment especially for children with long periods of institutionalization."

Loman et al. (2013) performed an interesting study on the effect of early deprivation on executive attention in middle childhood by comparing three groups of children who were adopted with a history of institutional care, adopted with a history of foster care and non-adopted children. Children were tested for two executive attention tasks on the neurological test (Go/No-go and Flanker) and revealed that behavioural performance of children who were adopted after institutionalization had more problems with sustained attention.

Further, available evidence indicates that children under institutional care significantly differ from children in family care, in terms of overall mental health as well as across all subscales. The mean score of mental health of children under institutional care was much lower than the mean score of mental health of children in family care. This implies that the children under institutional care are in need of more mental health services along with other welfare measures meant for them, which had been stressed by previous studies (Hermenau, Hecker, Elbert, & Ruf-Leuschner, 2014; Padmaja, Sushma, & Agarwal, 2014).

Hermenau et al. (2011) found that institutional care had detrimental effects on the development of children. Several studies further observed that children under institutional care are more anxious and had other problems too when compared to the children in family care as the mean score of the latter is higher than the children cared for in institutions. For example, van IJzendoorn, Schuenge and Bakermans-Kranenburg (1999) have reported that the psychological well-being of children was disturbed by the institutional environment. Palacios, Moreno and Roman (2013) found that children living in institutions had more problems with peers, poorer social skills and socio-economic status than the children in family environments. The presence of problems with peers could be the result of absence or negligence of adults in guiding the children to have healthy relationships with the peers.

Nevertheless, there is a positive impact of staying in an institution with other children. Children living in institutions develop more pro-social behaviour than children living in family care. Children in institutions belong to mixed age groups; they either help young children in everyday activities or are said to do so by the institutional staff. Older children help younger ones to take bath, wash their clothes, keep their things safely and so on. Thus, the pro-social behaviour is directed by the staff and is continued till they are in the institution. A study with children in family care responded that such children showed more hyperactive symptoms than the other groups as the mean score was higher than the children under institutional care. Post institutional care children showed difficulties with hyperactivity as noted in the earlier study (Kumsta et al., 2010).

A recent study in Puducherry covering 26 institutions disclosed that half of the children (48%) need mental health support services. The reasons behind the same are inadequate individual attention to the children, lack of trained manpower, non-availability of counsellors or psychologists and engagement of limited staff on multiple activities resulting in poor care to the children, and stress among staff caused by workload (Bhuvaneswari, 2017). Another study also corroborated the findings of the Puducherry study, that is, there is a need to appoint adequate staff with skills in the institution and arrange mental health support services in terms of individual counselling and group therapy (Sagar, Patra, & Gupta, 2017).

Older children reported more mental health challenges as compared to the younger ones, especially the children who could not perform well in studies. So far as the gender issue is concerned, with respect to the status of mental health, female children had greater difficulties than male children. Around 59% of the children in the Puducherry study fell in the category of slightly raised difficulties (25%), high difficulties (12%) and very high difficulties (22%) in the measure of SDQ. This probably could be due to the lack or no availability of mental health care professionals, resulting in unattended challenging behaviours prevailing among children in institutions. The pro-social behaviour of children in institutional care was close to average. The probable reason could be the fact that children spend most of the time with their peers and other children. Also, due to the shortage of staff, older children were made to help and extend support in daily activities and thus children were tuned to be pro-social in institutions. Conduct problems and hyperactivity were in the range of close to average whereas emotional problem and peer problem were on the slightly high on the difficulty range. Externalizing behaviour viz. conduct problem and hyperactivity, which were very much explicit, were controlled and monitored by the staff but children found the latter two really difficult to manage (Bhuvaneswari, 2017).

Children who were staying in the institutions for longer periods of time had higher mental health needs on account of higher behaviour difficulties than the children who had stayed relatively for a shorter period of time (Bhuvaneswari, 2017).

5.6.1 Resilience Capacity of the Children Under Institution Care

Resilience capacity plays an important role in adjusting to different situations in life. A child with higher resilience experiences lesser adjustment problems as compared to a child with low resiliency capacity. One study disclosed that about half of the children in institutions (45%) have a greater need to improve their resilient characteristics (Bhuvaneswari, 2017). As a few institutions restrict the children's mobility into the community environment, children lack the knowledge of family dynamics, tradition, culture and customs that are being followed in the society. Therefore, increasing the frequency of meeting the family members and allowing the child to be in their own community during festivals and holidays will pave way for the child to understand the community better than staying in institutions alone.

Resilience and mental health are significantly related and this positive relation was reported in previous studies (Sood, Bakhshi, & Devi, 2012). A positive correlation is also observed in resilience and general positive affect (Sood et al., 2012). Educational performance was found to be related to the resilience capacity. Children who reported having 'good' academic performance had high resilience capacity. Perception of safety and mental health were significantly related. Children who expressed that they felt they were in a safe environment had higher mental health. Lower perception of safety was related to low pro-social behaviour, high difficulties and lower resilience capacity.

5.7 Institutional Care: A Situation Analysis

Out of home children are placed in different types of care: adoption, foster care and institutional care. Adoption is opted for younger children who are abandoned, surrendered or orphaned. Foster care is for a temporary period and the child is taken care either by relatives or significant others or by any other family interested in taking care of child under supervision by the Government. Institutional care is given for either temporary or permanent periods. Among all these, out of home placement and institutionalization of children for long duration may yield maladaptive developmental changes along with adaptive skill development.

Most of the institutions were formed during the period of 1966–1975 (18.13%) and during 1996–2005 (14.67%) in India to cater to the children from underprivileged section ("Database on Orphanages under Women's and Children's Institutions (Licensing) Act, 1956," n.d.). All Institutions working for the welfare of children need to be registered under the JJ (Amendment) Act, 2006.

Wide ranges of developmental aspects were studied and the findings confirm the presence of intrapersonal, interpersonal and educational problems among children in institutional care. Children, who are exposed to early institutional neglect, reflect emotional bias which may act as risk factors for internalizing disorders (Stellern, Esposito, Mliner, Pears, & Gunnar, 2014). Children with lower scores on cognitive development were found to be less secure and had difficulty in understanding emotions than children reared in family (Vorria et al., 2006). Research reinstates the high level of mental health needs to be met for youths who were in institutional care (Gearing, MacKenzie, Schwalbe, Brewer, & Ibrahim, 2013).

5.7.1 Unmet Basic Needs/Needs at Low Standard

Unfortunately, the presence of warm, sensitive and responsive care was not observed in most of the institutions. Provision of basic physical essentials, that is, adequate food and safety are also not available in some of the institutions (McCall, Groark, & Rygaard, 2014). Absence of standard basic care has been reported in many of the institutions. Children of some of the institutions were admitted to hospitals with complaints like fever, vomiting and abdominal pain ("10 girls of a home suffer from food poisoning", 2015). In some institutions, children are never allowed to ask for second servings while in some institutions they were forced to make wrong statements about quality of care and support services ("The Pastor at the home loved to torture them," 2014; "We were tutored to say that we are treated well," 2014).

Skin-related diseases are vivid among children in institutional care as reported by a number of Newspapers ("Yet another children's home in Trichy violated rights", 2016; "Private children's homes aided by corrupt system", 2014). Malnourishment of children is not uncommon in most of the institutions ("Yet another children's home in Trichy violated rights", 2016).

5.7.2 *Status of Infrastructure in the Institutions*

Infrastructure varies from institution to institution. Few institutions have good infrastructure to meet the basic needs of children in a systematic manner while others lack minimum infrastructure. Therefore, there is a need to ensure minimum infrastructure facilities for those institutions which lack the same. In some institutions, timely renovation of the buildings is required to arrest further deterioration of infrastructure. Both Government and Non-governmental institutions are in need of additional buildings and/or renovation of existing infrastructures.

5.7.3 *Basic Facilities*

Sanitation facilities are not available in a good number of institutions. Therefore, in those institutions, girl children take bath in the open. Less number of dresses is also an issue. The children are provided with few sets of dresses which are insufficient. In addition, poor security system, dirty kitchens, cooking near a pool of sewage, crumbling and unpainted walls are some of the major constraints for most of the institutions. The girls defecate in the open which was admitted by the warden of the homes. As a result, sometimes they become vulnerable to sexual abuse. In yet another home, the children were compelled to bathe and relieve themselves in the garden despite the availability of the toilet ("The Pastor at the home loved to torture them", 2014).

5.7.4 *Physical Abuse*

Disciplining children is necessary and it should be done in a manner which will not cause any harm to them. However, sometimes disciplinary methods are so harsh that it causes physical harm. Physical abuse under the pretext of disciplining the children is rampant across institutions. Corporal punishment is an accepted form of disciplining the children because people are not aware of positive disciplining of the children. Rampant use of physical punishment in the institutions across the country has been reported by various agencies. For example, a six-year-old boy was branded with a hot iron rod for nocturnal enuresis ("Children make 'damning' statements against persons running the home", 2015). A reporter from Times of India helped in rescuing a 10-year-old boy who was selling soap bubbles on the streets. When the reporter met the child after two days, as a follow-up, the boy alleged that the caretaker of the home beat him repeatedly for not taking his daily routines (eating, sleeping and bathing). The report also revealed that the child had bruises on the face ("Boy rescued from street says he was beaten by caretaker," 2015). Children in government homes are beaten up, harassed by the staff of the institutions ("Horror stories from shelter for runaway kids", 2012). A 13-year-old boy was allegedly beaten up with a PVC pipe for refusing to clean the toilets ("Teen abused, assaulted in Bangalore Govt-run home", 2014). Many physical abuses go unnoticed or unreported.

5.7.5 Sexual Abuse

Like physical punishment, children of juvenile justice homes such as observation homes, children homes and shelter homes often report incidents of sexual abuse. Surprisingly, very few incidents of sexual abuse in institutions are reported and many go unreported.

> … the juveniles in conflict with law and children in need of care and protection, have become India's hell holes where inmates are subjected to sexual assault and exploitation, torture and ill treatment apart from being forced to live in inhuman conditions …..—stated by Mr. Suhas Chakma, Director of Asian Centre for Human Rights

Regarding sexual abuse of children in different institutions, various agencies reported information. For instance, a girl child, aged 14, delivered a baby girl and was rescued from an unregistered home ("Officials' ignorance adds to children's woes", 2015). The death of a boy inside a state-run rescue home raised the suspicion of sodomy as he had nail marks in his neck ("Boy found murdered at rescue home, sodomy suspected", 2015). An adolescent girl, aged 14, was sexually abused by the husband of the female warden of the home, repeatedly, followed by pregnancy and abortion ("Child Welfare panels fail, abuse continues at homes", 2014). A girl with hearing impairment was sexually abused and she also became pregnant, in a shelter home ("Nari Niketan rape case: Ex-staff held", 2015).

Children as young as two and three were illegally cared by a home and they were kept in a separate house where an elderly woman claimed that they were her grandchildren, which she was not able to prove ("Child rescued from unlicensed home, fourth in 3 days", 2015).

The situation of children in Institutional Care in India is depicted as Nobody's Children, Nowhere Children, Invisible Children (CRY, 2005). Two girl children aged 10 and 11 years were forcibly taken from the hostel and were sexually abused in Pollachi near Coimbatore, which is a bright example of the lack of safety for children under institutional care (Sairam, 2014). Hence, there arises a necessity to study the functioning of Child Welfare Committees, the prospects and challenges of children who are placed in institutional care, perception of service providers in institution and the parents of the children.

5.8 Perception of Children About Institutional Care and Support Services

Literature provides mixed perception about institutional care. It is mostly negative, from the point of view psychological development. As discussed earlier, abuse, neglect and maltreatment of children in the institutions are very common. Since children are the beneficiaries, it would be worthwhile to have children's perception about the nature and quality of services received by them from the institution. In this regard, a recent empirical study carried out in Puducherry, covering 26 institutions, captured the perspectives of children of care and support services (Bhuvaneswari, 2017). By and large, the findings provide the real picture.

In this section, an effort has been made to share their perception with respect to different issues, systematically, so that one can have a holistic perceptive of institutional care and support facilities as perceived by the children. So far as nutrition is concerned, almost all the children reported receiving food thrice a day while about 90% were of the opinion that they got adequate food. A majority of the children stated that the quality of the food was good. However, the remaining percentage possessed opposite views.

Regarding cleanliness of the institution, 85% of the children remarked that the environment around them was 'very clean' whereas 12% of the children expressed that it was 'not so clean' and 2% felt that it was 'not at all clean'. With respect to other basic needs, about two-third (72%) of the children's basic needs were fulfilled by the institution, which include, dress, soap and other essential items. In case of 28% children, the family members supplied the basic essential items.

Another very encouraging picture, which emerged from the study is, almost all the children were studying in different categories of schools and they were happy about the quality of education. For example, nearly 46%, 37% and 16% of the children were attending Government schools, government-aided schools and private schools, respectively.

In connection with relationship of the children with the caregivers of the institutions, an overwhelming number of the children (84%) reported having good relationships with their service providers whereas 10% of them stated that their relationship was not good while the remaining 5% perceived it to be 'not at all good'.

Shockingly, more than half of the children (58%) under institutional care indicated that they had undergone abuse in one form or another—physical abuse (35%) or psychological abuse (49%). Some children (4%) expressed that there is prevalence of sexual abuse from their peers and senior children within the same institution. Such sexual abuse was mostly experienced by the male children. Despite the presence of difficult circumstances and abuse, the children considered the institution to be a better place for them. It might be that their family environment was much worse than that of the institutions or a child did not have any parents or any other place to stay (Bhuvaneswari, 2017).

5.8.1 Leisure Time Activities

Children reported enjoying their leisure time through games and sports and other outdoor activities with children of same age group and gender. The institution which has open spaces and facilities for games and sports made the children very happy and in turn, it was good for physical health and releasing stress and anxiety and overcoming loneliness. Therefore, outdoor activities are always beneficial for children. The primary research carried out in Puducherry further disclosed that about two-thirds (67%) of the children could spend their leisure time playing with other children. The remaining percentage of the children was deprived of the same facilities in some institution for shortage of space or non-availability of sports items.

Regarding physical health, almost all the children (97%) were physically fit and received treatment as and when required. Few of them expressed their dissatisfaction about quality of treatment since they had reoccurrences of the disease (skin infection). So far as personal issues are concerned, they mostly preferred to share the same with their friends in the institutions (53%). The rest of the children shared the same with school friends and family members.

Nearly 89% of the children had visitors, who were either parents or family members who are their guardians, while 10% of the children had no visitors for the past three months. More than half of the children (68%) in institutional care did not want to continue their stay there and wanted to go back to their families.

Children in most of the institutions were engaged in extra-curricular activities during the weekends apart from the regular tuition classes which were carried out by part-time staff. The nature of extra-curricular activities included sports, music, dance, drawing, during the weekends. A good number of the children had attended dance classes (34%), sports (18%), drawing (24%) and music lessons (16%) (Bhuvaneswari, 2017).

5.8.2 Educational Performance of the Children

Education is essential for every child. Only education can bring change in their lives. The findings of Puducherry study disclosed that most of the children were motivated in studies, to perform better in academics as their family's economic condition was extremely poor and through good performance, they wished to become independent, so that they can support their family financially. Some children manifested their interests towards learning new subjects. Some children felt discouraged by their poor academic performance and expressed concern over their subjects such as inability to master certain mathematics. Some of them were found to be upset by poor memory, bullying by peers and friends, prejudice shown by school authorities towards children coming from institutions.

Supportive academic environment, teachers with helping attitudes and good peer relationships created a positive academic ambiance for motivation of some children in studies as stated. According to some of the students,

"Our teachers are helpful" – a 15 year old boy

"Our teachers explain the concept in simple language" – a 13 year old girl

"I like to go to school since I get a chance to teach junior students" – a 15 year old boy

"My classmates are helpful and they share the notes with me if I miss my class" – a 14 year girl

"I enjoy the school since I get a chance to play with other children" – a 12 year old boy

5.8.3 Negative Perception About Institutions in Puducherry

Nevertheless, some children are not happy in the institutions and in schools because of various challenges and they include poor quality food, lack of support from the staff of the institution, lack of encouragement from teachers, individual disinterest in some subjects, strict disciplinary measures, peer bullying, discriminatory attitude of some of the teachers and so on. The following verbatim responses of some of the children are clear illustrations of their negative attitude towards the institution and school:

"Food is not good" – a 12 year old male child

"Some of the staff are not friendly. They scold us for minor mistakes" – a 11 year old girl

"I find maths to be a difficult subject and that is why I am not interested to study the same subject" – a 15 year old boy

"My classmates bully me" – a 12 year old boy

"Some children use abusive words and that is why I do not like to go to school" - a 13 year old boy

"I do not like to study since I am very poor in communication skills" – a 13 year old boy

5.8.4 Perception of Children About Overall Institutional Ambiance

So far as institutional overall environment is concerned, a good number of children expressed their happiness and satisfaction about the institutions with special reference to their relationship with friends and caretakers. They experienced a sense of belongingness, sharing and safety. They also received sufficient food, accepted positive disciplinary measures, spent a lot of time on studies, special coaching, spiritual teaching, extra-curricular training, etc. For instance,

"I have got about 10 good friends in this institution. So I am very happy here" - a 13 year old boy

"My house is nearby. Therefore, my parents visit me every month, so I like to stay here" – a 14 year old boy

"We got good training in the institution about disciplined behavior in addition to learning a lot of skills from the staff" - 14 year old girl

"The location of the institution is good for me" – a 12 year old girl

On the contrary, the rest of the children expressed their dissatisfaction over living in institutional care as they had felt lonely, unhappy, insecure and burdened with bundle of negative emotions. The following verbatim responses reveal that children learn many skills have a conducive environment for getting education, and like to stay in institution:

"I miss my parents" – a 10 year old boy

"I experienced physical abuse for committing a minor mistake" – a 16 year old girl

"I do not have any touch with my biological parents. That causes me a feeling of insecurity in life" – a 12 year old girl

"I am unable to share my feelings with others" – a 11 year old girl

Replying to a question about whether they wish to go back to their own family, most of them expressed their desire to go back to family. The main reason for the same is that they were missing not only their parents but also their childhood friends, relatives and other neighbours. Some of the children also stated that they could perform better in studies had they been with their family members. Psychological distress owing to separation from the family members was clearly reflected in views of some of the children. For example,

"Life could have been much better if I could live with my parents" – a 13 year old girl

"I terribly miss my parents and siblings" – a 15 year old boy

"My mother used to take care of all my needs when I was with her" – a 14 year old girl

"I am unable to share my psychological sufferings with anybody in the institution" – a 11 year old girl

Regarding basic needs of the children, the majority of the children responded that they get adequate food and opined that the quality of it is good. These findings are parallel with the previously documented study by Embleton et al. (2014) where it was pointed that group care homes were more likely to meet the basic needs. The probable reason behind the basic needs of the children being met by the institution could be due to the State Advisory Board as well as the District Advisory Board formed by the Department of Social Welfare in the year 2015, to inspect the different institutions in Union Territory of Puducherry. In addition to the inspection made by the Board, periodical monitoring by the Integrated Child Protection Scheme staff and Child Welfare Committee might have helped to improve the quality of care in institutions in Pondicherry. Despite the satisfaction and happiness in institutions, more than half the children expressed their opinion that they want to stay with the family, especially the female children. The presence of warm, sensitive and responsive care in some of the institutions was noted in the review study by McCall, Groark and Rygaard (2014). The probable reason for the positive response in the current study could be that the children belonging to adolescence and they spent quality time with their peers and related less with the 133 of 185 service providers. Hence, their response regarding their relation with service providers was very casual (with not much thinking).

Finally, it may be concluded that although the overall findings of Puducherry study were positive in terms of quality of care as perceived by most of the children, this may not be the scenario in other institutions across the country.

5.9 Perception of Parents and Guardians About Institutional Care and Support Services

Limited research has been carried out on perception of parents or guardians about the quality of care and support services extended to the children under institutional care, which necessitated to address the issue. Most of the children under institutional care in Puducherry either had both or one parent or at least an extended family member to take care of them. About 150 parents were covered in the Puducherry study and they were covered following their availability during the field visit. Most of the parents were of the view that they are aware of the services related to the children (Bhuvaneswari, 2017). According to most of the parents covered in the study, children are safe in the institutions. Some of them even added that the institution is much safer for protection of children from sexual abuse than their own family or local community. This statement is contradictory to the experience of some of the children living in different institutions in Puducherry. Perhaps children did not share their experience of abuse with their parents or guardians out of feeling of shame or embarrassment.

Also, some parents expressed that the ambience is safer for the boys in the institution so far as their dependence and maladaptive behaviour is concerned. In the community, a large number of adolescent boys become dependent on alcohol, smoking and antisocial activities under peer pressure. Institution also facilitates an academic environment for study by arranging special coaching/guidance for the children after the school hours as remarked by some parents. Therefore, considering the overall circumstance, by and large, parents perceive institution as a safer and better environment for their children's overall welfare and well-being, especially the children who are coming from extreme backward families and children without biological parents.

It is a fact that care and support services for children and their safety in all the institutions are not similar. It depends upon a number of factors like leadership, availability of infrastructure and resources, attitude of the support staff of an institution, proper planning of annual or regular activities, delegation of responsibilities, close monitoring of the regular functioning of the institutions and taking corrective and proactive measures for improving the situation and creating a culture of good human values, and so on. Although some parents were happy with the care and support services available for the children in some institutions, the picture was not similar in other institutions as reported by a number of parents.

However, some parents of children from one particular institution recorded their dissatisfaction about the restricting rules on visits by the family and also about home visits for the children. Some parents told that children wished to go home, to visit their community and spend time with family during holidays and festivals. This is supported by the recent study (Sagar, Patra & Gupta, 2017) that revealed that rare exposure of the children to the outside world, closed environments and absence of open spaces will lead to a feeling of captivity in children.

Lack of awareness about the benefits of different institutional activities among parents caused dissatisfaction among some parents in Puducherry. Some family members are concerned about shelter, food and education. They are not much aware of the other rights meant for the children as outlined in the UNCRC, 1989. Therefore, there is an urgent need to sensitize the parents about the other rights of the children including right to safety so that parents do not indulge in disciplining the children through corporal punishment.

Some parents were found to be indifferent about child welfare and well-being and they visit their children in the institutions. Therefore, parents need to be communicated about the importance of family connectedness for the development of their children, significance of parental love for the child especially for very young children, the dynamic need of parental guidance during adolescence, availability of sponsorship programs for the children through the Integrated Child Protection Scheme (ICPS) wherein the family will receive an amount of Rs. 2000 per month to take care of the children in the family environment till the completion of 18 years.

5.10 Protection of the Rights of Children and Abuse Experienced, as Revealed by Puducherry Study

Along with positive perception about institutional care and support services in Puducherry, there are areas which need immediate attention of the concerned authority, especially about the safety of children. So far as abuse and exploitation is concerned, as discussed before, more than half of the children under institutional care in Puducherry expressed that they experienced abuse either in the form of physical abuse or psychological abuse or both. Psychological abuse in the form of reprimand, use of vulgar words, prejudiced behaviour by the staff for not carrying out day-to-day activities and, for managing challenging behaviours (Bhuvaneswari, 2017). The presence of emotional abuse was in line with the findings by Fitzpatrick et al. (2010) where it was mentioned that post-institutionalized adult survivors of severe emotional abuse had better coping skills than the survivors of physical and sexual abuse. Children had responded that many a times, they get scolded for no fault of their own. Physical abuse prevailed in a majority of the institutions in the form of corporal punishment. The current study reiterated the fact that the use of corporal punishment as a way of handling maladaptive behaviour was common and acceptable in institutions. The findings of the committee by Better Care Network, specific to India, revealed that despite efforts at prohibition of corporal punishment by law, it continues to be widely applied in families and in alternative care systems (Better Care Network, 2014). A Government research report confirms the practice of corporal punishment under institutional care (Kacker, Varadan, & Kumar, 2007) saying 56% of children experienced the same. The same is confirmed by some newspaper reports ("4 lakh in childcare: State NGOs make a killing through donations", 4 lakh in childcare: State NGOs make a killing through donations 2014; "Children make 'damning' statements against persons running the home", 2015; "Horror stories from shelter for runaway kids", 2012; "Teen abused, assaulted in Bangalore govt-run home", 2014). In addition, the consequence of physical abuse also damages the development in children. The profile of post-institutionalized adult survivors of 134 out of 185 physical abused showed that they required more intensive service than emotional abuse survivors (Fitzpatrick et al., 2010). India committed to prohibit corporal punishment in alternative care settings ("South Asia Initiative to End Violence against Children, SAARC Apex Body for Children", 2014) and the punishment for the same is mentioned in Section 82 of JJ Act 2015, particularly for institutional care. Service providers and other stakeholders need to have a massive and intensive training in positive disciplinary techniques which is more important than becoming aware of the law prohibiting corporal punishment. In addition, the earlier study pointed out that the percentage of children experiencing physical abuse could be higher than that of the revealed data and children in the age group of 5–12 years were more vulnerable to physical abuse in institutions (Kacker, Varadan, & Kumar, 2007). A study has shown a decrease in maltreatment by caregivers after restructuring the institution and training the staff in positive caregiving strategies (Hermenau et al., 2011; Nooreyezdan & Mehta, 2016). Children in institutions are those, who were difficult to manage by family members and whose families had very less time or no time for communication and caregiving. Hence, appointing sufficient number of staff in the institution is also a major factor in reducing maltreatment by the service providers, in the pretext of disciplining children. Some children expressed that there is a presence of sexual abuse by the peers and senior children of the same institution, particularly by male children. These findings are in line with the report by Asian Centre for Human Rights (2013) wherein it is documented that the presence of sexual assault in Juvenile Justice Homes in India is prevalent. Despite the presence of difficult situations, children felt safe in the institution and were happy about their stay in institutions. Also, the presence of homosexuality was recorded in the institutions by Mukhopadhyay and Bhalla (2016).

It is believed that a child within 18 years of age cannot commit any crime and even if they commit any offence or crime, they do the same without realizing its consequences. That is why they need behaviour modification in juvenile homes. However, given the increasing involvement of children of upper age groups in heinous crimes, latest legislation in India brought down the upper age limit of children from

18 to 16 years and if any child above 16 years of age is found to be a part of any crime, they will be tried in criminal courts. Therefore, it is important to have some idea about the nature of offences and/or criminal activities committed by children.

5.11 Nature of Offences Committed by Juvenile Delinquents

Consciously or unconsciously, some disadvantaged and/or street children, especially those who are out of school, get involved in socially undesirable activities under the influence of peer group or sub-cultural group members, violent movies and games, extreme poverty, compulsive situation and, a desire to probe their potential before the peer group members. Finally, these acts are termed as delinquent acts as per the law. Analyzing the secondary data, Agarwal (2018) observed an increasing trend of involvement of the juveniles in heinous crimes. Data in Table 5.1 clearly indicate the increasing trend of crimes committed by the children.

Data provided in Table 5.2 highlights the total number of registered cases across India for juveniles under different categories. These figures are shocking and they give a hint to take up the issue seriously and carry out more diagnostic studies to ascertain the factors responsible for committing such serious offences at such young ages. Mental health professionals like Psychiatrists and Psychologists were of the view that easy access to pornographic materials on the internet and WhatsApp are solely responsible, in addition to hormonal changes. Lack of supervision of children's whereabouts, especially the children who become school dropouts, problems in the family, lack of emotional bondage among family members and poor social network are other contributory factors for the same.

With the passage of time, there is a rapid change in the lifestyle of the younger population along with changing social structures and urbanization. Nowadays, the younger population is more home-bound. This often occurs due to parents' feeling of insecurity regarding their child's safety. Some parents do not allow their children to go

Table 5.1 Cases registered against Juvenile in conflict with law and crime rate under IPC during 2015–2016

Year	Registered cases against Juveniles in conflict with law	Under total cognizable IPC crimes	Percentage cases of Juvenile in conflict with law to total cognizable crimes
2011	25,125	2,325,575	1.1
2012	27,936	2,387,188	1.2
2013	31,725	2,647,722	1.2
2014	33,526	2,851,563	1.2
2015	31,396	2,949,499	1.1

Table 5.2 Cases registered in India against Juvenile in conflict with law under different crime heads of IPC during 2015

S. No.	Type of crime	No.
1.	Murder (Section 302 IPC)	853
2.	Attempt to commit murder (Section 307 of IPC)	980
3.	Culpable Homicide not amounting to murder (Section 304 IPC)	36
4.	Attempt to commit Culpable Homicide (Section 308 IPC)	60
5.	Rape (Section 376 IPC)	16,988
6.	Kidnapping and abduction	1630
7.	Dacoity	193
8.	Robbery (Section 392 To 394, 397 And 398 IPC)	1358
9.	Criminal Trespass/Burglary (Section 457 to 460 IPC) (Total)	2605

to the field for playing with the neighbour's children and sometime, non-availability of open field for games and sports also contribute. The consequences of less outdoor activities are active involvement in playing games on mobiles and on the TV. Most of the games which children usually like are violent in nature, which instills violence as normal in the young minds, in addition to developing aggressive attitude among them. For minor issues, sometimes they argue with their parents and/or fight with other children. Some parents overlook the engagement of children in mobile and TV games as they are busy, resulting in the development of compulsive behaviour among children, that is, they feel restless if they are unable to play the game one day. Engagement in video and mobile games has a detrimental effect on their studies.

Data provided in Table 5.3 are alarming when we look at the nature of heinous crimes committed by a good number of young children. For example, in 2015, 1092 children were involved in murder. Out of them, 13 were below 12 years of age while 283 were aged between 12 and 16 years. A total of 1841 children were charged for rape. Among them, 14 were below 12 years while 490 and 1337 belonged to 12–16 years and 16–18 years of age group respectively. Likewise, 1508 were involved in kidnapping and abduction.

5.12 Causes Behind Juvenile Delinquency

Various psychosocial, cultural and biological factors are responsible for juvenile delinquency. More specifically, they include:

1. **Poverty**: Poverty is one of the root causes behind juvenile delinquency. A larger number of parents, living below the poverty line, are unable to provide education to their children. Instead, they prefer to engage their children in some economic activities for survival. A good number of them have never been to school or became school dropouts and loiter most of the time and thus become vulnerable to

Table 5.3 Juveniles apprehended under IPC and SLL crimes by age groups and sex during 2015

S. No.	Nature of crime	Below 12 years	12-16 years	16 to 18 years	Total
1.	Murder (Sec. 302 IPC)	13	283	796	1092
2.	Attempt to commit murder (Sec. 307 IPC)	10	342	1008	1360
3.	Rape (Sec. 376 IPC)	14	490	1337	1841
4.	Kidnapping and Abduction	11	288	1209	1508
5.	Dacoity	0	45	256	301
6.	Robbery (Sec. 392 to 394, 397 and 398 IPC)	22	431	1385	1838
7.	Criminal trespass/burglary (Sec. 457 to 460 IPC) (Total)	81	1288	2263	3632

exploitation and abuse. Sometimes they are used by different criminal groups for their vested interests and engage them in unlawful activities like pickpocketing, smuggling and so on.

2. **Dysfunctional Family Environment and/or Family Violence**: A healthy and happy family environment is prerequisite for a child's healthy emotional, social, physical and personal development. A child feels insecure if the family environment is hostile and/or tensed. Unhealthy family environment is discouraging for children's concentration in studies. Parents from those families fail to discharge their duties towards proper child upbringing. As a result, children from those families gradually get attracted to sub-cultural groups and get involved in socially undesirable activities with or without knowledge.
3. **Peer Group Influence**: During childhood and adolescence, peer group influence is very strong. Every child wishes to get recognition to peer group members for their strengths and some specialties of their personality or quality. Peer group influence become more dominating when interpersonal relationship with parents and siblings are not strong. Some children are benefitted by positive peer group influence while some get involved in antisocial activities.
4. **Out of School**: Children and adolescents, who discontinue education, remain idle and loiter in the community without any specific purpose or activities. While loitering, they draw attention of the bad company and fall in their trap and gradually get misguided in life.
5. **Situational Affairs**: Adversities in life indulge some children to become a part of criminal groups for earning quick money. Adversities include child sexual abuse, physical or verbal abuse, sudden death of main earning members in the family, family violence, alcoholism and so on.

6. **Role of Internet and Mobile**: Easy access to adult sites, violent movies and computer games instigate some children to experiment the same in reality. Excessive uses of mobiles and internet are primarily responsible for hostile behaviour among some children.
7. **Psychological Characteristics of an Individual**: An individual with low-stress tolerance capacity, poor locus of control, poor self-concept, cognitive distortion, mental disorders and substance dependence are more at risk of getting involved in socially undesirable activities. For example, there exists a strong link between psychological condition of the youth and delinquent tendencies. A study of female inmates in Bangladesh showed "very high incidence of psychiatric disorder among the offenders of a Female Juvenile Center" (Maruf et al., 2015). These offenders also found to be dependent on substance abuse.
8. **Social and Cultural Factors**: When a child is living in a locality where a large number of people are engaged in unlawful activities, from childhood, he/she has been observing the same activities and gradually a child start accepting these activities as a normal phenomenon for survival. As a result, the child also becomes a part of the same society and does similar activities. In this regard, Brandt (2006) discussed the role of the social and psychological factors behind delinquent activities of children in a society like India. He argued that social environment has a significant impact on deviant behaviour of a child. Further, Chung and Lawrence (2006) remarked that when the neighbourhood ties are weak, children become more vulnerable to delinquent tendencies. Weak neighbourhood and ineffective parenting make some children highly vulnerable to antisocial activities.
9. **Biological Factors**: So far as biological factors are concerned, any individual is influenced by their biological as well as genetic makeup. Further, the hormonal changes in the body of the juveniles make them more impulsive and rebellious, resulting in involvement in socially undesirable activities under the slightest influence of peer group members. Finally, a combination of social, psychological, cultural and biological factors plays an important role and/or creates a situation for committing crimes/offences by children and adolescents.

5.13 Behaviour Modification of Juvenile Delinquents

The broad objective of behaviour modification, a psychological technique, is to change a particular behaviour or reaction. In other words, it is a method to replace undesirable behaviours with more desirable ones through positive or negative reinforcement. It is basically based on the concept of conditioning which is a kind of learning. Conditioning may be categorized into two groups viz., classical conditioning and operant conditioning. Classical conditioning depends on a particular stimulus or signal. An example of this would be a family member visiting a religious place every day when the morning bell is heard. Operant conditioning is another type, which involves using a system of rewards and/or punishments.

Different methods of behaviour modification are (i) Positive reinforcement; (ii) Negative reinforcement; (iii) Punishment; (iv) Flooding; (v) Systematic desensitization; (vi) Aversion therapy; and (vii) Extinction.

Numerous studies have been conducted on behaviour modification of juvenile delinquents. Findings of some of the studies are discussed in this section. Evidence suggests that "cognitive behavioural therapy reduces recidivism in both juveniles and adults" (Landenberger & Lipsey, 2005). The therapy assumes that people can have control over their emotions and behaviour through self-consciousness and then make positive changes in their thoughts which translate into positive behaviour. Research has unearthed the fact that "in most cognitive behavioural therapy programs, offenders improve their social skills and thinking becomes more rational, which facilitates self-control, impulse management and self-efficacy."

In a meta-analysis study covering findings of 548 studies carried out during 1958–2002, Lipsey examined the effectiveness of various approaches to intervention with young offenders (Lipsey 2009). All these studies were related to intervention policies, practices and programs for behaviour modification of offenders. After reviewing the findings of all these studies, Lipsey grouped evaluations into seven categories viz., counseling, deterrence, discipline, multiple coordinated services, restorative programs, skill-building and surveillance. Lipsey observed that "the interventions which were based on punishment and deterrence appeared to increase criminal recidivism." He also noticed that "therapeutic approaches based on counseling, skill-building and multiple services had the greatest impact in reducing any further criminal behavior." In another meta-analysis study, Landenberger and Lipsey (2005) noticed that "programs based on cognitive behavioural therapy are effective with juvenile and adult criminal offenders in various criminal justice settings, including prison, residential locales, community probation and parole".

In a single case study based research by Lasher, Webb, Stinson and Cantrell (2017) social anxiety of the offender was addressed through individualized treatment approach following rational emotive behaviour therapy and time-limited dynamic psychotherapy. The findings disclosed "an increased understanding of his anxiety and improved mental health in his social interactions, both in the context of treatment groups and with female staff, and was willing to continue follow-up care in the community indicating supportive evidence for individualized treatment of incarcerated offenders as opposed to exclusively utilizing manualized psycho-educational interventions".

Further evidence suggests the benefits of family-based treatments for behaviour modification of serious juvenile offenders. However, evidence concerning benefits of these treatments in case of the youths is scanty. Keeping this limitation in mind, Dopp, Borduin, White and Kuppens (2017) performed a meta-analysis to summarize the findings of the research on family-based treatments for serious juvenile offenders. The results disclosed that "across studies, family-based treatments produced modestly, yet long-lasting, treatment effects, relative to comparison conditions".

Juvenile offenders with mental health challenges need special attention from professionals for improving their mental health status, so that they do not indulge themselves in the similar offence again and again. Underwood and Washington (2016) indicated that "interrelated problems of youth for being involved in deviant activities need a dynamic system of care that extends beyond mere treatment within the juvenile justice system".

Other than behaviour modification of juvenile delinquents, a number of other measures need to be adopted and they include the following:

- Sensitizing the parents about their roles and responsibilities in upbringing of the children with quality care and listening to their voices and giving them quality time.
- Improving resilience capacity of children through school-based orientation program.
- Sensitizing school teachers to teach in a child-friendly manner and not to resort to physical punishment and humiliating children for minor mistakes.
- Encouraging students for better academic performance.
- Extending individual, family and group counselling to parents and their children as situation demands.

5.14 Measures Taken by International Agencies for Protection of Child Rights

5.14.1 The United Nations Convention on the Rights of Children (UNCRC, 1989)

The United Nations Convention on the Rights of Children, formulated in 1989 and ratified by the Government of India, has around 52 articles focusing on the survival, development, protection and participation of every child all around the world. Article 3, 4, 5, 12, 13, 14, 16, 17, 18, 19, 20, 21, 26, 27 and 30 of UNCRC lay importance on strengthening family care both directly and indirectly.

5.14.2 The UN Guidelines for the Alternative Care of Children

The guidelines for the Alternative Care was formulated by the United Nations in the year 2009 as the UNCRC emphasized on children to be reared in family and placed the responsibility of upbringing on parents and family members. Alternative Care, whether beneficial or not so beneficial, takes a child away from family and his/her parent.

The UN Guidelines for the alternative care of children, which is based on UNCRC, has two main core principles—the necessity principle and the suitability or appropriateness principle.

The principle of necessity states only in case of compulsion, children should be placed in alternative care for best interest of the child while the necessity principle focuses on improving existing living condition of a child for ensuring improved quality of life.

The principle of appropriateness talks about suitability of a place for proper care and upbringing of a child from the point of view of availability of basic facilities as well as contact with parents and specific needs of a child.

5.14.3 UN Guidelines for the Alternative Care of Children on Family-Based Care Includes

- "The family being the fundamental group of society and the natural environment for the growth, well-being and protection of children, efforts should primarily be directed to enabling the child to remain in or return to the care of his/her parents, or when appropriate, other close family members" (Paragraph 3).
- "Removal of a child from the care of the family should be seen as a measure of last resort and should, whenever possible, be temporary and for the shortest possible duration" (Paragraph 14).
- "The use of residential care should be limited to cases where such a setting is specifically appropriate, necessary and constructive for the individual child concerned and in his/her best interests" (Paragraph 21).
- "While recognizing that residential care facilities and family-based care complement each other in meeting the needs of children, where large residential care facilities (institutions) remain, alternatives should be developed in the context of an overall deinstitutionalization strategy, with precise goals and objectives, which will allow for their progressive elimination" (Paragraph 23).

5.14.4 UN Guidelines for the Alternative Care of Children on Residential Care Include

- "Facilities providing residential care should be small and be organized around the rights and needs of the child, in a setting as close as possible to a family or small group situation. Their objective should generally be to provide temporary care and to contribute actively to the child's family re-integration or, if this is not possible, to secure his/her stable care in an alternative family setting, including through adoption or kafala of Islamic law, where appropriate" (Paragraph 123).
- "Measures should be taken so that, where necessary and appropriate, a child solely in need of protection and alternative care may be accommodated separately from children who are subject to the criminal justice system" (Paragraph 124).

- "The competent national or local authority should establish rigorous screening procedures to ensure that only appropriate admissions to such facilities are made" (Paragraph 125).
- "States should ensure that there are sufficient caregivers in residential care settings to allow individualized attention and to give the child, where appropriate, the opportunity to bond with a specific career. Caregivers should also be deployed within the care setting in such a way as to implement effectively its aims and objectives and ensure child protection" (Paragraph 126).
- "Laws, policies and regulations should prohibit the recruitment and solicitation of children for placement in residential care by agencies, facilities or individuals" (Paragraph 127).

5.15 Social Measures Taken by the Government of India for Child Welfare

5.15.1 The National Policy for Children 1974, 2013

The National Policy for Children 1974 had given much importance to family for optimal growth of children and society has to support the family.

The Government of India reframed the policy and the new National Policy for Children in 2013 affirmed the government's commitment to the right-based approach in addressing the dynamic needs and challenges of children. The policy made survival, health, nutrition, development, education, protection and participation as the undeniable rights of every child as well as providing it the highest priority.

Reaffirmation in the policy includes—protection of all rights of children in terms of growing a peaceful and happy family environment with parental love and affection and quality care.

5.15.2 Integrated Child Protection Scheme (ICPS)

ICPS is a centrally sponsored scheme introduced in 2009 for care and protection of children under Ministry of Women and Child Development. One of the major objectives is to strengthen child protection at family and community level. The guiding principles of ICPS include child protection and safety of children for which parents are primarily responsible, followed by government, civil society and local community. In addition, children should not experience any discrimination and enjoy equality in all respect so that they can grow with quality education, dignity and skills.

Following are the care, support and rehabilitation services by ICPS

- Emergency Outreach Services;
- Open Shelters;
- Family-based non-Institutional Care through Sponsorship, Foster Care, Adoption and Aftercare;
- Institutional Services;
- General Grant in Aid.

Need for Child Welfare

As the growth and development of child is affected, irrespective of the severity of the consequence, it gets reflected in the society, both during the childhood as well as when the child grows into an adult. When deprived of care and protection from the family or community, the child may succumb to physical illness or psychological disturbance, which in turn, makes the child vulnerable to exploitation and maltreatment. When the child grows into an adult, long-term consequences are again reflected in the family and in society - they either maltreat the family members or get involved in antisocial activities. This complicated unhealthy vicious circle needs to be modified as healthy circles. Hence, fulfilling the need of the child is vital, for breaking the circle. The greater need for mental health policy is the needs of children and the service for them are noted in countries with higher population of children in the world (WHO, 2005).

Institutional Care became a major pathway for welfare of very young children as well as adolescents, as family disorganization gradually amplified due to various factors ranging from individual's incapacity to war in the nation.

5.16 Conclusion and Implications

Although a larger number of children across countries are benefitted by the institutions for their overall growth and development, there is a need to improve the quality of services by appointing more qualified and training manpower for implementing the care and support services effectively. There is also a need to establish more number of institutions for accommodating all the children in need of care and protection, especially the children who are abandoned by their parents and have no place to stay. Mental health needs of the children require special attention from the professional psychologists for which every institution should appoint at least one professional and trained psychologist. Mental health support services, along with guidance for study, will give confidence to the children to perform better in academics. Vocational training programs should be arranged on such areas which has a job prospect or where the skill would help the children to earn money and lead a life with dignity.

For strengthening institutional care in developing countries like India, the Government should allocate more funds towards this end and develop appropriate mechanisms for periodic monitoring and evaluation of services rendered to the children.

Close monitoring of the functioning of the institutions can ensure safety and quality care and support services. In this regard, cooperation from the available parents and the larger society and corporate sections are essential. In case of shortage of funds, those institutions can think of approaching the corporate bodies for funding under corporate social responsibility. Neglecting institutions, where poor and orphan children reside, would result in non-utilization of human resources and violation of their fundamental rights.

Strengthening institutional care has many implications. First, rendering justice to all disadvantaged children as an obligation of any nation. Second, quality care and education to disadvantaged children will contribute to national growth and development in the long run. Third, crime rate will go down. When a disadvantaged child will get the opportunity for education and basic facilities, they will not indulge in socially undesirable activities for survival.

5.17 Ensuring Quality Care in the Institutions

- An institution governing board should comprise of an educationist, a doctor, a legal professional, a social activist and local public representatives who can contribute in any possible manner for effective functioning of the institution. There should be a clear vision and mission of the institution along with good infrastructure. Effort should be made to develop networks with other allied organizations for referral and support as and when required. Close network with relevant government departments and international welfare organizations should be developed and their suggestions should be sought.
- Appointing staff at all levels based on their skills, aptitude and interest in taking care of the children. In this regard, house mothers could be widows or a woman without a child.
- Ensuring safety for all the children by installing CCTV cameras in different places of the institution.
- Ensuring that all the institutions are registered and followed all the government regulations.
- An institution should have adequate space for games and sports and group activities, including space for gardening and agriculture where children could be engaged.
- Every institution should have a qualified doctor on a regular basis or as a part-time basis, one professional psychologist, qualified teachers with maths and science as subjects, trained social workers and staff for vocational training and other support staff.
- There should be a system of periodic review meeting among all the staff to discuss about issues and challenges and find out the solutions.
- Emphasis should be given on value education, hygiene sense and character building.

- Special workshop should be organized for the children on life skills, child rights, health and hygiene, mental health, stress management and so on.
- Children should be engaged in different cultural, sports and group activities in which all the children should be encouraged for participation and their performance should be appreciated.
- Making every effort for generating funds for running all the programs. In this regard, a goodwill ambassador may be appointed.
- An institution should also make an effort to tap experienced human resources from the neighbouring community for running all the programs. For example, retired teachers could be approached for teaching the children.
- Sensitization program should be organized for all the service providers to ensure child-friendly environment in the institution instead of abusing them physically and psychologically for doing minor mistakes. Safety of the children from all forms of abuse and neglect should be ensured. In this regard, latest legislative measures like The Protection of Children from Sexual Offences Act, 2012 and the Juvenile Justice (Care and Protection) Act (2015) should be referred. These laws clearly defined the punishment for abusing children in different forms. Children should be trained properly for formation of good behaviour and continuous reinforcement in this regard will be beneficial.
- Recent study in Puducherry disclosed that about half of the children were facing mental health challenges and/or behaviour difficulties. Therefore, there is an urgent need to recruit trained psychologists for mental health screening and support services as per need, that is, individual counselling, group therapy, play therapy and family counselling.
- Special effort to be taken to appoint part-time teachers for children for guiding them in some subjects like English, Maths and Science for further improvement of academic performance.
- There is a need to arrange vocational training programs for some children who are not good in studies and have discontinued regular education.
- For improvement of overall quality of services in the institutions, there is a need to arrange periodic training and/or manpower development training for the service providers and administers.
- Aftercare program and follow-up of the adolescents who leave the institution after the age of 18 years would be beneficial to maintain records concerning their status and if possible, support could be extended for getting any job.
- There is a need for organizing awareness programs on Child Rights for all Stakeholders of the institutions, including Children.

5.18 Recommendations for Government Prior to Issuing License and Periodic Monitoring and Evaluation

Based on secondary data, a number of steps are recommended for ensuring the best interest of the children under institutional care. The recommendations include

- Ensuring basic infrastructural facilities for the children so that they can leave without any difficulty, prior to giving approval to any non-government welfare organization.
- Ensuring overall safety measures for all the children in institution.
- Ensuring minimum manpower for running the institution smoothly. Manpower is needed in administrative, teaching staff, vocational trainers, health professionals (doctors and psychologist or counsellor), support and security staff.
- Periodic visit of the institutions by the respective government social welfare staff for monitoring of the activities of the institution and providing feedback from time to time for improving the quality of care and support services.
- The Government should carry out evaluation study of the institutions from time to time so that need-based feedback could be offered.
- Inspection report should be the basis prior to renewal of license.

5.19 Recommendations for Parents

Parents and guardians should be sensitized to visit their children under institutional care periodically. Periodic meeting with parents and siblings will be beneficial for mental health needs of the children, that is, emotionally they will feel better and in turn they would be able to concentrate in studies. Apart from this, their interpersonal relationship with other children and service providers would be better because of emotional stability.

5.20 General Recommendations

- It is also important to monitor the functioning of Observation Homes and Shelter Homes.
- Community participation and sensitization in matters related to juvenile delinquency is important. Sensitization of community members about the issue of neglected children and children in distressed conditions will help to draw attention of childline for rescue and rehabilitation of these children.

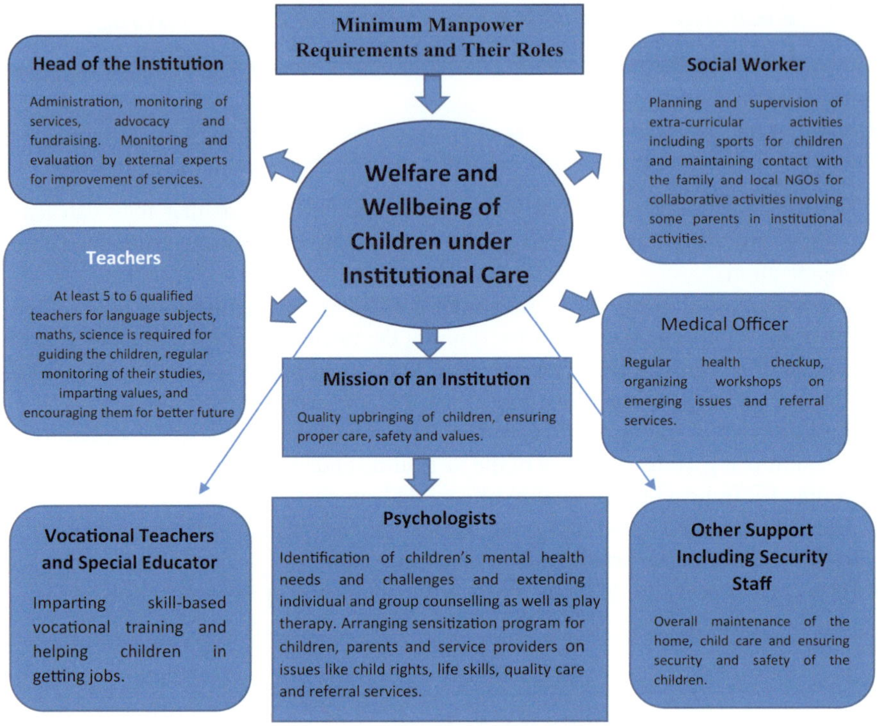

Model 5.1 A conceptual model for an effective institution

5.21 Proposed Conceptual Model for Child Care and Safe Protection of Children in the Institution

Based on the field-based evidence, a conceptual model of better care and support services to the children under institutional care has been proposed (Model 5.1).

5.22 Proposed Conceptual Model for Prevention, Intervention and Rehabilitation of Juvenile Delinquents

A conceptual model has been proposed to ensure welfare and well-being of every child in the society. A number of measures have been proposed for prevention of juvenile delinquency based on the first-hand field experience of the first author while working with disadvantaged children. Further guidelines for the children who are already engaged in deviant social activities have been proposed. Until there is occupational rehabilitation, there is every possibility that a child may go back to his/her

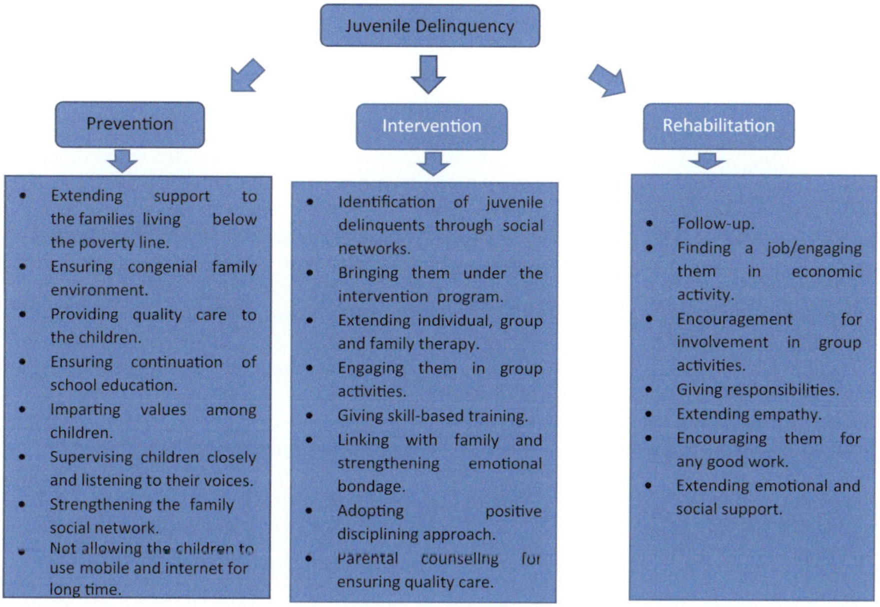

Model 5.2 A conceptual model for prevention, intervention and rehabilitation of juvenile delinquents

previous activities. Therefore, a number of measures are suggested for meaningful rehabilitation of juvenile delinquents (Model 5.2).

References

Abou-Khadra, M. (2012). Sleep of children living in institutional care facilities. *Sleep Breath, 16*(3), 887–894. https://doi.org/10.1007/s11325-011-0592-z.

Agarwal, D. (2018). Juvenile delinquency in India—Latest trends and entailing amendments in Juvenile Justice Act. *People: International Journal of Social Sciences, 3*(3), 1365–1383.

Asian Centre for Human Rights. (2013). *India's hell holes: Child sexual assault in juvenile justice homes*. Asian Centre for Human Rights.

Ayaz, M., Ayaz, A., Basgul, S., Karakaya, I., Sismanlar, S. G., Yar, A., et al. (2012). Prevelance of mental disorders and associated factors in institutionalized 3–5 year old children. *Turkish Journal of Psychiatry, 23*(2), 82–88.

Berridge, D., Blehal, N., & Henry, L. (2012). *Living in children's residential homes*. (No. DFE-RR201). Department for Education, UK.

Better Care Network. (2014). *Country care review: India*. Retrieved from http://tbinternet.ohchr.org/_layouts/treatybodyexternal/Download.aspx.

Bos, K. J., Zeanah, C. H., Smyke, A. T., Fox, N. A., & Nelson, C. A. (2010). Stereotypies in children with a history of early institutional care. *Archives of Pediatrics and Adolescent Medicine, 164*(5), 406–411.

Boy rescued from street says he was beaten by caretaker. (2015, February 2). *The Times of India*, p. 3.
Boy found murdered at rescue home, sodomy suspected. (2015, January 24). *The Times of India*, p. 9.
Bowlby, J. (1952). *Maternal care and mental health*. Geneva: World Health Organization.
Bhuvaneswari, K. (2017). *Mental health of children under institutional care: An empirical investigation.* Thesis submitted to Pondicherry University in partial fulfillment of the requirement for the Award of the Degree of Doctor of Philosophy.
Brandt, D. (2006). *Delinquency, development, and social policy*. London: Yale University Press.
Child rescued from unlicensed home, fourth in 3 days. (2015, June 25). *The Times of India*, p. 3.
Child Welfare panels fail, abuse continues at homes. (2014, August 28). *The Times of India*, p. 5.
Children make "damning" statements against persons running the home. (2015, November 29). *The Hindu*, p. 7.
Chung, Le Hen, & Lawrence, S. (2006). Relations between neighborhood factors, parenting behavior, peer deviance and delinquency among juvenile offenders. *Development Psychology, 42*(2), 319–331. https://doi.org/10.1037/0012-1649.42.2.319.
Crime in India Reports (2005–2015). Ministry of Home Affairs, Government of India.
CRY. (2005). The Right to a home and a family… a dream. For India's Most Invisible Children. Retrieved November 12, 2015, from http://www.cry.org/projects/storiesofhopeq.html.
Database on Orphanages under Women's and Children's Institutions (Licensing) Act, 1956. (n.d.). NIPCCD—A Compilation.
Dopp, A. R., Borduin, C. M., White, I. I., Mark, H., & Kuppens, S. (2017). Family-based treatments for serious juvenile offenders: A multilevel meta-analysis. *Journal of Consulting and Clinical Psychology, 85*(4), 335.
Embleton, L., Ayuku, D., Kamanda, A., Atwoli, L., Ayaya, S., & Vreeman, R. (2014). Models of care for orphaned and separated children and upholding children's rights: Cross-sectional evidence from western Kenya. *BMC International Health and Human Rights, 14*(9), 1–18.
Escueta, M., Whetten, K., Ostermann, J., O'Donnell, K., & POFO. (2014). Adverse childhood experiences, psychosocial wellbeing and cognitive development among orphan and abandoned children in five low income countries. *BMC International Health and Human Rights, 14*(6), 1–13.
Euser, S., Alink, L., Tharner, A., IJzendoorn, M., & Bakermans-Kranenburg, M. (2013). The prevalence of child sexual abuse in out-of-home care: A comparison between abuse in Residential and in Foster Care. *Child Maltreatment, 18*(4), 221–231.
Fischer, S., Dölitzsch, C., Schmeck, K., Fegert, J. M., & Schmid, M. (2016). Interpersonal trauma and associated psychopathology in girls and boys living in residential care. *Children and Youth Services Review, 67,* 203–211. https://doi.org/10.1016/j.childyouth.2016.06.013.
Fitzpatrick, M., Carr, A., Dooley, B., Flanagan-Howard, R., Flanagan, E., Tierney, K., et al. (2010). Profiles of adult survivors of severe sexual, physical and emotional institutional abuse in Ireland. *Child Abuse Review, 19*(6), 387–404. https://doi.org/10.1002/car.1083.
Gearing, R., MacKenzie, M., Schwalbe, C., Brewer, K., & Ibrahim, R. (2013). Prevalence of mental health and behavioral problems among adolescents in institutional care in Jordan. *Psychiatric Services, 64*(2), 196–200.
Gleason, M. M., Fox, N. A., Drury, S. S., Smyka, A. T., Nelson, C. A., & Zeanah, C. H. (2014). Indiscriminate behaviors in previously institutionalized young children. *Pediatrics, 133*(3), e657–e665.
Hermenau, K., Hecker, T., Elbert, T., & Ruf-Leuschner, M. (2014). Maltreatment and mental health in institutional care—Comparing early and late institutionalized children in Tanzania. *Infant Mental Health Journal, 35*(2), 102–110. https://doi.org/10.1002/imhj.21440.
Hermenau, K., Hecker, T., Ruf, M., Schauer, E., Elbert, T., & Schauer, M. (2011). Childhood adversity, mental ill-health and aggressive behavior in an African orphanage: Changes in response to trauma focused therapy and the implementation of a new instructional system in. *Child and Adolescent Psychiatry and Mental Health, 5*(29), 1–9.

Hindustan Times, New Delhi (2019, January 17). *CBI registers cases against 2 more shelter homes in Bihar for abuse of minors.*

Horror stories from shelter for runaway kids. (2012, July 3). *The Times of India*, p. 3.

Jiménez-Morago, J. M., León, E., & Román, M. (2015). Adversity and adjustment in children in Institutions, Family Foster Care, and Adoption. *The Spanish Journal of Psychology, 18*. https://doi.org/10.1017/sjp.2015.49.

Kacker, L., Varadan, S., & Kumar, P. (2007). Study on child abuse: INDIA 2007. Ministry of Women and Child Development, Government of India. Erişim Adresi: http://www.unodc.org/pdf/india/publications/htvs_miniweb/childabuse_.

Kumsta, R., Kreppner, J., Rutter, M., Beckett, C., Castle, J., Stevens, S., et al. (2010). Deprivation specific psychological patterns. *Monographs of the Society for Research in Child Development, 75,* 48–78.

Lasher, M. P., Webb, J. R., Stinson, J. D., & Cantrell, P. J. (2017). Addressing social anxiety concurrently with prison-based sex offender treatment: A case of individual needs in an era of manualized treatment. *Journal of Correctional Health Care, 23*(3), 271–282.

Landenberger, N. A., & Lipsey, M. W. (2005). The positive effects of cognitive–behavioral programs for offenders: A meta-analysis of factors associated with effective treatment. *Journal of Experimental Criminology, 1*(4), 451–476.

Lipsey, M. W. (2009). The primary factors that characterize effective interventions with juvenile offenders: A meta-analytic overview. *Victims and Offenders, 4*(2), 124–147.

Loman, M. M., Johnson, A. E., Quevedo, K., Lafavor, T. L., & Gunnar, M. R. (2014). Risktaking and sensation-seeking propensity in post institutionalized early adolescents. *Journal of Child Psychology and Psychiatry, 55*(10), 1145–1152. https://doi.org/10.1111/jcpp.12208.

Loman, M. M., Johnson, A. E., Westerlund, A., Pollak, S. D., Nelson, C. A., & Gunnar, M. R. (2013). The effect of early deprivation on executive attention in middle childhood: Early deprivation and executive attention. *Journal of Child Psychology and Psychiatry, 54*(1), 37–45. https://doi.org/10.1111/j.1469-7610.2012.02602.x.

Maruf, M. M., Rahman, F., Khan, M. Z. R., & Jahan, N. (2015). Socio-demography, substance abuse and offence among inmates with psychiatric disorders in female juvenile centre, Bangladesh. *People: International Journal of Social Sciences, 1*(1).

McCall, R. B. (2012). The development and care of institutionally reared children. *Child Development Perspectives, 6*(2), 174–180.

McCall, R. B. (2013). The consequences of early institutionalization: Can institutions be improved? Should they? *Child and Adolescent Mental Health, 18*(4), 193–201. https://doi.org/10.1111/camh.12025.

McCall, R. B., Groark, C. J., & Rygaard, N. P. (2014). Research, practice, and policy issues on the care of infants and young children are at risk: The articles in context. *Infant Mental Health Journal, 35*(2), 87–93.

Merz, E. C., & McCall, R. B. (2010). Behavior problems in children adopted from psychosocially depriving institutions. *Journal of Abnormal Child Psychology, 38*(4), 459–470. https://doi.org/10.1007/s10802-009-9383-4.

Muhamedrahimov, R. J. (1999). New attitudes: Infant care facilities in St. Petersburg, Russia. In: J. D. Osofsky, H. E. Fitzgerald (Eds.), *WAIMH Handbook of infant mental health. Vol. 1. Perspectives on infant mental health* (pp. 245–294). New York: Wiley.

Muhamedrahimov, R. J., Agarkova, V. V., Vershinia, E. A., Palmov, O. I., Nikiforova, N., McCall, R. B., et al. (2014). Behavior problems in children transferred from a socio-emotionally depriving institution to families in St Petersburg, Russian Federation. *Infant Mental Health Journal, 35*(2), 111–122.

Mukhopadhyay, T., & Bhalla, V. (2016). Case study on compliance of juvenile justice (care and protection of children) rules, 2007 by juvenile institutions in Kolkata. *Institutionalized Children Explorations and Beyond, 3*(1), 29. https://doi.org/10.5958/2349-3011.2016.00003.7.

Nari Niketan rape case: Ex-staff held. (2015, December 14). *The Times of India*, p. 8.

Nelson, C. A. (2007). A neurobiological perspective on early human deprivation. *Child Development Perspectives, 1,* 13–18. https://doi.org/10.1111/j.1750-8606.2007.00004.x.

Nooreyezdan, M., & Mehta, D. (2016). Need for legal aid: Reflections on child welfare committees. *Institutionalized Children Explorations and Beyond, 3*(1), 46. https://doi.org/10.5958/2349-3011.2016.00004.9.

Officials' ignorance adds to children's woes. (2015, November 29). *The Hindu*, p. 7.

Oriol, X., Sala-Roca, J., & Filella, G. (2014). Emotional competences of adolescents in residential care: Analysis of emotional difficulties for intervention. *Children and Youth Services Review, 44,* 334–340.

Padmaja, G., Sushma, B., & Agarwal, S. (2014). Psychosocial problems and wellbeing in institutionalized and non-institutionalized children. *Journal of Humanities and Social Science, 19*(10), 59–64.

Palacios, J., Moreno, C., & Roman, M. (2013). Social competence in internationally adopted and institutionalized children. *Early Childhood Research Quarterly, 28*(2), 357–365. https://doi.org/10.1016/j.ecresq.2012.08.003.

Parwon, S. T. (2006). Orphanage Assessment Report Submitted to Hon. Vivian J. Cherue, Deputy Minister for Social Welfare, Ministry of Health and Social Welfare.

Private children's homes aided by corrupt system. (2014, August 25). The Times of India, p. 6.

Provence, S., & Lipton, R. C. (1962). *Infants in institutions*. Oxford: International University Press.

Sairam, R. (2014, June 13). Two minor girls raped at knifepoint. *The Hindu*. Pollachi. Retrieved from http://www.thehindu.com/todays-paper/tpnational/tp-tamilnadu/two-minor-girls-raped-at-knifepoint/article6109593.ece.

Smyke, A. T., Koga, S. F., Johnson, D. E., Fox, N. A., Marshal, P. J., Nelson, C. A., et al. (2007). The caregiving context in institution-reared and family-reared infants and toddlers in Romania. *Journal of Child Psychology and Psychiatry, 48,* 210–218. https://doi.org/10.1111/j.1469-7610.2006.01694.x.

Save the Children. (2014). Institutional care: The last resort policy brief. Retrieved from http://www.thinkchildsafe.org/thinkbeforedonating/wpcontent/uploads/Institutional-Care-The-Last-Resort-Save-The-Children.pdf.

Sagar, R., Patra, B. N., & Gupta, P. (2017). *Gap analysis in mental health care services in child care institutions: A Delhi-based study*. NCPCR. Retrieved from http://ncpcr.gov.in/showfile.php?lang=1&level=2&&sublinkid=949&lid=1283.

Sood, S., Bakhshi, A., & Devi, P. (2012). An assessment of perceived stress, resilience and mental health of adolescents living in border areas. *International Journal of Scientific and Research Publications, 3,* 176–179.

South Asia Initiative to End Violence against Children | SAARC Apex Body for Children. (2014). Retrieved December 1, 2016, from http://www.saievac.org.

Stellern, S., Esposito, E., Mliner, S., Pears, K., & Gunnar, M. (2014). Increased freezing and decreased positive affect in post institutionalized children. *Journal of Child Psychology and Psychiatry, 55*(1), 88–95.

Teen abused, assaulted in Bangalore govt-run home. (2014, August 23). *The Times of India*, p. 8.

The Juvenile Justice (Care & Protection) Act. (2015). *The juvenile justice care and protection of children act, 2015*. Ministry of Law and Justice, Government of India. Retrieved from http://www.indiacode.nic.in/acts-in-pdf/2016/201602.pdf.

The National Policy for Children, 2013. (2013). *Government of India, National Policy on Children*. New Delhi: Ministry of Women and Child Development.

The Pastor at the home loved to torture them. (2014, August 28). *The Times of India*, p. 5.

The St. Petersburg. (2008). USA Orphanage Research Team. The effects of early social emotional and relationship experience on the development of young orphanage children. *Monographs of the Society for Research in Child Development, 73,* 1–262.

UNCRC. (1989). *United Nations Convention on the Rights of the Child*. Geneva: High Commissioner for Human Rights.

Underwood, L., & Washington, A. (2016). Mental illness and juvenile offenders. *International Journal of Environmental Research and Public Health, 13*(2), 228.
van IJzendoorn, M. H., Palacios, J., Sonuga-Barke, E. J. S., Gunnar, M. R., Vorria, P., McCall, R. B., & Juffer, F. (2011). Children in Institutional Care: Delayed development and resilience. *Monographs of the Society for Research in Child Development, 76*(4), 8–30. https://doi.org/10.1111/j.1540-5834.2011.00626.x.
van IJzendoorn, M. H., Schuengel, C., &Bakermans-Kranenburg, M. (1999). Disorganized attachment in early childhood: Meta-analysis of precursors, concomitants, and sequelae. *Development and Psychopathology*. 11:225–249. https://doi.org/10.1017/s0954579499002035.
Vorria, P., Papaligoura, Z., Sarafidou, J., Kopakaki, M., Dunn, J., van, IJzendoorn. M.H., & Kontopoulou, A. (2006). The development of adopted children after institutional care: A follow-up study. *Journal of Child Psychology and Psychiatry, 47*, 1246–1253. https://doi.org/10.1111/j.1469-7610.2006.01666.x.
We were tutored to say that we are treated well. (2014, August 28). The Times of India, p. 5.
Wiik, K., Loman, M., Ryzin, M., Armstrong, J., Essex, M., Pollak, S., et al. (2011). Behavioral and emotional symptoms of post-institutionalized children in middle childhood. *Journal of Child Psychology and Psychiatry, 52,* 56–63.
WHO. (2005). *Atlas: Child and adolescent mental health resources: Global concerns, implications for the future*.
Whetten, K., Ostermann, J., Pence, B. W., Whetten, R. A., Messer, L. C., Ariely, S., & The Positive Outcomes for Orphans (POFO) Research Team. (2014). Three year change in the wellbeing of orphaned and separated children in institutional and family-based care settings in five low- and Middle Income Countries. *PLoS ONE, 9*(8), e104872. https://doi.org/10.1371/journal.pone.0104872.
Yet another children's home in Trichy violated rights. (2016, January 25). *The Times of India*, p. 6.
Zeanah, C. H., Nelson, C. A., Fox, N. A., Smyke, A. T., Marshall, P., Parker, S. W., et al. (2003). Designing research to study the effects of institutionalization on brain and behavioral development: The Bucharest Early Intervention Project. *Development and Psychopathology, 15,* 885–907. https://doi.org/10.1017/S0954579403000452.
Zeanah, C. H., Smyke, A. T., & Settles, L. (2006). Children in orphanages. In K. McCartney & D. Phillips (Eds.), *Blackwell handbook of early childhood development* (pp. 224–254). Malden, MA: Blackwell Publishing.
10 girls of a home suffer from food poisoning. (2015, November 16). *The Hindu*, p. 5.
4 lakh in childcare: State NGOs make a killing through donations. (2014, August). *The Times of India*, p. 6.